Communication for
Development
One World, Multiple Cultures

THE HAMPTON PRESS COMMUNICATION SERIES

Communication, Culture and Social Change

Josep Rota, series editor

Communication and Development: One World, Multiple Cultures
Jan Servaes

forthcoming

Communication Research in Europe
Manual Parés i Maicas (ed.)

Communication for Development
One World, Multiple Cultures

Jan Servaes

Katholieke Universiteit Brussel

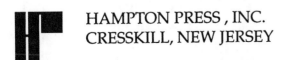

HAMPTON PRESS , INC.
CRESSKILL, NEW JERSEY

Printed in the United States of America

Library of Congress Cataloging-in-Publication Data

Servaes, Jan.   1952-
    Communication for development : one world, multiple cultures /
Jan Servaes
        p.   cm. -- (The Hampton Press communication series)
    Includes bibliographical references and indexes.
    ISBN 1-57273-197-4. ISBN 1-57273-198-2 (pbk.)
    1. Communication in development.   I. Title.   II. Series
HD76.S475   1999
302.2--dc21   98-56037
                                                                            CIP

Hampton Press, Inc.
23 Broadway
Cresskill, NJ 07626

With love to

Yai
Fiona
Lisa

Contents

LIST OF FIGURES

LIST OF TABLES

x Contents

Foreword
Culture as a Mainstream

Jan Pronk
Dutch Minister of Development Cooperation

The lessons we learn from our past mistakes are never a sufficient guide for the present. History moves fast, and today faster than ever before. The globalization of markets, self-accelerating technological change, and the political upheavals in so many nations in the former East, West and South of this world are revolutionizing our societies. All over the world economic and social structures are being shaken up. We are witnessing a cross-fertilization of cultures. Cultural values turn out to be chameleon-like, changing according to newly emerging patterns of economic dominance. Social norms are giving way to fears of intrusion by what are perceived as threatening alien cultures.

We thought that we finally properly understood the role of culture in the development of our societies. We had been mistaken about that role when we began to produce theories about development in an effort to steer the process of development in a harmonious way. We learned that culture was neither irrelevant to development nor an impediment to it. We also learned that culture was neither sacred nor conservative, that development would not destroy culture but itself be affected by and adapted to the cultural context in a society. We learned it the hard way, after making many mistakes, sometimes with consequences opposite to those which we originally had in mind. However, 40 years after the launch of the first development plan—Point Four, in 1949—we knew better. Point Four was basically a program of top-down, technical assistance, provided by a supposedly superior culture to backward, underdeveloped societies. But gradually we came to understand the mutually enriching relationship between culture and development, accepting culture as the heartbeat of development and discovering development as a process far richer than simply economic growth or technological progress.

Forty years after Point Four the world had reached a point of no return. The end of the Cold War in 1989 was a revolution, not only in the East, but also in international relations. It released forces in the South aiming at the emancipation of individuals, peoples, and cultures. It also challenged the rationale behind many of the choices that had been made by the West.

These forces had major cultural consequences. Economic globalization on the basis of technological change has given rise to a global culture. The end of the dominant ideological contest in the second half of the 20th century—the battle between capitalism and communism—unleashed a new cultural dispute: a conflict between cultural diversity in an open society, on the one hand, and on the other cultural self-containment in closed bodies, uniform guilds rather than communities, characterized by static conventional wisdoms instead of a quest for a common but diversified good.

This is the main characteristic of the 1990s: a new ideological conflict within a young global culture. A completely different setting for development. That is why the lessons we have learned do not provide sufficient guidance. We had learned to see cultural change in a society, economic development of a nation, and political emancipation of individuals within the state as mutually enriching processes, working together in harmony. However, the harmony turns to discord if local cultures are increasingly affected by alien values, economic development is being controlled by forces on the global market rather than by domestic supply and demand, and social and polical emancipation is being thwarted by a culture of exclusion rather than integration. Such circumstances will not produce harmony between culture and development. Instead, it is a recipe for conflicts, often of a violent nature.

So this is a new era, indeed. An era of unprecedented opportunity due to the emergence of the global market. An era, too, of new conflicts because in this global market there are many forces tending toward economic, social, and cultural exclusion.

A GLOBAL CULTURE

A world market for new goods, material and nonmaterial alike, is forming rapidly. Although substantially dictated by Western tastes, products are responding to the growing cultural "métissage" of the world, and designers cater to the need of as many as 10 different skintones. The same is true for music, in which different styles weave themselves into a world pattern that is accessible to almost everyone.

The global market is not restricted to material goods. An electronic highway is in the making in the nonmaterial world. This form of infrastructure enables individual consumers to watch films and TV programs, consult libraries, or go shopping, at home in their armchairs, at any moment of the day. Transport on this electronic highway is provided by telephone, television, and computer. The image is that of virtual reality. Instead of us going into the world, the world will come to us.

A worldwide computer information network has been set up, called the Internet, which allows users to consult databases, store information and send electronic mail. Friends are being made and partners selected via this network. The public exchange of views and ideas is carried out via newsgroups, a kind of electronic notice board on which everyone can leave messages. The Internet provides thousands of fields of interest, varying from serious science to trivia. This is cyberspace, the elusive world of global computer communication.

Information can reach virtually all corners of the world. The media have become a valuable tool for educational purposes and a source of amusement for people who have little or no access to other entertainment. A world culture is in the making, influenced by the West, but not exclusively: culture with the universal commodity as a basis, heading for globally shared tastes and fashions. It is one step on the way to a world community.

A CULTURE OF EXCLUSION

The opportunities are there, but who can grasp them? To what extent are people likely to participate?

Today's reality presents a grim picture. The numbers of the poor are on the increase, while at the same time a minority of the population with access to knowledge and capital is becoming richer. The demarcation line runs through developed and third world countries alike. The poor are faced with tantalising visions of wealth that are broadcasted all over the world. But like mirages, they retreat when you approach them.

In January 1994, the first global advertisement was broadcast simultaneously in every part of the globe. The message was not "love thy neighbor" or "thou shalt not kill." It was "Drink Coke." On a symbolic level this was a neat encapsulation of the main trend in human communications worldwide: commercialization and consumerism. Advertisements manufacture needs: they exploit the desire individuals feel to define a distinctive identity. Advertising fuels rising expectations for poor people, rising like the prices that make a mockery of all such expectations.

The poor are also excluded from cyberspace. Originally designed as a form of communication for scientists, this medium only reaches an educated audience. The double handicap of being poor and poorly educated effectively bars participation of the majority of the population in any country. Children without access to computers in primary schools have a handicap in education and, later on, on the labor market.

Exclusion is not only an economic phenomenon. It has social and political consequences as well. And it has also major cultural dimensions. Exclusion of people results in a culture of neglect in 'thinking people away'. People are objects rather than human beings. This inevitably results in a culture of disdain—blaming people for their fate, their poverty, their foreigness rather than blaming the system. Today, the victims of the system are being blamed, not the system itself. One step further is a culture of alienation: people not belonging to a community, not being taken care off, not caring any more about the system, which becomes alien to them. That this may breed a culture of violence and oppression is well known today. It is one of the major dangers of the last decades of this century.

MANIPULATION OF CULTURE

It is not only the unequal opportunity of access to the new affluence that causes concern, but also the quality of what is provided. There is a growing resistance to tendencies toward uniformity, based on models and tastes that are a product of Western society. George Ritzer (1993) challenges the "McDonaldization" of society, the process by which the principles of the fast-food restaurant are coming to dominate more and more sectors of society. McDonaldization poses a threat to local cultures and dehumanizes the production process by putting emphasis on quantity rather than quality. Apart from satisfying hunger and thirst, the particular qualities of the family meal that impart feelings of security and well-being might be lost forever if food is "zapped" or "nuked" instead of cooked. Eating then becomes a refuelling rather than a dining experience. McDonaldization is no longer restricted to the food industry and has turned into a dehumanizing system that may become destructive of social relations.

The most powerful impact of commercialization has been in the realm of the media. A sinister paradox is the result. Although technology permits the release of an inexhaustible stream of information, commercialization, fed by TV ratings, is limiting the scope of that information. The countervailing power of public broadcasting is under pressure. During the 1980s, governments deregulated or privatized TV programming in most of Western Europe. As the European Community became both a single market and a common broadcasting region, advertising time on European television became a hot commodity. Meanwhile, commercial television is quickly spreading outside the industrial countries. Perhaps half the world's people have access to commercial TV broadcasts.

The news is presented to us through a looking glass. It looks bigger, yet we see less. In our communication society it is becoming increasingly difficult to provide truthful information. All institutions, be they political, economic, social or cultural, have communication divisions for the purpose of manipulating the channels of information: press, television, and education. The world of communication that creates products for profit and the world of information that is seeking truth are slowly blending. The transfer and exchange of cultural values that take place in our channels of information are increasingly commercialized and manipulated by interest groups with economic power.

In his book *Who Stole the News?* Mort Rosenblum (1993) analyses the same phenomenon. Television news has become a consumer item that must be exciting and easy to understand. The distinction between news and entertainment, between fact and fiction, is fading away. In-depth analysis and background information are rare. The public at large is not supposed to be interested in investigative journalism, and large-scale commercial advertisement dictates what is offered to the public.

LOSS OF CULTURE

If we look beyond the scope of what the media offer us, what do we see? According to Robert Kaplan (1994), "A bifurcated world, part of the globe is inhabited by Hegel's and Fukuyama's Last Man, healthy, well fed, and pampered by technology. The other, larger, part is inhabited by Hobbes's First Man, condemned to a life that is poor, nasty, brutish, and short" (p. . 11).

In this divided world the social fabric of many communities is being destroyed. The differences in access to the global culture and the loss of cultural values due to the commercialization of the channels of information are the main culprits. Other investments in sophisticated technology can in the long term be almost equally disruptive. This is true, for instance, for major infrastructural works requiring resettlement of people, or for the lure of the big cities. Culture, which should serve as a mechanism for adjustment to change, is at a loss when the change is too rapid and drastic.

> When people are displaced, production systems may be dismantled, kinship groups are scattered, and long-established residential settlements are disorganized. People's lives are affected in very painful ways. Many jobs and assets are lost. Health care tends to deteriorate. Links between producers and their customers often are severed, and local labor markets are disrupted. Informal social networks that are part of daily sustenance systems . . . are dissolved. . . . Traditional community and authority systems can lose their leaders. Symbolic markers, such as ancestral shrines and graves, are abandoned, breaking links with the past and with peoples' cultural identity. (Ritzer, 1996, p. 157)

Urbanization is particularly destructive in developing countries.

> Large sections of people are drifting away from their social, moral and cultural moorings in the course of the dislocation which characterises modern city life. And in the midst of this flux, society is failing to create new structures and rules to replace the old ones. The West, of course, has been passing through a period of rising crime and family breakdown for many decades . . ., but the West has been able to absorb many of the stresses and strains placed on its social fabric by creating sophisticated services, institutions, counselling, advice centres and hotlines to help at least some of those in need. In a country such as India urban society is going through such an accelerated stage of transition that even sociologists have not quite mapped out the new landscape, there is no provision at all for such strains. Indeed, it is in this grey area between the loss of the old and the absence of anything new that anger, unchannelled and unfocused, is exploding, with little to contain it. (Rosenblum, 1993, p. 19)

Communities feel threatened by rapid societal changes with which they cannot cope. They may disintegrate and dissolve into bigger entities. Or they may search for and return to old values and traditions. The scope of interest narrows down to the family, the clan, or the tribe. An effort is made to preserve cultural identities.

Those who wish to do this deserve our support. We must see to it that cultures can survive. Not only will they provide a stable basis for their members, but cultural diversity is beneficial to us all. There is no hierarchy in cultures. The gains are reciprocal. As ANC lawyer Albie Sachs puts it, "The new South Africa would indeed be a charmless place if we were banned from hearing Bach or told that Swan Lake had been replaced by crocodile lagoon." However, the interaction between cultures should never become a one-way street, in which Western norms and values are a predominant force.

IDENTITY POLITICS

Taken to extremes, such introversion can degenerate into hostility toward everything that is foreign or simply different. Natural distinctions between different cultural identities may then lead to a climate in which the line between "them" and "us" can no longer be crossed. This is the seedbed that political leaders, at a loss to resolve the problems facing them, can harvest by inciting to violence as a smokescreen.

By itself, cultural, religious, or ethnic identity is hardly ever sufficient to provoke a conflict. In the present, postideological era, however, elites feel ever more tempted to politicize cultural and ethnic differences when trying to solve disputes over access to power or scarce resources. Lately we have seen an upsurge of this kind of identity-related conflict, in which the accumulation of political and ethnic antagonisms erupt into an uncontrollable stream of violence.

It seems to make little difference whether those in question represent a minority group or a dominant culture. The projected image of a culture under threat appears to be a highly effective rallying cry to mobilise people who would otherwise never dream of butchering their neighbor.

Identity-related conflicts are especially troubling for two reasons. First, they are by nature couched in absolute terms and therefore leave little room for compromise. Second, they appeal to basic instincts that can bring about great personal violence and cruelty. In both these ways Rwanda and Bosnia are two of a kind.

Identity politics does not merely look back to the past to reclaim a sense of community, lost in the course of modern times. It also utilizes the instruments of modern technology, which are available on an ever-more accessible world market. In Serbia ethnic cleansing was preceded by years during which fallacies about people of different origins or creeds were deliberately propagated on television. In Rwanda it is a radio station, "Mille collines," which is instrumental in spreading a gospel of ethnic fear and hatred.

TOWARD AN OPEN SOCIETY

Today's leaders are faced with the challenge of steering between the global culture, as it evolves, and traditional cultures at regional and local levels. On the one hand, progress, both material and spiritual, seems to point in the direction of global interaction, nurtured by basic and universal norms and values. Universal values are sometimes challenged. The advocates of cultural relativism run the risk of playing into the hands of dictatorial regimes. It is my conviction that there are universal values that should not be questioned, no matter to what culture one belongs. The right to life is one of them.

However, there are and there should be regional and local variations in the global pattern. These differences can be an enrichment for all who are liberal enough to question their own supposed cultural supremacy. A globalization that did not respect such variation would be a body without a soul. It would meet the fate of the red shoes in Andersen's fairy tale, which keep on moving, regardless of the wearer's wishes.

Our ultimate goal should be an open society, based on individual freedom, in which different cultural communities can peacefully coexist. A society whose members respect their neighbors and care for them, even if they don't belong to the same "tribe." The best way of achieving this goal is to strengthen the social fabric and remove fear. People should start by regaining certainties. They should be able to give direction to their own lives. They should feel themselves not excluded from society but part of it. They should harvest the crops of their own little plot of land, or earn a salary, or have access to credit to create their own income. Education is a valuable tool in increasing mutual understanding, as are literature, music, and sport.

Second, there is the element of space. That implies seeing the significance of man-made boundaries in proportion. It also refers to the need to foster local cultural autonomy and diversification. It requires a willingness to delegate political responsibilities from the national to the local level in order to eliminate the dichotomy between political elites and the people.

Third, there is the element of time. Developed nations have needed hundreds of years to build democratic societies. Their cultures have slowly adapted to new situations. Other nations, however, particularly in the more remote parts of the world, have matured and survived through centuries of isolation and seclusion. We cannot expect that within 10 or 20 years those cultures will have adjusted to or have come to terms with external forces, without losing their proper identity. Let's give them time.

Finally, human rights should be respected. In the course of time, when societies strive toward more openness, more autonomy, and more diversification, new conflicts may arise. The development of the state, the nation, the market, the city, cannot take place without conflict. It is in itself a form of conflict. Conflicts cannot be prevented; they can only be managed and limited, with the help of a democratic process starting with one basic point of departure: the preservation of human rights. That is the best guarantee for building a society within which we can prevent conflicts from escalating into violence.

Culture is like a river. It meanders and follows its own course. It is a source of life. We bathe in it and drink its water. Without the river, the land grows barren. The river is fed by little streams which provide fresh water. They should not be cut off, for then the river would become turbid and stagnant. If the river develops into a torrent and floods, it can be a devastating force. It should then be canalized to save lives. We must steer cautiously and slowly in the middle and be aware that culture, although not a panacea, should always be a mainstream.

NOTES

CERNEA, M. M. *Resettlement and development,* unpublished report, World Bank, Washington, 8 April 1994.

INDIA TODAY, 31 May 1994, pp. 132-136.

KAPLAN, R. D. "The coming anarchy", *The Atlantic Monthly,* February 1994.

RITZER, G. (1996) *The McDonaldization of Society: An Investigation into the Changing Character of Contemporary Social Life.* Pine Forge Press, Thousand Oaks.

ROSENBLUM, M. (1993). *Who stole the news?,* John Wiley, New York.

Acknowledgements

Although only my name appears on the cover of this book, it has to be seen as the end-product of a group process in which many people took part—people who have been and continue to be of great support to me in both intellectual and emotional ways. As the references suggest, great intellectual debts are owed to many who have written about the same or related issues. Others have read and commented on portions of the book, *One World, Multiple Cultures. A New Paradigm on Communication for Development*, published by the Belgian Academic Press Acco in 1989, which can be considered the first draft for the present one. The present volume attempts to clarify some of the misconceptions and shortcomings identified by some readers. It also provides illustrations in the form of case studies.

First and foremost I would like to express my warm and deep appreciation for the unfailing assistance and cooperation of Patchanee Malikhao and Randy Arnst, who have been co-authoring articles that formed the basis for the present text. I thank my wife Patchanee for introducing me into Thai culture. *Khob khun mak, krap!* Randy assisted in my struggle to come to grips with distinct research methodologies. They will notice that many of their ideas and arguments have been included in this text. I would like also to express my sincere appreciations to Jan

Pronk and Naowarat Pongpaiboon for granting me permission to publish their writings.

Sincere thanks are also due to James Anderson, Joe Ascroft, Choy Arnaldo, Njoku Awa, Kwame Boafo, Renuka Berry, Andrew Calabrese, Brenda Dervin, Salag Dhabhanandana, Shalmali Guttal, Cees Hamelink, Alan Hancock, Staf Hellemans, Tom Jacobson, Tim Kennedy, Ulla Kivikuru, John Lent, Rico Lie, Khor Yoke Lim, Daniel Mato, John Mayo, Daniele Mezzane, Francis Nyamnjoh, Manfred Oepen, Syed Rahim, Mina Ramirez, Ev Rogers, Rafael Roncagliolo, the late Kukrit Pramoj, Arvind Singhal, Sulak Sivaraksa, Sara Stuart, Mike Traber, Pradip Thomas, and Bob White for the stimulating discussions and the exchange of ideas and critical arguments; to members of the Participatory Communication Research Network for locating relevant references and providing theoretical clarification toward a theory of participatory communication; to the graduate students at Antwerp University, Chulalongkorn University, Cornell University, Nijmegen University and Thammasat University for asking the right questions; to the Series Editor Josep Rota and Publisher Barbara Bernstein for their patience and warm and consistent support in getting this manuscript published; and to so many others whom I met at conferences, meetings, in the field, or who just were there to share their time, ideas, and experiences. Only I am responsible for what I have written, but this book could not have appeared without their encouragement, support, participation, advice, and critical interest. As I consider this book part of an ongoing research project, I welcome any comments, suggestions, and criticisms from the readers.

Jan Servaes

Important Note: In all cases in which gender is not implicit, I have attempted to combine feminine and masculine pronouns. However, as English is not my mother tongue, I apologize to the reader if he or she still finds errors.

Moving at Last

A hawk shifts its wings in the sunlight—
A sudden chill in the fiery firmament.
A shuddering of leaves—
Evidence of a wind at work.

The ripple of a wave says
This is water, not a mirror.
A flash of the eye says
There's a heart inside.

A tearing of chains
Proclaims the agony they caused.
A flash of light in the sky
Shows there's yet a way to go.

Hand clenched in sweating fists
Their flesh boiling—
Gasping and falling
Show feeling is not dead.

The movement of a finger yet
Proclaims a strength long hidden.
The grass among the stones
Show how it has been crushed.

Forty empty years—a nation silent;
Forty million people dared not move an inch;
Earth to sand and wood to stone all broken,
All asleep, all paralyzed in heart and eye.

Birds in the sky, ignorant of air,
Fishes in the deep know no wet.
Earthworms blind to earth
And maggots happy with their filth.

So the rot set in
As it must in what is still,
Until, amid the murk
A lotus bloomed.
And then a little movement,
Fair and free of filth
Unclear, still dulled
And yet a sign of life.

Then the drum sounded
And the great day came.
The guns resounded
And the people fought to win.—Naowarat Pongpaiboon

(trans. by Michael Wright)
Bangkok, October 14, 1973

Introduction

The unfolding dialectic of world history is entering its most comprehensive and perhaps most problematic phase—at once unnerving
and creative. It heralds a process of mutation in the history of the
human species, with far-reaching changes in the arrangement of
human affairs: in the structuring of global power relations, in the
encounter of civilizations, in several other areas such as class, region,
ethnicity, and religion. And yet few, if any, seem to have a clue to
the real nature of this transformation.
—Rajni Kothari (1984:323)

"Moving at Last" or "Mere Movement" won the 1980 Southeast Asian
Writer's Award. The Nominating Committee was unanimous in its
appreciation that the work of Naowarat Pongpaiboon is one of the most
articulate expressions of the conscience of contemporary Thailand. It
was stated that Naowarat's poetry is unique in the sense that it combines the particular with the universal, that it conveys passionate feelings with grace and dignity.

This poem was written on the evening of the popular uprising
of October 14, 1973. On that day, mass demonstrations by students and
workers destabilized the dictatorial regime of Prime Minister Thanom

Kittikajon. He fled the country, and in the more liberal period which followed close links were forged between students, farmers, and workers, and hopes for greater political and social consciousness expressed. Concerted efforts were made by newly established interest groups to tackle the wide-ranging social and economic problems that affected the rural and urban poor—landlessness and debt, unemployment, labor migration from the countryside to the capital of Bangkok, harsh working conditions, and the inadequate provision of health care, education, and welfare facilities.

Unfortunately, all these efforts were brought to a violent stop when, on October 6, 1976, student demonstrations at Bangkok's Thammasat University were brutally suppressed by police and right-wing vigilante groups. A coup d'état on the same day returned military factions to power. They would stay in power until the early 1990s.

Thailand is one of those countries most Western tourists fall in love with, especially those who just stay for a few weeks, as there is so much to see and experience of an unusual nature. However, if they would stay a bit longer they might soon discover that their first impressions were very superficial and not well considered. Even foreigners who live in the "land of smiles" for a longer period of time very often do not understand Thai culture and society. Many of them do not even try and, often implicitly and unintentionally, instead stick to their ethnocentric views on other cultures and societies. They, therefore, very often get upset by typical Thai working habits that pay much less respect to Western efficiency, rationality, and ethics. They do not succeed in unmasking the Thai smile.

In the social science literature, Thailand often is labeled as "unique." The two main reasons for this are the country has never been colonized, and Buddhism is present in all facets of everyday life. Armed with more of these statements, researchers then attempt to get to the bottom of Thai society. They decide, very early on, that the Thai people are very individualistically oriented and that the social structure is very loose (the so-called "loosely structured system theory"). Arguments to demonstrate this theorem are there for the taking: Thai modern history is a chain of coups and countercoups, the Thai political scene is rather unpredictable, and on every street corner one can, in the course of a few minutes, observe situations of that Thai individualism.

In my opinion, this vision of the Thai culture is very superficial. These researchers focus attention on the study of the formal structures of a given society in general, or the Thai society in particular. By so doing, however, they mask attention to the informal rules, values, and norms that underlie these structures and the way in which the Thai explain their roles and relationships in society. To understand the process underlying the structure one has to seek the "logic" that defines every-day living. Like Naowarat's poetry one has to penetrate beneath the surface of things and symptoms in order to search for deeper meaning.

The Thai context is featured as one of the points of reference on the issues under discussion in this volume. But the Thai case could very well serve as a vivid reflection of what has been happening to so-called Third World societies in general. As the main issues involved are actually global in character, they all share a similar cultural source of "development" being "forced" on them, all in the name of modernization and progress. Apart from the issue of power, most scholars point to the lack of a unifying concept of development and the absence of a cultural perspective as explanatory factors. A unifying concept of development is not just a planning technicality, but fundamentally it is a question of political will, determination, and persistence. In similar ways, the (re)discovery of culture as a major factor for development implies a fundamental rethinking of old ways of seeing. Culture may not be a panacea but should, as Jan Pronk eloquently argues in his foreword, always be a mainstream.

In Search of a New Paradigm

It is fashionable today to maintain that the problem of communication and development must be studied in its social context and that there are no generally valid blueprints available for "development." It is also often stated that it no longer suffices to analyze and describe, but that strategies for a solution must be proposed. Obviously, such a task demands a multidisciplinary approach.

These theses are of relatively recent date. More specifically, the cultural and communication dimensions of development have long been given short shrift. Only in the last 15 years or so has it been realized that culture and communication could well have a fundamental impact on the entire question of development.

It is generally agreed that thinking about development and communication as a distinct discipline emerged after World War II. Since that time the problematique has become increasingly complex, mainly due to changes in the societal and world system on the one hand, and the interdisciplinary nature of development and communication theory on the other.

In addition to this interdisciplinary character of development theory, Bjorn Hettne (1982, 1990) perceives three more reasons for its complexity: First, more than conventional economics, sociology, or political science, development theory is concerned with structural change. Second, in order to find solutions, development theory has been closely related to development strategy. And third, development theory is more explicitly normative than social sciences in general.

In my opinion, the same is true for communication theory when analyzed at the macro level, that is, at the level of communication as a social function in society. This can be illustrated by quoting two international communication scholars. Kaarle Nordenstreng (1981: 280) states

> the global trends in the field of mass communication research can be expressed in terms of two interrelated tendencies on change: a tendency toward a more holistic framework and a tendency toward policy orientation. The holistic approach, for its part, may be seen to imply two sub-aspects: a stressing of the processional approach covering simultaneously various stages of the communication process and a stressing of the contextual approach tying the particular communication phenomena into wider socio-politico-economic settings.

Cees Hamelink (1981: 7) adds

> no pertinent theoretical framework for the study of international communication has yet been developed and as a result there is continuing dependence on: mass media theories (usually fragmentary, and based on obsolete psychological and sociological notions) political science theories on international relations (usually inadequate descriptions of status quo situations); imperialism/dependencia theories (usually too narrowly confined to the transfer of mechanisms).

At the risk of over-simplification, I would like to take Karl Erik Rosengren's (1981) typology as my starting point. Rosengren returns to the old but still basic question of the relationship between culture and social structure. He distinguishes between two extremes: social structure influences culture versus culture influences social structure. For my purposes, I read social structure as social change or development, and culture as communication (both software and hardware, thus including technology). Next, Rosengren puts these basic propositions in a cross-tabulation in order to classify the four main types of the relationship: cultural autonomy, culture creates social structure (idealism), social structure creates culture (materialism), and the interdependence or mutual influence between both (cf. Figure I.1).

So far the discussion on the relationship between development and communication has concerned mainly the materialism-idealism axis. But it may well be, Rosengren argues, that in the coming years the focus of attention will be that of interdependence-autonomy and that it will be moving from a holistic, overall perspective to a more differentiated one.

Development influences communication

		YES	NO
Communication influences	YES	Interdependence	Idealism
development	NO	Materialism	Autonomy

FIGURE I.1. Types of relations between culture (communication) and society (development)

Three Paradigms on Communication for Development

Most authors who are concerned with the problem of development set two views, schools, or *paradigms* next to or in opposition to each other: modernization and growth versus dependency and underdevelopment. Whereas the first paradigm can be considered the oldest and most deeply rooted view in Western thought, the dependency theory came from Latin America. However, because paradigms in the social sciences tend to build on each other rather than reject each other radically, a new vision has been emerging over the last few years that focuses on the elements neglected by the previous paradigms. Therefore, it can be argued that the social sciences are in a *pluri-paradigmatic state,* thus emphasizing that the multiplicity of viewpoints and associated methodological approaches are the norm rather than the exemption. I describe this new paradigm for the time being as another and multidimensional development, or, in short, the *multiplicity* paradigm.

During the late 1940s and 1950s most development thinkers stated that the problem of underdevelopment or "backwardness" could be solved by a more-or-less mechanical application of the economic and political system in the West to countries in the Third World, under the assumption that the difference was one of degree rather than of kind. This mainly economic-oriented view, characterized by endogenism and evolutionism, ultimately resulted in the modernization and growth theory.

As a result of the general intellectual "revolution" that took place in the mid 1960s, this Euro- or ethnocentric view on development, which is generally referred to as *modernization,* was challenged by Latin

American social scientists, and a theory dealing with dependency and underdevelopment was born. This dependency approach formed part of a general structuralistic reorientation in the social sciences. The so-called *dependistas* were primarily concerned with the effects of dependency in peripheral countries, but implicit in their analysis was the idea that development and underdevelopment must be understood in the context of the world system.

This need for a more global perspective has been strengthened as the present worldwide crisis shows the degree to which the world economy has become a reality. Therefore, the need for a more contextual analysis becomes apparent. "The question of communication and change in society is by no means solely a Third World problem," Goran Hedebro (1982:10) argues, "it is a highly general one, with many basic similarities among all countries no matter what their states of development." Contrary to the more economics and political-oriented views of the modernization and dependency theories, the central idea in the multiplicity paradigm is that there is no universal path to development, that development must be conceived as an integral, multidimensional, and dialectic process that can differ from one country to another. In other words, every society must define development for itself and find its own strategy.

At the same time, this also implies that the problem of development is a relative one. Therefore, according to this paradigm, no part of the world can claim to be developed in all respects. Furthermore, the discussion on the degree and scope of inter(in)dependence is connected with the content of development. As I try to explain, according to this view "another" development could be defined as need-oriented, endogenous, self-reliant, ecologically sound, and based on participatory democracy and structural transformations.

The Constraints of the Framework Under Study

Before giving a more detailed overview of these paradigms, I make a number of preliminary remarks.

First, the chronological approach applied here has a certain bias in creating the impression that later theoretical contributions replace earlier ones. Although new innovations often were stimulated by the shortcomings of previous theorizing on the one hand, and, according to Kuhn (1962), theoretical changes in the social sciences are different from positive sciences on the other hand, these three paradigms still do find support among academics, policymakers, and the general public. Today, both paradigms still have their proponents and opponents, and are thus used in specific circles by policymakers, and the public at large. In general, in theory the modernization vision was dominant until the second half of the 1960s, but it has yielded ground since then to the dependency theory. This dominance is more readily discerned in the scientific area than in Western policymaking institutions and public opinion. The latter were and are sensitive to the paternalism, with respect to non-Western cultures, that characterizes the modernization theory.

Because in the social sciences "paradigms" tend to accumulate rather than to replace each other (Janos, 1986), I like to conceive of paradigms as *frames of meaning* that are mediated by others:

> The process of learning a paradigm or language-game as the expression of a form of life is also a process of learning what that paradigm is not: that is to say, learning to mediate it with other, rejected, alternatives, by contrast to which the claims of the paradigm in question are clarified. The process is itself often embroiled in the struggles over interpretation which result from the internal fragmentation of frames of meaning, and from the fragility of the boundaries that separate what is 'internal' to the frame from what is 'external' to it, that is, belongs to discrete or rival meaning frames. (Giddens, 1976:144)

Therefore, "a paradigm is what the members of a scientific community share, and conversely, a scientific community consists of men [and women!, JS] who share a paradigm" (Kuhn, 1970:172). Such paradigms are constructs identifying broad relationships between two or more general categories, together with some basic assumptions concerning the nature of a larger universe. So defined, these paradigms are not theories, for they do not provide explanations, only instructions as to where to go for explanations. "Accordingly, they allow us to organize research and, by structuring intellectual curiosity, provide an appropriate focus for scientific disciplines" (Janos, 1986:1).

Consequently, in each time period one can make a distinction between a dominant and an alternative perspective on development. Moreover, each paradigm can be further subdivided into what can be called its "mainstream" of thinking and its "counterpoints." As pointed out earlier, the modernization paradigm continues to be influential at the political level although it no longer enjoys the widespread theoretical endorsement that it did up until the mid-1960s. However, broadly speaking, the *beliefs* on which it is built—that is, economic growth, centralized planning, and the explanation for the state of underdevelopment as sought in chiefly internal causes that can be solved by external (technological) "aid"—are still shared by many governments, development agencies associated with the United Nations, the World Bank, and so on, and, of course, transnational companies. Also, the majority of Western public opinion sticks to the ethnocentric and paternalistic views that are present in the modernization theory.

Another observation concerns the evolution in thinking of certain theorists and researchers. As has been argued previously, paradigms in the social sciences build on one another rather than break fundamentally with previous theories. As a consequence, many individual thinkers deepen and widen their views in an evolutionary, sometimes dialectic way. Thus, it might occur that their earlier work can be viewed as an eloquent evidence of the modernization or dependency theory, whereas their later publications are more in line with the multiplicity paradigm. This is the case with the work of Samir Amin (1979, 1985). In the communication field one can observe that much of the early work of the so-called ILET-group dealt with dependency topics, whereas now their collaborators have become famous for their attempts to define the concept of democratization in communication theory (see, e.g., the work of Matta, 1979 or Somavia, 1977). However, a related and less likely aspect, which can be considered to be one of the major flaws in many well-intended policy recommendations, concerns the mixing of these paradigms in a rather contradictory fashion. Very often, reports of academicians and policymakers are heaped with all sorts of fashionable recommendations. As Van Nieuwenhuijze (1982:56) cynically observes:

> At no time has a change of fashion in development approaches resulted in the elimination of the previous approach. Even if the next fashion is introduced as a corrective to, or because of proven inefficiency of, the preceding one, elements of previous approaches do linger on—if only because it is not always possible to undo their institutionalization.

This is, as is discussed later, the case with much of the technology debate.

Furthermore, an important characteristic of the development theory is involvement in policy (Booth, 1994; Boudin, 1991; Sztompka, 1993). These paradigms, in other words, have practical applications to policy. And, inversely, one may state that that application requires knowledge. As Peter Kloos (1984) indicates, there are different kinds of knowledge:

> Unlike the natural sciences, there are two kinds of knowledge in the socio-cultural sciences, namely the culture-specific and the generally valid. Further, the possession of the necessary knowledge does not yet mean that this knowledge is actually used. That is not a question of knowledge but of power. (my translation, JS)

In other words, some regularities in human behavior can be explained on the basis of culture-specific laws, others on the basis of generally valid laws. Culture is a phenomenon whose content differs from society to society, generally because the living conditions of the societies differ. Because their epistemological status differs, these two kinds of knowledge also imply two kinds of rules. In the case of culture-specific rules, one speaks of moral rules that have a normative character; the generally applicable laws have a more natural-scientific character. The laws of the forms of production, for example, cannot be changed; the laws that underlay the production relationships, however, can well be changed. Because the development theory is concerned with processes of social change, I would venture to say that each development paradigm itself already implies a policy recommendation. Therefore—and also supported by extensive research conducted by Geert Hofstede (1980, 1991)—I would argue that the solutions of development problems are culture-bound and cannot be transplanted to other societies with other values.

Another related topic deals with the problem of power and the legitimization of power relationships. Each social order can be characterized by an interrelated division between a (economic) base and a (ideological and symbolic) superstructure. According to Pierre Bourdieu (1979), the dominant classes call upon an ideological and symbolic preponderance, not only to maintain their position in the social hierarchy but to justify it. This system has a "symbolic power" because it is capable of construing reality in a directed manner. Its symbolic power does not lie in the symbolic system itself but in the social relationships between those who exercise the power and those who are subject to it. Symbolic power functions mainly unconsciously as the legitimation criterion for the existing social and economic power relationships, and it creates myths and ways of life. So, in reality, not only normative but also—and especially—power factors play a role in policy and planning, and this is certainly the case when it comes to confirming and carrying out policy recommendations.

A New Perspective on Culture

The above discussion is directly related to the definition of culture. Raymond Williams (1981) said that it is one of the two or three words that are the most difficult to define. One of the first critical reviews of concepts and definitions of culture cited 164 different definitions (Kroeber & Kluckhohn, 1952). According to Michael Thompson and his colleagues (Thompson, Ellis, & Wildavski, 1990) two families of definitions vie for supremacy. One views culture as composed of values, beliefs, norms, rationalizations, symbols, and ideologies (i.e., mental products). The other sees culture as referring to the total way of life of a people, their interpersonal attitudes as well as their attitudes.

Therefore, I start with a *description* of how I perceive "culture" rather than a definition. In other words, what exactly constitutes a culture, or different cultures? Culture is the collective equivalent of personality and, consequently, is not amenable to simplistic classification or pigeonholing. Cultures have indistinct peripheries, and they shade off into one another in a quite indefinite way. We do not always recognize a culture when we see one. Cultures can overlap, absorb, encompass, and blend. They can be differentiated according to environment, custom, social class, worldview, or *Weltanschauung*. The tendency is to think of another culture as somewhat foreign or exotic, as existing outside one's national borders. However, some intranational communications can be far more cross-cultural than international communications. Often, for instance, in many developing nations there exists an easily discernable cultural gap between the ruling elite and the masses. In other words, culture varies with the parameters through which we choose to look at it (Berger & Luckmann, 1967).

The meaning of concepts and symbols, as well as the use of language as such, is culture bound. Culture is a complex phenomenon that can be interpreted in a narrow or broad sense. I reject the viewpoint that conceives of culture as only a partial phenomenon of social reality and thus considers cultural sociology a subdiscipline of the social sciences. Cultural sociology derives its special character not so much from a specific object field but rather from a specific perspective on society.

In this sense, cultures can be defined as social settings in which a certain reference framework has taken concrete form or has been institutionalized. It orients and structures the interaction and communication of people within this historical context. The classic distinction between structure and culture as an empirical duality becomes meaningless. All structures are cultural products and all culture gives structure. This intrinsic bond with a society in which actions are full of value makes all social facts cultural goods. Social facts, like institutions, behavioral patterns, norm systems, structures, and societal models, are construed and cultivated in the light of certain values, preferences, or options that have developed in a society in response to certain common needs or problems. Culture has material and immaterial aspects which are part of a certain way of life, passed on and corroborated via socialization processes (e.g., school, media, religion) to the members of that society.

The reproduction of any social organization entails a basic correspondence between processes of "subjection" and "qualification." This basic social functioning of *subjection/qualification* involves three fundamental modes of ideological interpolation. Ideologies impact and qualify subjects by expressing to them, relating them to, and making them recognize: (a) what exists and what does not exist (i.e., a sense of identity); (b) what is good and bad (i.e., normalization); and (c) what is possible and impossible (i.e., a logic of conservation versus a logic of change). Ideological interpolations are made all the time, everywhere, and by everybody. However, ideological interpolations tend to cluster at nodal points in the ongoing social process, which one could call *ideological institutions*, or *apparatuses*, and which are both discursive and nondiscursive.

This process through which meaning is transmitted is never linear. It is linked to power in conscious and unconscious ways; it is sporadic and ubiquitous and transcends spatial and cultural boundaries:

> Culture is the deposit of knowledge, experiences, beliefs, values, attitudes, meanings, hierarchies, religion, timing, roles, spatial relations, concepts of the universe, and material objects and possessions acquired by a large group of people in the course of generations through individual and group striving. (Samovar & Porter, 1988: 19)

It not only concerns decisions about good and evil and so on, but also the way we eat, live, or dress. Ideologies do function in rational as well as irrational, in conscious as well as unconscious forms. The latter, unconscious aspects are, in my opinion, more important though often overlooked. Joseph Campbell (1988) called them *myths or dreams* in the sense that a dream is a personal myth, and a myth is the public dream of a society. Myths are therefore culture-bound creations of the human mind and spirit:

> National cultures are structured around myths which explain the origins of the particular grouping, their specific national identities and their concepts of national destiny. Such national mythologies seek in grounding in broader cosmic myths, and thus gain a sacred, timeless character. Myths function more at the unintentional, symbol level, defining that what a national society is trying to become. Mythological functions are likely to be especially strong at times of national crisis, rapid change or external threat. (White, 1988: 19-20)

Culture can be taken as the way we perceive and interact with the world, and those with whom we share similar perceptions. It is precisely such shared, often unarticulated and sometimes inarticulable patterns of perception, communication, and behavior that are referred to as "a culture." Culture is subjective, and it is personal. Alder (1985: 413) believes the core "of cultural identity is an image of the self and culture intertwined in the individual's total conception of reality. This image, a patchwork of internalized roles, rules, and norms, functions as the coordinating mechanism in personal and interpersonal situations."

Therefore, various cultures also manifest different identities. Three empirical dimensions can be distinguished in such frames of reference: a worldview (Weltanschauung), a value system, and a system of symbolic representation and social organization. Worldviews are not static any more than the cultures that enshrine them, even though values and customs within worldviews can be and are inherited from one generation to another. Ideological institutions or apparatuses fulfill a key role here. They are forms of behavior that are crystalized on the basis of social acceptance into more-or-less standardized self-evident routines that can work as both negative-repressing and as positive-liberating. They exist in strategies of relations of forces supporting, and supported by, types of knowledge that are both discursive and nondiscursive. They form clusters of institutions that have an impact on and influence each other and that are distinct from others by their own identity. The term *cultural identity* refers to two complementary phenomena: an inward sense of association or identification with a specific culture or subculture and an outward tendency within a specific culture to share a sense of what it has in common with other cultures and of what distinguishes it from other cultures. Like all social processes, these processes are not purely rational or preplanned events. We therefore live, as Benedict Anderson (1983) eloquently puts it, in "imagined communities." In such communities culture must be seen as the unintended result of an interweaving of the behavior of a group of people who interrelate and interact with each other.

A Few Words on Definitions

Although most social scientists reckon that the concepts of power, culture, communication, development, and social change are essential for an understanding of social reality, the concepts are often not defined, and therefore, they are interpreted in different ways. This is mainly due to the complexity and multidimensionality of these concepts. Therefore, according to Lederer (1980:1),

> it is not true that the social sciences purposely aim at bringing forth ambiguous products, but rather that the objects of social sciences—social facts and processes—are more open to common experience and interest than the objects of other spheres of knowledge. Their ideas can quite easily be coopted by persons and institutions for public intervention irrespective of the scientific standing of the concepts used and of the quality of their application.

In other words:

> Communication is not a general abstract phenomena. Rather, as a
> social process, it is constituted in a specific spatial and temporal
> framework. How people communicate, where and why they com-
> municate, with whom they communicate, what and why they com-
> municate, is a function of historical processes. Communication is
> nothing more, and nothing less, than the articulation of social rela-
> tions between people. Consequently, a concern with the communica-
> tion process necessitates the identification of the web of social rela-
> tions within which the process of communication are interwoven.
> (Mahmud, 1981:2)

Therefore, "a definition of 'communication' is totally subject to the theoretical framework that is to be placed on social interaction" (Thomas,
1982: 80).

The same can be said of other concepts, for instance, *development*.

> The idea of development, if not the word, is as old as the expansion
> of Europe, and, interestingly enough, in all the interpretations it has
> been given, there has been present some notion of duty. What has
> changed has been the answer to the question to whom the duty is
> owned. (Mair, 1984:1)

Therefore, some authors argue that

> the overloading of 'development' has reached such a high level that
> we cannot hope to rescue the word for use to signify any particular
> concept or variable. If Development Studies are to develop (!) a more
> promising approach is onomasilogical: let us identify by definition
> the concepts that we need and then try to find suitable unambiguous
> terms for each. (Riggs, 1984:184)

However, some authors argue that this is no longer possible.
Consequently, they propose to get rid of the concept of development:

> The term, development, in its current usage lacks the rigorous epis-
> temological, conceptual, and at times, methodological power to be of
> much value in enhancing our understanding of some of the most
> complex historical, social, political, economic, and spiritual occur-
> rences of our times. (Mowlana, 1986:1)

Although I have great sympathy with these arguments, I do not see how another term could easily replace it in practice. Instead of disputing terminologies, we examine the very policies in order to find out what development actually is, while being aware that these policies may overtly express the latent aspirations of the societies. Stöhr (Taylor & Stöhr, 1981:453) summarizes:

> Consideration of development 'from above' or 'from below' is in essence a consideration of the nature of development itself and everyone, it seems, knows what development is except the experts! This is perhaps not surprising because in the ultimate sense development is a reflection of personal values, conditioned by the societal framework in which one lives. The value a society holds, which themselves change over time, are the ultimate standard by which development or lack of it will be judged. It is perhaps obvious but worth re-stating that an outside view of a society's 'development' may be very different from an assessment made by that society itself.

In sum, it is safe to say that today scholars as well as policymakers look upon development as an ethical-political process of social change.

In the following chapters, I summarize this evolution in postwar thought about development and communication (Part I) and identify the various options in communication policymaking and communication research (Part II). In the third part of this book I also provide case studies to exemplify the major theoretical arguments. For obvious reasons, I must limit myself to a global sketch. Therefore, I am only able to outline the framework within which I think that the issue of communication for development needs to be discussed.

Part I
From Theory . . .

1

Two World(view)s Apart?
Modernization Versus
Dependency

For the first time, the history of imperialism and its culture can now be studied as neither monolithic nor reductively compartmentalized, separate, distinct. True, there has been a disturbing eruption of separatist and chauvinist discourse, whether in India, Lebanon, or Yugoslavia, or in Afrocentric, Islamocentric, or Eurocentric proclamations; far from invalidating the struggle to be free from empire, these reductions of cultural discourse actually prove the validity of a fundamental liberationist energy that animates the wish to be independent, to speak freely and without the burden of unfair domination. The only way to understand this energy, however, is historically.
—Edward W. Said (1993: XX-XXI)

In Chapters One and Two the general concepts that are normally referred to in discussions on development are presented. I address the topic from a historical perspective: as a shift from modernization and dependency theories to more normative and holistic approaches (Chapter 1). These new insights are grouped together as the multiplicity paradigm (in Chapter 2).

The *modernization paradigm*, dominant in academic circles from around 1945 to 1965, supported the transfer of technology and the sociopolitical culture of developed societies to "traditional" or "under-developed" societies. The *dependency paradigm* was widely accepted among scholars as a relevant framework for analyzing international relations from the mid-1960s to the early 1980s. Since then the emerging *multiplicity paradigm* is gaining ground in academic circles (Melkote, 1991; White, Nair and Ascroft, 1994).

At the more limited level of communication for development one can distinguish between two basically different models that build on these more general development paradigms: the mechanistic *diffusion model* (Chapter 1) versus the organic *participatory model* (in Chapter 2).

MODERNIZATION AND GROWTH

Historical Context

After World War II, the founding of the United Nations stimulated relations among sovereign states, especially the North Atlantic nations and the developing nations, including the new states emerging out of a colonial past. During the Cold War period, the superpowers—the United States and the former Soviet Union—tried to expand their own interests to the developing countries. In fact, the United States was defining development as the replica of its own political-economic system and opening the way for transnational corporations. Christopher Simpson (1994) and Rohan Samarajiva (1987), who examined the beginnings of the development communication concept, found that the seminal work by Daniel Lerner (1958) and Wilbur Schramm (1954) was a spin off from a large and clandestine audience research project conducted for the Voice of America by the Bureau of Applied Social Research. Some of their research reports still remain classified by the CIA. Both Simpson and Samarajiva note the strong influence exerted by the demands of psychological warfare, in the context of the Cold War, on the early studies of development communication in the United States: "Exploratory work on the early period suggests the following pattern of net influence flows: marketing research to communication research; marketing and communication research to psychological warfare; from psychological warfare to communication and development" (Samarajiva, 1987:17). Similar observations have been made by other scholars (see, e.g., Ambrose, 1983; Schiller, 1969, 1976; Smythe, 1981; Smythe & Van Dinh, 1983; or Tunstall, 1977).

At the same time, many developing countries saw the "welfare state" of the North Atlantic nations as the ultimate goal of development. These nations were attracted by the new technology transfer and the model of a centralized state with careful economic planning and centrally directed development bureaucracies for agriculture, education, and health as the most effective strategies to catch up with the industrialized countries.

Growth and Progress

Thus, the oldest development paradigm is rooted in Western economic history and, consequently, structured by that rather unique, though historically important, experience. Development is one of the oldest and most powerful of all Western ideas. It can be found in the works of 19th-century philosophers such as Condorcet, Comte, Durkheim, Saint-Simon, Spencer, and even Karl Marx. The central element of this perspective is the *metaphor of growth* and the identification of growth with the Western idea of *progress*. Development is thus conceived as organic, immanent, direct, cumulative, irreversible, and goal-oriented.

The modernization paradigm considers underdevelopment in terms of perceptible, quantitative differences between rich and poor countries. Development means bridging the gaps by means of imitation processes between traditional and modern, retarded and advanced, or barbarian and civilized sectors and groups to the advantage of the latter. Accordingly, developing countries must gradually meet the "qualities" of industrialized countries because

> despite geographic, historical, and cultural heterogeneity, the countries in this group have one outstanding characteristic in common. They are without exception transitional societies in which the process of social, economic, and political modernization has proceeded far enough to profoundly disturb or even completely shatter traditional customs and institutions without, however, proceeding far enough to set them on the path of continuous and effective development. (Adelman & Morris, 1967: 203)

This paradigm thus conceives of development as a spontaneous, irreversible process that every society passes through. As criteria for comparison are a number of quantitative, predominantly economic, growth indexes such as income, volume of savings, and levels of investment. As thinking about modernization proceeded in the 1950s and 1960s, and as the one-sided economic strategy of "unbalanced growth" did not solve the problem, various so-called "noneconomic" factors, including attitude change, level of education, mass media, and institutional reforms, were introduced. However, in my opinion, the economic root has always remained the essence of the modernization paradigm. This can be illustrated with the following definition of what constitutes a *modern society* (Almond & Coleman 1960: 532):

> A modern society is characterized, among other things, by a comparatively high per capita income, extensive geographical and social mobility, a relatively high degree of commercialization and industrialization of the economy, an extensive and penetrative network of mass communication media, and, in general, by widespread participation and involvement by members of the society in modern social and economic processes.

This process takes place in a number of successive stages or phases, each of which presumes a higher degree of development. Development implies structural differentiation and functional specialization and is stimulated primarily by endogenous factors.

Consequently, the means of modernization were the massive transfer of capital, ideology, technology and know-how, a world-wide Marshall Plan, and a green revolution. The measures of progress were Gross National Product, literacy, the industrial base, urbanization, and the like: all quantifiable criteria. Everett Rogers (1976a:124) wrote that although:

> India, China, Persia, and Egypt were old, old centers of civilization . . . their rich cultures had in fact provided the basis for contemporary Western cultures . . . their family life displayed a warmer intimacy and their artistic triumphs were greater, that was not development. It could not be measured in dollars and cents.

Empiricism and Positivism

Empiricism and positivism are largely derived from Western thought, from an Aristotelian heritage in Western or European culture that embodies a fundamental desire to change reality and sees that reality is concrete, measurable, and manipulable. These assumptions and methods, formulated under a totally different social, cultural, economic, and political situation, were absolutized and intended to be transferred to the rest of the world. Western mentality tends to see humanity as an *object*, an entity formed by external forces, a passive body that reacts to external stimuli and influences in a predictable fashion. "It postulates a duality between man [and woman] and nature. Hence, there is an obvious disparity between the metaphysical and epistemological underpinnings of functionalism and the ethos that surrounds Asian cultures" (Dissanayake,1986: 8).

The Take-off Model

A related characteristic of underdevelopment, which soon caught the attention of researchers, was the "dualistic" nature of underdeveloped nations: the co-existence of an advanced or modern sector with a backward or traditional one. These two sectors, *the traditional and the modern*, were conceived as two stages of development, co-existing in time, and, in due course, the differences between them were to disappear because of a natural urge toward equilibrium. The problem was to remove the obstacles or barriers, which were to be found only in traditional society. The removal of these barriers can be organized through at least five mechanisms: (a) *demonstration*, whereby the developing world tries to catch up with the more developed by adopting more advanced methods and techniques; (b) *fusion*, which is the combination and integration of distinct modern methods; (c) *compression*, whereby the developing countries attempt to accomplish the task of development in less time than it took the developed world; (d) *prevention*, that is, learning from the "errors" made by the developed countries; and (e) a*daptation* of modern practices to the local environment and culture.

Another characteristic of modernization thought is the emphasis on *monodisciplinary explanatory factors*. The oldest is the economic variant, associated with Walter Rostow (1953): a traditional society changes itself in successive phases into a modern society after a leap to self-sustaining growth based on a combination of industry-promoting, financial, and infrastructional measures. Rostow outlined five stages through which, in his opinion, all societies have to pass: (a) the traditional society, (b) the pre take-off stage, (c) take-off, (d) the road to maturity, and (e) the mass consumption society. In fact, Rostow's stages were basically derived from the distinction between "tradition" and "modernity," which is well known from the classical sociology of Durkheim, Tönnies, the Weberian analysis of ideal models, and especially Parsons's (1960) pattern variables: particularism versus universalism, ascription versus achievement, and diffuseness versus specificity. This sociological variant was the phase theory in which a traditional society changed into a modern society by changing norms, values, and role orientations. Society went through development or modernization as particularism, ascription, and diffuseness were replaced by universalism, achievement, and specificity.

The political variant of this view predicted the creation of a modern society after it passed through more primitive stages of various political-administrative developmental and participation processes. This theory dominated Western social sciences in the 1950s and 1960s.

Therefore, referring to the advocated unilinear and evolutive perspectives, and the endogenous character of the suggested development solutions, critics argue that the modernization concept is a veiled synonym for *Westernization*, namely, the copying or implantation of Western mechanisms and institutions in a Third World context. Nowhere was this as clear as in the field of political science. The political modernity, which was to be achieved by "political development," was modeled on a British type parliamentary democracy or a presidential democracy of the U.S. type. Many U.S. scholars started from the assumption that the American political system was the touchstone for the rest of the world. The rationale for President John F. Kennedy's Peace Corps Act was totally ingrained in this belief.

A more psychological explanation was also available. It claimed that the development of the individual needs of businessmen and policymakers would accelerate the modernization process. As each discipline within the social sciences approached the modernization process from its own point of view, the scholarship on modernization became increasingly specialized. Therefore, according to Tehranian (1977), the orthodox modernization theories fall into one or a combination of the following four categories: stage theories, index theories (of mainly economic variables), differentiation theories (largely advanced by sociologists and political scientists), and diffusion theories (advanced primarily by social psychologists, this theory suggests that the development process starts with the diffusion of certain ideas, motivations, attitudes, or behaviors).

Modernization in East and West

This progress paradigm was avowed at both ends of the ideological spectrum, both by the classic liberal and neo-liberal theorists like Keynes and by the classic Marxist thinkers. Both ideologies have a lot in common. The differences in approach lie on the level of the means, the relative role that is assigned to the market versus the state. But the objective is the same: development on the basis of the Western vision of growth and progress (Mehmet, 1995; Souchou, 1994). The obstacles for development are indicated only in the traditional sectors and are initially only attacked with economic means. Where liberals try to achieve development by means of a massive transfer of capital technology to the Third World, the classic Marxists argue for state intervention, the stimulation of the public sector,

and the establishment of heavy industry as an initial step in the development process—in other words, development according to the Soviet
model. Some scholars (see, e.g., Banerjee, 1985; Cheung, 1996; Kin Chi,
1994; Wong, 1979) claim that even in Mao's China this view on development was of great importance. Since the revolution, there have been two
ideological "lines." The first stands for a highly centralized, technocratic
guidance of society toward modernization; the second is based on the
elimination of the so-called *Three Great Differences* (i.e., city versus country, mental versus manual labor, worker versus peasant), a collective
functioning on the basis of mass democracy, and self-reliance. These
authors state that these lines continue to guide the Chinese development
process in apparently nonantagonistic contradiction.

The Two Step Flow of Communication

In the course of the 1950s, more sociological, psychological, political, and
cultural factors were considered in the view of modernization. The place
and role of communication processes in the modernization paradigm
was also further examined, with the American presidential election campaigns functioning as the theoretical framework.

    These models saw the communication process simply as a mes-
sage going from a sender to a receiver. This hierarchic view of communication can be summarized in Laswell's classic formula: "*Who says What
through Which channel to Whom with What effect?*" (Laswell, 1948) Out of a
study in Erie County, Ohio, of the 1940 U.S. presidential election came the
idea of the so-called "two step flow of communication" (Lazarsfeld,
Berelson, & Gaudet, 1944). Although the researchers expected to find that
the mass media (radio and press) had a great influence on the election,
they concluded that voting decisions were chiefly influenced by personal
contacts and face-to-face persuasion. The first formulation of the two-step-
flow hypothesis was the following: "Ideas often flow from radio and print
to opinion leaders and from these to less active sections of the population"
(Lazarsfeld et al., 1944:151). Thus, two elements are involved: (a) the
notion of a population divided into "active" and "passive" participants, or
"opinion leaders" and *"followers"*; and (b) the notion of a *two step flow of
influence* rather than a direct contact between "stimulus" and "respon-
dent" (or the so-called bullet or hypodermic needle theory). Since that
time the concept and role of "personal influence" has acquired a high status in research on campaigns and diffusions, especially in the United
States. The general conclusion of this line of thought is that mass communication is less likely than personal influence to have a direct effect on
social behavior. Mass communication is important in spreading awareness
of new possibilities and practices, but at the stage at which decisions are

being made about whether to adopt or not to adopt innovations, personal communication is far more likely to be influential.

The Diffusion of Innovations

Everett Rogers (1962, 1983; Rogers & Schoemaker, 1973) is said to be the person who introduced diffusion theory in the context of development. Modernization is here conceived as a process of diffusion whereby individuals move from a traditional way of life to a more complex, more technically developed, and more rapidly changing way of life. Building primarily on sociological research in agrarian societies, Rogers stressed the adoption and diffusion processes of cultural innovation. This approach is therefore concerned with the process of diffusion and adoption of innovations in a more systematic and planned way. He distinguishes between five phases in the diffusion process: awareness, interest, evaluation, trial, and adoption. The role of the mass media is concentrated in the first stage of the process, whereas "personal sources are most important at the evaluation stage in the adoption process" (Rogers, 1962: 99). In the second edition of his work (Rogers & Schoemaker, 1973), there are only four crucial steps left in the process of diffusion and adoption: the knowledge of the innovation itself (*information*), the communication of the innovation (*persuasion*), the decision to adopt or reject the innovation (*adoption or rejection*), and the *confirmation* of the innovation by the individual.

Psychological, Institutional and Technological Explanations

Apart from the diffusion model one can distinguish among three more approaches: a psychosociological, institutional, or technological interpretation of communication and modernization.

The psychosociological or behavioristic perspective on communication and modernization is particularly concerned with individual value and attitude change. Rokeach (1966) defined *attitude* as "a relatively enduring organization of beliefs about an object or situation predisposing one to respond in some preferential manner." "Attitude change" would then be "a change in predisposition, the change being either a change in the organization or structure of beliefs, or a change in the content of one or more of the beliefs entering into the attitude organization" (Rokeach, 1966:530). Central in the view of Daniel Lerner (1958), one of the main representatives of this communication for modernization paradigm, is the concept of *empathy*, that is, "the capacity to see oneself in the other fellow's situation, . . . which is an indispensable skill for people moving out of traditional settings." The major hypothesis of his study was that "high empathic is the predominant personal style only in modern society, which is distinctively industrial, urban, literate and participant" (Lerner, 1958:50). Central in his research design was the individual-psychological capacity of people to adjust to modern environments. Emphatic persons had a higher degree of mobility, meaning a high capacity for change, and were more future oriented and rational than so-called traditional people. Therefore, according to Lerner, mobility stimulates urbanization, which increases literacy, and consequently, economic and political participation as well. Moreover, the role and function of the mass media is carefully examined in this context: "He (i.e., the modern man, JS) places his trust in the mass media rather than in personal media for world news, and prefers national and international news rather than sports, religious or hometown news" (Inkeles & Smith, 1974:112). In other words, the media stimulate, in direct and indirect ways, mobility and economic development; they are the motivators and movers for change and modernization.

Wilbur Schramm (1964), building on Lerner's theory, took a closer look at the connection between mass communication and modernizing practices and institutions. The modern communication media supplement and complement as *mobility multipliers* the oral channels of a traditional society. Their development runs parallel to the development of other institutions of modern society, such as schools and industry, and is closely related to some of the indices of general social and economic growth, such as literacy, per capita income, and urbanization. So Schramm (1964: 263) claimed that "a developing country should give special attention to combining mass media with interpersonal communication." In Schramm's opinion, mass media perform at least three functions: they are the "watchdogs," "policymakers," and "teachers" for change and modernization.

A third, technologically deterministic approach, sees technology as a value-free and politically neutral asset that can be used in every social and historical context. Within this perspective at least four different points of view can be distinguished. A first rather optimistic view shares the conviction that the development and application of technology can resolve all the varied problems of humankind. The second view is at the opposite extreme; namely, technology is the source of all that goes wrong in societies. A third variant expresses the view of technology as the prepotent factor in development; it sees technology as the driving force of development. The fourth variant was popularized by Marshall McLuhan (1964). It views technology as an inexorable force in development, an irresistible as well as an overwhelming force. As McLuhan (1964: VIII) puts it: "Any technology gradually creates a totally new human environment," or, in other words, the medium is the message.

Critique out of Latin America

Under the influence of the actual development programs in most Third World countries, which did not turn out to be as optimistic as the modernization paradigm predicted, early criticisms began to be heard in the 1960s, particularly in Latin America. One of the first scholars who questioned Rostow's model was the Jamaican economist, W.G. Demas. In a review of Rostow's (1953) book Demas wrote:

> The impression made by this book on the present reviewer is that it throws considerable light on the process of the economic evolution in the Western world since the British industrial revolution. Whether it throws light on the problems facing the less developed countries is a more debatable point. (Demas, 1953:188)

In a famous essay, the Mexican sociologist, Rodolfo Stavenhagen (1966), argued that the division into a traditional, agrarian sector and a modern, urban sector was the result of the same development process. In other words, growth and modernization had brought with them greater inequality and underdevelopment. Stavenhagen tested his theses against the situation in Mexico, whereas others came to similar conclusions for Brazil and Chile.

The best known critic of the modernization theory is, without doubt, Gunder Frank (1969). His criticism is fundamental and three-fold: the progress paradigm is empirically untenable, has an inadequate theoretical foundation, and is, in practice, incapable of generating a development process in the Third World. Moreover, critics of the modernization paradigm charge that the complexity of the processes of change is too often ignored; that little attention is paid to the consequences of economic, political, and cultural macro-processes on the local level, and that the resistance against change and modernization cannot be explained only on the basis of traditional value orientations and norms, as many seem to imply. The critique did not only concern modernization theory as such, but the whole (Western) tradition of evolutionism and functionalism of which it is part.

A Plea for a 'Phenomenistic' Communication Orientation

One of the first to criticize the underlying assumptions of the two-step-flow theory was a student of Lazarsfeld and Merton, Joseph Klapper (1960). He made the following tentative generalizations:

1. Mass communication ordinarily does not serve as a necessary and sufficient cause of audience effects, but rather functions among and through a nexus of *mediating factors* and influences.
2. These mediating factors are such that they typically render mass communication a contributory agent, but not the sole cause, in a process of reinforcing existing conditions. Moreover, regardless of the condition in question, and regardless of whether the effect in question is social or individual, the media are *more likely to reinforce than to serve change.*
3. However, on such occasions when mass communication does function in the service of change, one of two conditions is likely to exist. Either the mediating factors will be found to be inoperative and the effect of the media will be found to be direct; or the mediating factors, which normally favor reinforcement, will be found to be themselves impelling toward change.
4. There are certain residual situations in which mass communication seems to produce direct effects, or directly and of itself to serve certain psychosocial functions.
5. The efficacy of mass communication, either as a contributory agent or as an agent of direct effect, is affected by various aspects of the media and communications themselves or of the communication situation (including, e.g., aspects of textual organization, the nature of the source and medium, the existing climate of public opinion, and the like).

Consequently, Klapper recommended and described a new orientation which he named *phenomenistic:* "It is in essence a shift away from the tendency to regard mass communication as a necessary and sufficient cause of audience effects, towards a view of the media as influences, working amid other influences, in a total situation" (1960:5).

A Critical Assessment of the Modernization Paradigm

Since the 1960s, communication and modernization have come under attack from distinct sides in different parts of the world. The most important points of this criticism of the modernization view of communication can be summarized as follows:

1. *Empirically,* what has been studied are primarily specific, quantitatively measurable, short-term, and individual effects that are generalized in a questionable manner. When testing Lerner's thesis, for instance, sever-

al scholars, including Schramm and Ruggels (1967), found little evidence of any single pattern of mass media growth in relation to literacy, urbanization, and per capita income. Rather, the evidence showed that these patterns vary widely by region, environment, or culture. Therefore, Lee (1980: 21), after a detailed review of Lerner's hypotheses, concluded

> Lerner's model is, at least, an approximation of the Western experience and must not be accepted as a developmental inevitability. Lerner's attempt to generalize to a universal process from rather limited historical experience should be treated with great caution. The model is an ethnocentric identification of Western (especially American) middle-class values and images.

2. This approach starts from basic positivistic and behavioristic positions that presuppose a linear, rational sequence of events, planned in advance and with criteria of rationality determined externally. The assumption is that human behavior can be explained in terms of independent, isolated, and direct causalities, as has been the case with the behavioristic stimulus-response model. The process of communication through mass media is compared to the communication process in face-to-face situations. The *transmission of information is* viewed as an isolated and linear activity, with a beginning and an end. This concept, which is directly derived from the mechanistic information theory, is, in my opinion, difficult to transfer to processes of human interaction where the context, in which the transmission or communication process occurs, forms an integrated and substantial part of the overall process:

> There are just too many human and social variables imposing themselves to make for a neat experiment. How can we have a society working normally and realistically and at the same time proceed to isolate one variable (the mass media) and test its impact? We cannot do it—at least I have not been able to find a way. (Merrill, 1971:236)

3. *Positivism* assumes "reality" can be "objectively" and empirically grasped and rarely questions these assumptions. Indeed, the normal mode is to laugh off those who do, or request they empirically invalidate empiricism. In many cultures, however, the immeasurable (i.e., that which cannot be named, described, or understood through any form of reason) is regarded as the primary reality. Rather than a stimulus-response switchbox, people are regarded as active, creative, purposeful creatures. Writing about the Brahmin view of "oneness and subjectivity," Jayaweera (1986: 41) says such challenges

are not likely to be considered seriously by social scientists . . . who purport to live in the real world of empirical science. But then their 'real world' . . . is being shown up to be mostly a fiction, and that, by the most scientific among them, the high-energy physicists.

4. In most Sender-Receiver models the *social context* in which communication takes place is absent. Therefore, according to Thomas (1982:84), "the entire notion of a Sender-Receiver relationship may tend to obscure the process of information transmission as it occurs at the social level of behavior." The notion of *intentionality is* still considered to be a basic aspect of any definition of communication. This notion assumes implicitly—even explicitly in the "uses and gratifications" theory—that each human activity can be explained on the basis of a subjective definition provided by the actors themselves. In other words, human behavior is not conditioned by one's place in a social context (system or subsystem, social group or class), but by the individual's self-defined place and impact on his or her environment. Brown (1979: 9) places the problematique in a more culturalistic and philosophical perspective:

> The one way flow of information establishes an hierarchical relationship between the source (the communicator) and the receiver. The source becomes subject and the receiver object, since contemporary mass communications technology does not allow for immediate feedback from the receiver. This results in dominant and dominated man-man relationships that are consistent with the anti-historical dominant man-environment relationship that constitutes the Western world view of history.

More specifically, the two-step-flow hypothesis neglects the fact that a great amount of information flows directly from the media to users without passing through an opinion leader. Furthermore, the concept of *opinion leader* has proven to be far too simple. It can be said, for instance, that change can and should occur from below by those who need it on their own behalf. Therefore some suggest a so-called 'N-step-flow' model. Lin (1973:206), after a detailed analysis of the literature, concludes

> the overwhelming evidence relative to the indirect tests is that the first-step flow may be true and the second-step flow cannot be confirmed. Because one of the two low-level propositions tested was not confirmed, we may safely conclude that there has been no indirect confirmation of the hypothesis either.

5. As has been argued, little attention is given to sociological and contextual factors except for commercial and ideological reasons. By motivating individuals to aspire to mobility and higher standards of living, the media, in editorial material as well as advertising, are creating the kind of consumer demand that maintains the dependence of Third World economies on the West. Partly because of the high proportion of imported programs, and partly because of imitation, the dominant message of the media is *conservatism, materialism, and conformism.* Even schools and educational TV programs reinforce these kind of ideas. At the same time, by omitting advertising from their research and only concentrating on the content of editorial material, some researchers divert attention away from the principal intended object of the mass media, namely, to produce and market to advertisers the means to complete the marketing of consumer goods and services. Therefore, Dallas Smythe (1981: 250) argues that "in this way, they (that is, these researchers, JS) naturally protect from investigation the blind spot: the audience and its work."

6. As a result of the underlying ethnocentrism and endogenism, one takes for granted that results derived from U.S. campaigns can be extrapolated toward Third World settings, or that the media hardware as well as software has to be imported from "outside." This rather deterministic perspective has had very negative consequences, especially in the field of technology transfer. Therefore, one could argue for an integrated and multidimensional approach in which communication technology has to be considered as a complement to the development process. However, in reality, one often observes that technologies are under the control of those with power and are used in ways consistent with those interests.

7. The static and ahistorical manner of studying communication processes leads to the supposition of a stable social system in which social harmony and integration prevails and class struggle or social conflicts and contradictions are nonexistent. Rao (1986:202) says such research

> equals a long series of empirical-analytical, fragmentary, piecemeal studies, guided by the dichotomy of facts and values, directed by the interested to steer social technology for status-quo purposes, and epistemologically handicapped by the Kantian tradition of confining reality to predefined categories which are applied to it.

In practice, modernization accelerated the growth of a westernized elite structure and of urbanization. With the help of foreign aid, rural backward areas were developed with regard to agriculture, basic education, health, rural transportation, community development, and so on. As a result, government bureaucracies were extended to the major urban centers. The broadcasting system was used mainly for entertainment and news. Radio was a channel for national campaigns to persuade the people about specific and select health and agricultural practices. According to Robert White (1988:9):

> The most significant communication dimension of the modernization design in the developing world has been the rapid improvement of the transportation, which linked rural communities into market towns and regional cities. With improved transportation and sources of electric power, the opening of commercial consumer supply networks stretched out into towns and villages carrying with it the Western consumer culture and pop culture of films, radio and pop music. Although rural people in Bolivia or Sri Lanka may not have attained the consumption styles of American middle-class populations, their life did change profoundly. This was the real face of modernization.

DEPENDENCY AND UNDERDEVELOPMENT

Historical Context

The dependency paradigm played an important role in the movement for a New World Information and Communication Order from the late 1960s to the early 1980s. At that time, the new states in Africa and Asia, and the success of socialist and popular movements in Cuba, China, Chile and other countries, provided the goals for political, economic, and cultural self-determination within the international community of nations. These new nations shared the idea of being independent from the superpowers and moved to form the Non-Aligned Nations. *The Non-Aligned Movement* defined development as political struggle (Nordenstreng and Schiller, 1979).

At a theoretical level, the dependency approach emerged from the convergence of two intellectual traditions: one often called neo-Marxism or structuralism, and the other rooted in the extensive Latin

American debate on development that ultimately formed the ECLA (the United Nations Economic Commission for Latin America) tradition, in which the Argentine economist Raul Prebisch played an important role. Therefore, in contrast to the modernization paradigm, the dependency paradigm was born in Latin America. This does not mean, however, that the modernization paradigm was only debated in that region. For instance, one of the theoretical contributions that influenced the emergence of the dependency theory was provided by an American, Paul Baran (1957), who together with Magdoff (1969) and Sweezy (1981), was spokesperson for the North American *Monthly Review* group. He was one of the first to articulate the thesis that development and underdevelopment are interrelated processes, that is, they are two sides of the same coin. In Baran's view, continued imperialist dependence after the end of the colonial period is ensured first and foremost by the reproduction of socioeconomic and political structures at the Periphery in accordance with the interests of the Center powers. This is the main cause of the chronic backwardness of the developing countries because the main interest of Western monopoly capitalism is to prevent—or, if that is impossible—to slow down and to control the economic development of underdeveloped countries. As Baran uncompromisingly puts it, the irrationality of the present system will not be overcome as long as its basis, the capitalist system, continues to exist.

Beginning in the 1950s, investigations aimed at the theoretical and empirical elaboration of the process of underdevelopment began in Latin America in branches of the United Nations, such as the United Nations Conference on Trade and Development (UNCTAD) and the Economic Commission for Latin America (ECLA). The ECLA economists initially used a picture of the international economic world order that would bring about a polarizing structure between a group of central and peripheral economies, the former with its own dynamic and the latter with a dynamic dependent on the former. ECLA argued in the 1950s for a strategy of industrialization by import substitution, planning and state intervention, and regional integration as the appropriate route to development. This strategy turned out to be inadequate, for although it created a relatively small national middle class, social inequality was aggravated and led to other, more indirect forms of technical and financial dependency.

The "Dependistas"

Initially, the Latin American dependistas set out to unravel the deleterious effects of this relationship of dependency in the Periphery. The major ogre was the "imperialistic" Center. But as the discussion developed, differing theoretical points of view and analytical methods emerged. Some academics turned to French structuralism and also to the European Marxist research tradition, which had fossilized in the 1930s and had not been involved in any significant empirical research since the disappearance of the Austrian Marxist school. After a time, the dependency theories presented themselves as variants in the tradition of Marxist political economy, primarily oriented to the study of dependent and peripheral-capitalistic societies. After several years, a second division occurred. One group of dependistas studied capitalism as one comprehensive world system with mutually changing hierarchies. Others concentrated on the formulation of theories of limited range and empirical studies of important economic sectors and transnational companies, social classes, and so-called "internal colonialism," and political models with analyses of repressive bureaucratic and military regimes and populist experiments.

Some dependistas worked exclusively with economic variables, whereas others also took social and political factors into consideration in their research. Typically, the scientific divisions of economics, political science, sociology, history, and the like, which were a tradition of the West, were less rigidly distinguished in the Latin American division of scientific labor. Some stressed the sectoral and regional oppositions within the dependency system (e.g., Sunkel & Paz, 1970); others (e.g., Cardoso & Faletto, 1969) were more concerned with possible class oppositions. Opinions also differed about one of the central elements in dependency theory, that is, the specific relationship between development and underdevelopment. Whereas Frank (1969) observes what he termed "a development towards underdevelopment," Cardoso and Faletto argued that a certain degree of (dependent) capitalist development is possible.

Three schools of thought can thus be distinguished on the basis of the great variety within dependency theory: the *structuralists*, the *Marxists*, and the *dependistas*. Osvaldo Sunkel, for instance, tried to formulate a global framework with his thesis of transnational capitalism, whereas Cardoso understood the dependency viewpoint more as a specific method for the analysis of countries or regions. Frank sought the primary cause of underdevelopment externally, that is, in the relationship of dependency between the Center and the Periphery. He therefore focuses on analyses of the world system and modes of production. On the other hand, scholars such as Cueva (1977) and Vitale (1979), for instance, argue that the internal structure in the Periphery determines its relationship with the Center. Some Latin American classics that contain detailed analyses of the negative effects of the dependent situation in the Periphery are Cardoso and Faletto (1969), Marini (1973), and Sunkel and Paz (1970).

A Definition of Dependency

Although their approaches vary, all dependistas agree to the basic idea exemplified in the following definition by Dos Santos (1970: 231):

> Dependence is a conditioning situation in which the economies of one group of countries are conditioned by the development and expansion of others. A relationship of interdependence between two or more economies or between such economies and the world trading system becomes a dependent relationship when some countries can expand through self-impulsion while others, being in a dependent position, can only expand as a reflection of the expansion of the dominant countries, which may have positive or negative effects on their immediate development. In either case, the basic situation of dependence causes these countries to be both backward and exploited. Dominant countries are endowed with technological, commercial, capital and socio-political predominance over dependent countries—the form of this predominance varying according to the particular historical moment—and can therefore exploit them, and extract part of the locally produced surplus. Dependence, then, is based upon an international division of labour which allows industrial development to take place in some countries while restricting it in others, whose growth is conditioned by and subjected to the power centers of the world.

Hence, according to the dependency theory, the most important hindrances to development are not the shortage of capital or management, as the modernization theorists contend, but must be sought in the present international system. The obstacles are thus not internal but external. This also means that development in the Center determines and maintains the underdevelopment in the Periphery. The two poles are structurally connected to each other. To remove these external obstacles, each peripheral country should dissociate itself from the world market and opt for a self-reliant development strategy. To make this happen, most scholars advocated that a more-or-less revolutionary political transformation would be necessary. Paul Sweezy, for instance, concludes

> for the vast majority of the peoples of the periphery, dependent development yields not a better life and a brighter future but intensified exploitation and greater misery. The way forward for them is therefore through a revolutionary break with the entire capitalist system, a road that is already being traveled by a growing number of countries in the periphery. (Sweezy, 1981: 80)

Therefore, one may say that the dependency paradigm in general as well as in its subsector of communication, is characterized by a global approach, an emphasis on external factors and regional contradictions, a polarization between development and underdevelopment, a subjectivistic or voluntaristic interpretation of history, and a primarily economically oriented analytical method.

Global Exploitation

Whereas supporters of the modernization and communication paradigm take the nation state as their main framework of reference, dependistas believe in a predominantly international level of analysis. They argue that the domination of the Periphery by the Center occurs through a *combination of power components*—military, economic, political, cultural, and so on. The specific components of the domination of any nation at a given point in time vary from those of another as a result of the variations in several factors, including the resources of the Center powers, the nature or structure of the Periphery nation, and the degree of resistance to domination. Today the cultural and communication components have become of great importance in continuing the dependent relationships because, as many scholars argue, we stand within the rather paradoxical situation that, as the Third World begins to emancipate itself economically and politically, cultural dominance increases. Whereas the former colonialist was largely out to plunder economically profitable areas, the emerging technological evolution of the communication media contributes to a new cultural and ideological dependency. Dependistas not only place transnational communication media among the dominant ideological distributors, but also educational institutes (e.g., universities and research methodologies), political information and propaganda organizations (e.g., the U.S. Information and Communication Agency or the Peace Corps), security agencies (e.g., the Central Intelligence Agency), and even labor unions.

Cultural or Media Imperialism

A relatively old but still very appropriate definition of *media imperialism* is the one used by Oliver Boyd-Barrett (1977:117):

> The process whereby the ownership, structure, distribution or content of the media in any one country are singly or together subject to substantial external pressures from the media interests of any other country or countries without proportionate reciprocation of influence by the country so affected.

Building on this definition and Johan Galtung's (1980) discussion of imperialism, we can distinguish among four *mechanisms of imperialism:* exploitation, penetration through a bridgehead (i.e., the peripheral elite), fragmentation, and marginalization. Although exploitation is seen as the major source of inequality in the world, the three other mechanisms can be conceived as supporting factors. In other words, their influence can be both direct and indirect and of an objectively measurable or subjectively perceptible nature (for an elaboration, see Servaes, 1983). Therefore, we agree with Cees Hamelink (1983), who gives preference to the concept of *cultural synchronization* above the more common cultural imperialism idea. In his opinion, cultural imperialism is the most frequent, but not exclusive, form in which cultural synchronization occurs, for cultural synchronization can take place without any overt imperialistic relations.

Modes of Influence

One can distinguish between different modes of influence by the degree of intentionality which precedes them or with which they are accepted. According to Boyd-Barrett (1977, 1982), the international communication process consists of four major interrelated components: (a) the shape of the communication vehicle, involving a specific technology at the consumer end and a typical range and balance of communication contexts; (b) a set of industrial arrangements for the continuation of media production, involving given structural relationships and financial facilities; (c) a body of values about ideal practice; and (d) specific media contents. Lee (1980), among others, adds a fifth component by emphasizing the importance of historical analysis.

Those scholars who are particularly interested in studying the so-called *shape of the communication vehicle* argue that radio and television were mainly developed in the United States specifically as one-way communication media for domestic distribution. Yet neither of these features were absolutely necessary in technological or market terms. This one-way character of broadcasting media—that is, the goal of nonstop broadcasting, the orientation toward a large mass audience, and the striving for up-to-the-minute news—has become the dominant "shape" for the rest of the world. This standardization is sustained by a technological infrastructure developed largely in the United States. Although some developing countries have begun to manufacture their own receiver sets, all are dependent on imports for the expensive production and distribution technology supplied by transnational companies. In this respect, language also must be seen as more than a vehicle of communication. As is argued later, developing a national language is, very closely tied to the whole question of national identity.

The *organizational and financial structure,* which lies behind the shape of a communication vehicle, is equally subject to export and dissemination. The form of the export or dissemination is not always direct, but may be of an indirect nature through advertising, technology transfer, the control of banking facilities, the dissemination of values or contents, and so on.

It is in the software (programming), management, and evaluation domains where the threats to cultural autonomy and local adaptations are most acute because, once a nation accepts another's concepts of what constitutes "professional," "responsible," or "appropriate" use of any communication medium, its room for cultural adaptation and experimentation may be seriously compromised. *Values of practice* can be either explicit and visible rules of behavior in media organizations or implicit assumptions. Examples of values of practice include the idealized principles of "objectivity" and "impartiality" in newsreporting, assumptions about the most appropriate forms of technology for specific media tasks (e.g., encouraging the adoption of educational TV by developing countries), and assumptions about what constitutes a "good" TV series.

These Western values of practice can be exported and disseminated through at least three mechanisms: the institutional transfer, training and education, and the diffusion of occupational ideologies. The export and dissemination of media products, including form and content, is probably the most visible form of Western domination and penetration in the Periphery. It has resulted in a substantial body of research on general as well as more specific cases which attempt to explore how particular media structures and products function as an importer of cultural and consumption values and a promoter of (foreign, mainly Western) economic and political interests.

Another approach is to look at the genesis of the pattern of dependency. This work must begin with an examination of the role of the mass media in a general international framework of economic and political relations.

Three "Schools" of Cultural Dependency

As has been pointed out previously, the number of people who have been doing research within this dependency perspective is large. Some researchers focus on a particular medium, others on a specific geographic area. Both approaches can also be combined, either from a general standpoint or by way of a case study. However, the most outstanding work in this tradition, and the one that has had the greatest influence on the international scene, is the study by the *International Commission for the Study of Communication Problems,* chaired by Sean MacBride (1980).

We can distinguish among three "schools" within the cultural dependency theory, all of which stem from more general theoretical and methodological approaches within marxism: the culturalists, the political economists, and the structuralists.

First are the *culturalists*, who interpret culture, communication, and ideology rather idealistically and autonomously. They sympathize with the instrumentalist view which states that the media are actively engaged on behalf of a ruling class in suppressing or diverting opposition and reinforcing the ruling ideology. They attempt to establish with some empirical precision the links between state power and media. Representatives of this "conspiracy" theory in the communication field include the works by Tunstall (1977) and Schiller (1969, 1973, 1976).

Second, there are the *political economists*, who, as materialists, are more concerned with the political and economic base in which culture and communication occur. They work within a more structuralist view that analyzes how the economic forces in the media favor resistance to fundamental social change, mainly because of a combination of market forces, operational requirements, and established work practices. The key is ownership; its focus is thus more on economic structures than ideological content of the media. The publications of Hamelink (1977, 1982), Mattelart (1976, 1983), and Schiller (1981, 1984, 1989) exemplify this approach in the international communication field.

Third, there is a more *structuralist view* that concentrates on the ideology and content of the media itself. It differs from the other two schools, especially the political-economist, in the recognition of a greater degree of autonomy of the cultural superstructure from the economic structure. The argument that the superstructure is "only in the last instance" determined by the base, one of the well known statements by the French structuralists, was thoroughly discussed during the 1970s, and led to a number of subdivisions. Most of these theorists are close to the multiplicity paradigm. Therefore, they are presented in the next chapter.

Quantity Equals Quality?

Due mainly to the fact that research in the international communication area is still in its infancy and deals with rather complex realities, one may say that the media imperialism thesis needs further empirical examination. Two citations, derived from critical studies on the dependency approach, illustrate this. Michael Tracey (1985: 44), for instance, concludes that the level of analysis employed for understanding the implications of the mass media at the international, as opposed to the national and individual level, has remained frozen at the stage of intellectual development achieved by communications [sic] research in the first three or four decades of this century.

Ingrid Sarti (1981: 323) arrives at a similar conclusion:

The level of generality of most of the "cultural dependency" literature does not clarify the specific dynamics of the ideological process and its effects on Latin American peoples. The specification of how ideological action takes place, and whom it affects and how, is often overlooked.

Generally, research into cultural dependency patterns is limited to quantitative and objectively measurable results. This kind of study demonstrates *how much* information, entertainment, advertising, capital, software, and hardware are exported, and also the unbalanced communication flow between the Center and the Periphery, which also causes intraregional and intranational disparities (between rural and urban areas, linguistic and ethnic majorities and minorities, rich and poor classes, etc.). The qualitative impact and consequences of this dependency relationship, however, are often overlooked: how these unequal processes affect the culture, ideology, and identity of the local population in the long term. Some exception must be made for the problem of the production of news, which has been analyzed in detail, both quantitatively and qualitatively. But, in view of its specific character, the findings derived are difficult to generalize.

It goes without saying that quantitative research is useful. However, one also needs more detailed information on qualitative aspects, such as cultural and ideological components or the impact of external (mainly Western) influences on local communities. Many authors, among them advocates of the cultural imperialism approach as well, have recognized these shortcomings and urged that the approach be redefined and re-examined. Far from being only a top-down phenomenon, foreign mass media interact with local networks in what can be called a coercive/seductive way and, therefore, have radically different effects and meanings in different cultural settings. Far from being passive recipients, audiences are actively involved in the construction of meaning around the media they consume. Obvious illustrations can be found in studies on pop music and youth subcultures (see, e.g., Amit-Talai & Wulff, 1995; Dowmunt, 1993; Malm & Wallis, 1984; Robinson, Buck, & Cuthbert, 1992). This is one of the basic arguments about communication, as they are developed in the multiplicity paradigm.

Multiple Developments and Structures

One can observe a number of interrelated developments taking place in today's world. First, there is a tendency to import cultural content and develop local imitations. Second, many Third World communicators and organizations are using the imported media technologies to attempt to forge a more autonomous culture, independent of but at the same time borrowing from Western culture. The idea of an international media software convergence is, therefore, rendered weak. Furthermore, as is the case in the West, one observes that in spite of the better production quality, the majority of local audiences prefer programs produced in their own culture. This preference is based on, at least, language and cultural affinity. Therefore, imported media can have a "boomerang effect," conveying precisely the opposite consequence to that presumed by purveyors or observers of the surface. For instance, in his interesting analysis of the role of the Portuguese language during the era of Portuguese colonialism in Africa, De Sousa (1974:125) concludes that "in a dialectic process, the very Portuguese language that served the colonial power as an instrument of alienation was being used against it as a vehicle for ideas that preached emancipation from colonial domination."

At a more structural level, an important transition taking place in many countries is the strengthening of the traditional culture at grass-roots levels. "Traditional" should not be viewed here in a conservative-repressive way but in a progressive-emancipative one.

Therefore, one can observe the *growth of dualistic communication structures*. Adaptation of traditional media for education and social action are encouraged because of their cultural values and their inexpensiveness:

> Folk media are grounded on indigenous culture produced and consumed by members of a group. They reinforce the values of the group. They are visible cultural features, often strictly conventional, by which social relationships and a world view are maintained and defined. They take on many forms and are rich in symbolism. (Ugboajah, 1985:172).

A logical approach for societies and cultures that are concerned about the hegemony of culturally imperialistic Western media, therefore, could be to develop sets of "alternative," "countercultural," or "demythologizing" integrated media that use external media technologies and products for radically different purposes. Video and audiocassettes especially are explicitly mentioned for their "emancipative" potentials. They are rather cheap and consumer friendly, and are difficult to control and censor by authorities. Although they are correct in general, Boyd and Straubhaar (1985:19; see also Boyd, Straubhaar, & Lent, 1989) nevertheless warn about too much optimism:

> While the view of Third World audiences as passive may no longer be accurate, the concepts of media dependency on foreign sources and a one-way flow of information may be exacerbated by VCRs. Given an apparently widespread trend toward entertainment in audience choices, this apparently greater freedom of choice may turn out to be only a greater freedom to select from pirated Western-produced television or film material. Cassettes may extend the present imbalance in the flow of films and television programs from developed to developing countries, even in those countries where such imported content is banned or limited in broadcasting. The tendency of most cassette material to be pirated may also disrupt the existing levels of film and television production in the Third World. When copies are made illegally, no royalties are paid to the producer. This reduces the financial base of Third World production companies. Some Third World governments that count on maintaining political control, at least in part through control of communication media, are also discomfited by VCR's erosion of their control over television content. Not only might viewers ignore government-guided newscasts and development messages, but they may select illegally imported material that is considered immoral or politically subversive.

Intranational Contradictions

Another related problem, which already has been mentioned, concerns the absence of a so-called intranational analysis. Dependistas put too much emphasis on the contradictions at the international level and, accordingly, overlook the existing contradictions at the national level between the interests of the state and the media owners and between the government and the population. For example, in Latin America, Motta (1984: 384-385) points out that state intervention in national affairs has increased overall. This process of capitalist state intervention has produced authoritarian, mostly military, governments that have centralized decision making:

> First, the government controls the creation, distribution, and operation of mass media, as well as the flow of messages. The control takes many forms—station licensing, broadcasting regulations, and censorship. . . . This type of control seeks to depoliticize and demobilize society. Second, the government widely circulates official messages in order to mobilize the population towards state ends and to legitimize itself.

The political result of the dependency view, the critics state, is to turn attention away from these internal class relations and focus it on the Center, which is held responsible for existing social inequality and injustice. Therefore, Van den Bergh (1975:1) states that

> though these theories posit interconnections between international and intranational development processes, they in fact tend to present a uniform image of imperialist domination and dependence: the global "system" is analyzed in its past performance and present structure, but about the specific interconnections between global and domestic processes in the development of particular societies these theories have little to say.

One has to accept that "internal" and "external" factors inhibiting development do not exist independently of each other. Thus, in order to understand and develop a proper strategy one must have an understanding of the class relationships of any particular peripheral social formation and the ways in which these structures articulate with the Center, on the one hand, and the producing classes in the Third World, on the other. To dismiss Third World ruling classes, for example, as mere puppets whose interests are always synonymous with those of the Center is to ignore the realities of a much more complex relationship. The very unevenness and contradictory nature of the capitalist development process necessarily produces a constantly changing relationship.

A Critical Assessment of the Dependency Paradigm

Just as the dependency theory flows from dissatisfaction with the modernization paradigm, the critics of the dependency point of view charge that it is not capable of adequately explaining complex postcolonial reality. Some of the criticism of the more simplistic forms of dependency is even found among dependistas themselves.

Common criticisms are:

1. *A lack of internal class and state analyses within the Periphery that inhibit development of the productive forces.* It is impossible to develop explanatory models without looking at the development of the global framework of power relations as a whole. Cristóbal Kay convincingly shows that Frank's influential thesis—the development of the center countries is due to the exploitation of the peripheral countries and the underdevelopment of the peripheral countries is due to the development of the center countries—has to be abandoned. "Recent historical research has

shown that the development of the center countries was above all due to the internal creation, appropriation and use of the surplus and had less to do with the pillage or exploitation of the peripheral countries" (Kay, 1989: 205).

2. The excessive economic, static, and monolithic approaches are often unable to explain and account for changes in underdeveloped economies over time. This implicitly accepted static and ahistorical view largely ignores the historical manifestations of imperialism and is in danger of becoming mere empty and highly abstract formulae. It prevents dependistas from explaining why and how stages and phases succeed one another and encourages a *"third worldist" ideology* that undermines the potential for international solidarity by lumping together as enemies both the center and the periphery.

3. *A naïve view of production forms* that locates the force of capitalist development and underdevelopment in the transfer of the economic surplus from the Periphery to the Center and, therefore, fails to differentiate capitalist from feudal or other precapitalist modes of controlling the direct producer and appropriating the surplus.

4. An overemphasis on external variables as the cause of underdevelopment and dependency tends to focus on the metropoles and international capital (the so-called *existing international division of labor),* as they are "blamed" for poverty, stagnation, and backwardness, instead of on local class formation. This misdirects political action, leading to pessimism and political complacency on the part of actual or potential revolutionary or liberation movements.

5. *An erroneous evaluation of the internationalization of capital and production* which holds that industrialization and thus "development" cannot take place in the Periphery, in the face of growing evidence to the contrary. The existing obstacles to development are due less to imperialist-Third World relationships than to the internal contradictions in the Periphery itself.

6. Furthermore, Amin (1979) notes that a view of dependency translated in political terms primarily serves the interests and desires of the Third World *bourgeoisie.* While overstressing the contradictions on the international level the dependistas take little account of the contradictions on the national level between the nation-state and the media structure and the government and the public at large.

7. *Most dependistas overlooked the emergence of new social movements and the so-called civil society.* This is a rather sobering observation, especially in view of the traumatic experience of the authoritarian state in Latin America. New social movements, such as anti-authoritarian, religious, ethnic, feminist, regional, anti-institutional, and ecological movements, have emerged in Latin America and other parts of the world (Ekins, 1992; Wignaraja, 1993). These new social movements differ from the old class-based movements, which were the focus of attention of the dependency scholars.

8. In general, most of the dependistas take for granted that, together with the high volume of Western media messages and products, a conservative and capitalistic ideology and a consumption culture is transmitted and established simultaneously. In this sense, they challenge the points of departure of the modernists and, in particular, those of the diffusion theorists who assume that the media play an important role in processes of social change. For this reason, the dependency theory can, with its stress on external explanatory factors, be considered the antithesis of the endogenously oriented modernization paradigm. However, the difference is minimal in regard to the quality of development because both use *mainly economic variables.*

9. The emphasis on a macroperspective, moreover, diverts attention to and interest in the problem of policy. Because of their radicality, as well as the failure of a number of experiments in the 1970s, that were clearly inspired by the dependency point of view (in Chile under Allende, Jamaica under Manley, and Tanzania under Nyerere), the dependistas lost immediate contact in most cases with the state apparatus and influences over policy. On the international level the dependency view affected the discussion of collective self-reliance in the context of a *New International Economic Order* (NIEO) and a *New International Information Order* (NIIO). But some of the weaknesses of the dependency approach also crept into these debates: economic and political nationalism, the stress on external factors, and the lack of concrete development strategies. The counter-strategies for breaking through the situation of dependency and inequality kept step with this: supranational bloc formation, macroindustrial development strategies in one's own country and continent, world coalitions against imperialism, and the striving for world revolution. However, as Blomstrom and Hettne (1984:199) correctly observed, "the 'failure' of self-reliance must be understood in relation to structural and political changes in the world and should not only be explained by inbuilt weaknesses of national development strategies." Therefore, as Friberg and Hettne (1985:212) point out, "Self-reliance is a

difficult option in the context of the present world order." Because of this, McAnany (1983:4) characterized dependency theory as "good on diagnosis of the problem . . . but poor on prescription of the cure." Dependency addressed the causes of underdevelopment but did not provide ways of addressing that underdevelopment.

THE DIFFUSION MODEL

Similarities between Modernization and Dependency Perspectives

Whereas supporters of the modernization theory take the *nation state* as their main framework of reference, dependistas believe in a predominantly international level of analysis. They argue that the domination of the Periphery by the Center occurs through a combination of power components, that is, the military, economics, politics, culture, and so on. The specific components of the domination of any nation at a given point in time vary from those of another as a result of the variations in numerous factors, including the resources of the Center powers, the nature or structure of the Periphery nation, and the degree of resistance to domination. Today cultural and communication components have become of great importance in continuing the dependent relationships because, as many scholars argue, we stand within the rather paradoxical situation that, as the Third World begins to emancipate itself economically and politically, cultural dominance increases. Whereas the former colonialist was largely out to plunder economically profitable areas and showed often only moderate interest in political administration, the technological evolution of the communication media have contributed to a cultural and ideological dependence.

In many ways dependency is the *antithesis* of modernization, but at the level of national communication processes it is a *continuation of* it. As is argued later, communication theories, such as the "diffusion of innovations," the "two-step-flow," or the "extension" approaches, are quite congruent with both the modernization and dependency theory. According to Everett Rogers, one of the leading proponents of the diffusion theory, this perspective implies "that the role of communication was (1) to transfer technological innovations from development agencies to their clients, and (2) to create an appetite for change through raising a 'climate for modernization' among the members of the public" (Rogers, 1986: 49). In the modernization perspective these development agencies were mainly Western; from a dependency perspective they have to be indigenous. However, the role assigned to communication was basically similar: an elitist, vertical or *top-down* process.

A Sender- and Media-centric Model

The 1950s was the decade of the media-centered communication model. One of the earliest and most influential of these came not from the social sciences or humanities, but from information engineering. Shannon and Weaver's linear "source-transmitter-channel-receiver-destination" model eclipsed the earlier, more organic, psychological and sociological approaches. Lasswell, Hofland, Newcomb, Schramm, Westley and Mclean, Berlo, and others each devised a model of communication. For an overview, see McQuail and Windahl (1993). This profusion of communication models may be attributed to three reasons.

First, because they identified communication basically as the transfer of information (*the stimulus*), they were amenable to empirical methodology, thus establishing the basis for communication as a distinct and legitimate science. Second, theorists focused on the efficiency, or effects, of communication (the response), thereby holding vast promise for manipulation or control of message "receivers" by vested interests, or the "sources." Finally, the communication models fit neatly into the nature and mechanics of *mass or mediated communication,* an emergent and powerful force at that time.

Therefore, in these years the discipline of communication was largely, and most importantly, centered on its *effects.* The "bullet" or "hypodermic needle" effects of media were to be a quick and efficient answer to a myriad of social ills. Robert White (1982: 30) writes "This narrow emphasis on media and media effects has also led to a premise . . . that media information is an all-powerful panacea for problems of human and socioeconomic development," not to mention dilemmas of marketing and propaganda. Falling short of exuberant claims, direct effects became limited effects, minimal effects, and conditional effects, coached in a "two-step flow." White (1982:30) continues that the measure of

> successful communication is: . . . the degree to which the passive consumer accepts the message exactly as it is proposed by the source. If the receiver is not getting the message, then something is wrong . . . and research is conducted to increase the persuasiveness of the message or to explain the resistance to the rationality of the message in terms of the irrational attitudes of the receiver.

Therefore, we could characterize this era as sender- and media-centric. The new models, in conjunction with the obsession with the mass media, led to a conceptualization of communication as *something one does to another*. White (1984:2) argues this pro-media, pro-effects, and anti-egalitarian bias of communication theory "has developed largely as an explanation of the power and effects of mass communication and does not provide adequate explanation of the factors of social change leading toward democratization."

SYNTHESIS

1. Similarities characterize the progression of both development and communication theories. Modernization and "bullet," or unilinear communication approaches, both view their mission primarily as "us to them."

2. Derived from a worldview of dominance over one's environment, the Western conception of communication is overwhelmingly oriented toward persuasion. Akin to the modernization paradigm in both theory and ideology, the approach is unidirectional, from the informed "source" to the uninformed "receiver," as reflected in its models. The dependency paradigm adopts this perspective implicitly at the intranational level.

3. The diffusion and development support communication approaches are congruent with the earlier philosophy. They tend to assign responsibility for the problem of underdevelopment to peoples residing in those societies.

4. Mass media play the preeminent role in the campaign of development through communication, and early predictions were of great effects. Bidirectional models and strategies such as feedback were added to render the initial message more effective.

5. Development as modernization and communication as one-way persuasion reached their zenith through the diffusion of innovations, the two-step-flow, and other "social marketing" strategies of attitude and behavior change directed at "underdeveloped" peoples.

6. Mass audiences were "influenced" with predispositions toward development and social institutions. Such media technology has been taken either as the sole solution, the driving force, or as simply a value-free tool in the process of development.

7. Research of the diffusion approach, like the modernization and dependency theories, suffers from an overemphasis on quantitative criteria to the exclusion of social and cultural factors. As a result, the manner in which foreign media hardware and software interact within a cultural context is largely unexplored.

2

The Best of Both
World(view)s: Multiplicity

The hallmark of modern consciousness, as I have been insisting to the point of obsession, is its enormous multiplicity. For our time and forward, the image of a general orientation, perspective, *Weltanschauung*, growing out of humanistic studies (or, for that matter, out of scientific ones) and shaping the direction of culture is a chimera. Not only is the class basis for such a unitary "humanism" completely absent, gone with a lot of other things like adequate bathtubs and comfortable taxis, but, even more important, the agreement on the foundations of scholarly authority, old books and old manners, has disappeared. If the sort of ethnography of thought work I have here projected is in fact carried out, it will, I am sure, but strengthen this conclusion. It will deepen even further our sense of the radical variousness of the way we think now, because it will extend our perception of that variousness beyond the merely professional realms of subject matter, method, technique, scholarly tradition, and the like, to the larger framework of our moral existence. The conception of a "new humanism," of forging some general "the best that is being thought and said" ideology and working it into the curriculum, will then seem not merely implausible but utopian altogether. Possibly, indeed, a bit worrisome.
—Clifford Geertz (1983:161)

Since the demarcation of the First, Second, and Third Worlds is breaking down and the cross-over center-periphery can be found in every region, there is a need for a new concept of development that emphasizes *cultural identity, empowerment and multidimensionality*. The concept of "another development" was first articulated in the industrialized nations of northern Europe, particularly by the Dag Hammarskjold Foundation in Sweden and the Green political movement in Germany. This does not mean, however, that the "another development" concept and perspective is Western. It can also be traced back to Third World environments. For example, some countries may be dependent economically but have greater cultural "power" in the region. Therefore, one can observe changes and developments of a more cultural and moral nature. The present-day world, in general as well as in its distinct regional and national entities, is confronted with multifaceted crises. Apart from the obvious economic and financial crisis, one could also refer to social, ideological, moral, political, ethnic, ecological, and security crises. In other words, the previously held dependency perspective has become more difficult to support because of the growing interdependency of regions, nations and communities.

As a result, also at a more theoretical level changes are also apparent. In the Latin American context, for instance, Jesus Martin-Barbero (1993a:187) observes that

> over the last few years a Latin American movement, dissolving pseudotheoretical issues and cutting through ideological inertias, has opened up a new way of thinking about the constitution of mass society, namely, from the perspective of transformations in subalternate cultures. Communication in Latin America has been profoundly affected by external transnationalization but also by the emergence of new social actors and new cultural identities. Thus, communication has become a strategic arena for the analysis of the obstacles and contradictions that move these societies, now at the crossroads between accelerated underdevelopment and compulsive modernization. Because communication is the meeting point of so many new conflicting and integrating forces, the center of the debate has shifted from media to mediations. Here, mediations refer especially to the articulations between communication practices and social movements and the articulation of different tempos of development with the plurality of cultural matrices.

Therefore, from the criticism of these two paradigms, particularly that of the dependency approach, a new viewpoint on development is emerging. The common starting point here is the examination of the changes from bottom-up, from the self-development of the local community. The basic assumption is that there are no societies that function completely autonomously and are completely self-sufficient, nor are there any communities whose development is exclusively determined by external factors. *Every society is dependent in one way or another, both in form and in degree.* Thus, a framework was sought within which both the Center and the Periphery could be studied separately and in their mutual relationship.

Interdependency

The concept of *interdependency* again loomed up in this context. This, however, is an ambiguous concept that can be misleading. For some, the idea of interdependency evokes a kind of community, a striving for integration that underlies the modernization paradigm. This is, for instance, very apparent in the so-called Brandt Report (1980) on the North-South relationships. For others, it is a more elaborated view of dependency expressing a more explicit structure that transcends the Center-Periphery dichotomy. The factors that made this elaboration necessary are, for example, the increased tensions within the Center (the so-called *interimperialistic rivalry)*; industrialization in the Periphery and the accompanying deindustrialization until a certain degree and in certain sectors in the Center (e.g., labor intensive sectors); the rise of regional powers such as Brazil and India, and the changes in capital flows; the international investment pattern, and technical developments. In particular; the role of transnational enterprises and national states within a superstructural world system urgently required rethinking. Rosenau (1980:2) observes:

> Ironically, in other words, the trend toward interdependence has highlighted the virtues of historic values associated with interdependence, thereby giving rise to two powerful and yet contradictory processes on the global scene: an integrative process whereby societies are becoming increasingly dependent on each other and a disintegrative process whereby groups within societies are increasingly demanding autonomy for themselves.

He adds: "Whichever of these processes ultimately prevails (or even if they both remain equally powerful for decades), it seems clear that they represent a transformation, even a breakdown of the nation-state system as it has existed throughout the last four centuries." For a more detailed discussion on globalization and localization issues, see Albrow & King (1990), Held (1995), King (1991), Miller (1995), Servaes & Lie (1997), Sklair (1991).

Imagined Communities and Nationhood

As discussed earlier, the notion of *imagined communities* (Anderson, 1983) emphasizes the centrality of the idea that nationhood exists as a system of cultural signification. From this perspective, nationhood is at the point of intersection with a plurality of discourses related to geography, history, culture, politics, ideology, ethnicity, religion, materiality, economics, and the social. Therefore, the *discourse of nationhood* can best be understood in relation to boundedness, continuities and discontinuities, unity in plurality, the authority of the past, and the imperatives of the present.

It moves along two interesting axes: space and time. In terms of the space axis, the dominant question is territorial sovereignty; for the time axis, the central question is the velocity of history, the continuity with the past. The way these two axes interact produces results that bear directly and challengingly on the problematic of nationhood. In other words: "What is important to bear in mind is that the manifold issues related to these axes are man-made and not natural givens. They are human constructs seeking the status of the natural" (Dissanayake, 1994:IX). Though Wimal Dissanayake borrows heavily from Anderson, he is not blind to his conceptual weaknesses: "That it (Anderson's theory, JS) pays inadequate attention to the materialities and overlooks discontinuities of history; it also gives short shrift to the political character of nationhood and the role ethnic loyalties and religious affiliations may have played in the construction of nationhood" (Dissanayake, 1994: xii). Therefore, Dissanayake complements his thinking on nationhood with the contributions of a number of other contemporary thinkers: Elie Kedourie, Ernest Gellner, Eric Hobsbawm, Anthony Giddens, and Partha Chatterjee. He acknowledges that their diverse formulations and theorizations of nationhood only serve to underline the complex and contested discursive terrain that it undoubtedly is, and he concludes that "national identity" needs to be discussed at four interconnected levels: the local, national, regional, and global.

Integral Development

At the same time, one can also observe changes and developments of a more cultural and moral nature. The present-day world, in general as well as in its distinct regional and national entities, is confronted with multifaceted crises. Apart from the obvious economic and financial crises, there are social, ideological, moral, political, ecological, and security crises.

In contrast with the more economical and politically oriented approach in the modernization and dependency paradigms, the central idea here is that there is no universal development model, that development is an integral, multidimensional, and dialectic process that can differ from society to society. In other words, each society must attempt to delineate its own strategy to development. This implies that the development problem is a relative one and that no one nation can contend that it is "developed" in every respect. Therefore, I believe that the scope and degree of interdependency must be studied in relationship with the content of the concept of development. Where the previous paradigms did not succeed in reconciling economic growth with social justice, the attempt is now being made to approach problems of freedom and justice from the relationship of tension between the individual and the society, and limits of growth are seen as inherent to the interaction between society and nature.

In what follows, three interrelated dialectic-analytical trends are discussed in more detail. Together, these trends, in my opinion, constitute the essence of the future debate on communication for development: (a) the analysis of the many faces of power, culture and ideology with regard to communication and development; (b) the relationships between distinct local, national and extern-national levels, social actors and sectors; and (c) the search for communication for development with "another" content.

The different communication for development approaches that build on the multiplicity paradigm can be grouped together under the participatory model.

TOWARD A "MULTIDIMENSIONAL" DEVELOPMENT AND COMMUNICATION MODEL

The impetus for a globalization of the development theories in the context of a worldwide research approach came from discussions conducted in the dependency school and from those Marxist circles that, under the influence of structuralism and anthropology, again took up the themes of forms of production, the so-called internalization of capital, and the ideological debate.

Multiplicity in One World

I briefly overview two interdisciplinary theories, which are substantial for our topic: the mainly economic world-system analysis and the anthropological "coupling" of production forms approach.

Although even some dependistas moved from the analysis of dependency to the study of *global accumulation or* world accumulation, the best known representative of the world-system analysis is Immanuel Wallerstein (1979, 1983). Like the dependistas, Wallerstein describes the world system in a rather static way by arguing that the fundamental traits of the capitalist world system since the 16th century have remained virtually unchanged. At the same time, however, he transcends the dependency framework when he states that a small number of Center countries enter into functional relationships with peripheral and semi-peripheral nations, that the developmental dynamic is determined internally and not externally, and that the hope for fundamental changes in certain states can be called almost nonexistent so long as the world capitalist system does not collapse. The latter, he immediately adds, is a long-term perspective due to "the limited possibilities of transformation within the capitalist world-economy" (Wallerstein, 1979: 66).

A number of Marxists, on the other hand, continue to examine the class struggle within national borders; the varying, contiguous forms of production; the distinction between industrial and commercial capital, populist, and nationalist trends; and the functioning of ideologies as social processes. Confronted with the findings of dependistas and world-system analysts, which question their basic ideas about, for instance, relations between classes and nations, some admit that these issues "remain largely unexplored and hence unresolved problems in sociological theory" (Vogler, 1985: XI). Few, however, reach the conclusion to substantially adjust their theoretical framework. Those who do, like Taylor (1979), point out the major shortcomings in classic Marxist approaches, which are considered to be too mechanistic and deterministic. They therefore advocate research that concentrates on the so-called articulation of modes of production:

> The contemporary reality . . . must be analyzed from within historical materialism as a social formation which is dominated by an articulation of (at least) two modes of production—a capitalist and a non-capitalist mode—in which the former is, or is becoming, increasingly dominant over the other. (Taylor, 1979:101-102)

Therefore, one returns to the old discussion on Asiatic or precapitalist modes of production.

It is not surprising that this view prevails among anthropologists, especially those who are doing research in Africa (Monga, 1994; Nyamnjoh, 1994). These authors criticize the interpretations of the first group because it seems to stress onesidedly the dynamic of the capitalist system as a universally explanatory principle. From their point of view, however, it is more a matter of a multiple dynamic: in the margin of the capitalist system, all kinds of pre- or noncapitalist organizational patterns maintain their own coherency and significance.

In Africa, old forms of organization, however much transformed, still seem to present a real obstacle to the effects of capitalist relationships. These forms of economic organization and production are often defined by the term *conviviality*. In this respect, two research areas from the work of the anthropologists are important: their studies on the organization and development of local groups, communities, and social structures in general; and their analyses of the so-called "informal sectors" in society. They stress the special autonomy of superstructural institutions in the precapital forms of production and also the coupling of forms of production and its particular role after decolonization has gained the upper hand. From this position, it appears that all kinds of noneconomic factors—such as cultural principles like kinship and religion, which gave shape to the old forms of production—still have a direct influence on this coupling (for a critical overview, see Coquery-Vidrovitch & Nedelec, 1991; De Villers, 1992; Kabra, 1995; Kelsall, 1995).

A fascinating integration of the two viewpoints is given by Oswaldo Sunkel and Edmundo Fuenzalida (1980). Their *transnationalization thesis* can be summarized in four points:

1. The capitalist system has evolved in recent decades from an international to a transnational or global system with the transnational corporations as the most significant actors.
2. The most striking feature of the actual system is the polarized development of transnationalization on the one hand, and national disintegration on the other.
3. Of particular interest is the emphasis on culture, which is the main stimulator of a new transnational, community of people from different nations but with similar values and ideas, as well as patterns of behavior.
4. The ultimate result is the parallel existence of varying sectors within the same national borders. In other words, the national societies are generating a variety of counter-processes that assert national and/or subnational values, sometimes reactionary and sometimes progressive.

It is the concentration on this dialectic interaction between (mainly transnational and/or global) integration and (mainly national) disintegration that leads to liberating as well as oppressive processes on the various levels of the societal system. In Servaes (1987), I combined an adjusted version of Sunkel and Fuenzalida's transnationalization thesis with Johan Galtung's (1980) six types, or aspects, of (possible) dependent relationships in order to achieve a conceptual framework for the analysis of relationships among *processes of integration, disintegration, and reintegration* at the various levels of a specific societal system, and for the study of the internal versus external variables and/or positive versus negative factors that determine the processes of power and empowerment in society. In a later publication Sunkel arrived at similar observations (see Sunkel, 1993).

Power and Interests

As noted earlier, another important aspect of the development debate is the concept of *power*. Although most social scientists reckon that the power concept is essential for the understanding of social reality, it is often not defined and, therefore, it is differently interpreted. This confusion is mainly due to the multidimensionality of the concept of power . itself.

The traditional interpretation of the power concept refers to material or immaterial perceived possessions in a narrow as well as a broad meaning, that is, a property or *possession* that is handled by actors in a mainly intentional, direct, or indirect manner. Max Weber's (1983) definition, which describes power as the capability of one individual or social group to impose its will, despite the objections of others, is often quoted in this context. One can find such a static perception in different functionalist as well as classic-Marxist theories. In such definitions power is onesidedly situated with the so-called "powerholders." Their position of power rests on a conflict relationship that can only be "resolved" by consensus on one side or by struggle on the other.

Critical social-philosophers and poststructuralists have pointed out the limitations of such a power concept. Michel Foucault, Anthony Giddens, and Jürgen Habermas, for example, state that the relationship between power and conflict is of an accidental nature. While not denying the fact that the exercise of power is an asymmetrical phenomenon, they instead believe that power is "all embracing" and "all mighty" and has to be coupled with the concept of 'interest'. Power and conflict often go together, so they argue, but this union is not because one logically implies the other, but because power has to be seen in concert with the pursuit of interest. Although power is a characteristic of every form of human interaction, contrapositions of interests are not, meaning that power is a dual concept that can be interpreted in two ways.

Looking at power in a *static* way, there are those who have power and those who endure power. But if interpreted in a *dynamic* way, one could say that even the powerless exercise power over the powerful. Thus, power concerns the possible effectuated and asymmetrically divided ability of one actor (*powerholder*) to put into order, inside a specific interaction system, the alternatives of actions of one or more actors (*power subjects*). Power centers around the capability to regulate and structure the actions inside asymmetrical relations. In other words, to exercise power is not the same as suppression.

With regard to this topic, three general problem areas can be discerned: (a) the mutual dependency between the macrolevel of the society or a given structure and the microlevel of the social actions involved; (b) the position and the autonomy of organized subjects; and (c) the relationship of domination, dependency, and subordination versus liberation, selective participation, and emancipation of power and interest contrapositions. These problem areas have been heavily debated in present social-scientific and social-philosophical circles and have resulted in a variety of disciplines and theories. One, substantial problem area, the debate on ideology is explored later.

To illustrate that power can be exercised in positive-liberative as well as negative-repressive ways, on the one hand, and to interpret the earlier discussion in the context of my topic on the other, I elaborate on the work of two important scholars—Pierre Bourdieu and Jurgen Habermas—who both extensively studied the relationship between society and culture.

The two basic concepts of Habermas' (1981, 1985, 1986, 1988) research program are *rationality* and *communication*. Habermas contends that the fundamental question of how a social order is possible can be answered by referring to the common definitions of reality that are created in everyday communication. Normative elements play a role here in two ways. First, these common definitions of reality are not only related to the objective data of the situation in which the social actors are located but to the norms that apply obligatorily to them and the veracity of their expressions. Second, mutual agreement is developed in everyday intercourse by the introduction of reference frames that are, in principle, open to criticism. *Communicative action is*, thus, internally related with symmetrical, power-free argumentation and with discussion on the tenability of points of departure.

Modern societies are characterized by polarization of two domains: first, the "life world" (Lebenswelt)—the private spheres, which depend on communicative action and dialogical discourse—and, second, the "systems" of the economy and the state, which rest on goal-oriented, rational action and are dominated by money and power. The independence of the two domains with respect to each other that has emerged in Western societies and seems to be spreading throughout the world must, according to Habermas, be judged in principle positively because this independence forms the basis for the material reproduction of societies. Under capitalist relationships, however, this independence of the economy and the state with respect to the life world has been matched by a kind of *colonization* of the life world by these independent subsystems. Habermas intends by this that the economy and the state violently penetrate the life world and intervene with money and power in problems that only can be resolved by communicative action, that is, by means of dialogical discourse and mutual accord.

The new social movements in the West, such as the women's movement, the environmental movement, and the peace movement, are, according to Habermas, not primarily oriented to problems that concern the distribution of material wealth but resist this colonization of the life world. They advocate a society in which the blind dynamic and the imperialism of the independent subsystems of economy and state are subject to the normative restrictions of a life world in which communication processes can again develop in full freedom.

With respect to the role of mass media, the theory of communicative action reveals the ambivalent character of mass communication. On the one hand, these media create an hierarchicalization of the communicative processes because they create lines of communication from the Center to the Periphery and from top to bottom. But, on the other hand, the mass media are directly linked to the rational structure of the communicative action. They are not detached from it, like the subsystems of power and money, but they embody generalized forms of communication. In so doing, they remain, for their functioning, ultimately dependent on bipolar positions of communicatively gifted actors. Herein, according to Habermas, lies their ambivalence, which was not perceived by the Frankfurt School. A pluralistic and democratic use of mass media is far from being achieved at this time, he states, but it does belong to the real possibilities of the mass media.

Habermas' theory of communicative action could provide possibilities for shifting the frontier to interactive planning, which explicitly takes up the problem of the relationship between authority and society. More particularly, it envisions a number of new, collective decision-making forms. In this sense, this theory offers no task that is strictly and forever defined. Rather, it must be seen as a directive for a new political praxis, a criterion against which the organization of both the political and the social life can be tested and judged. (For critical assessments of Habermas' work, see Forester [1988, 1989, 1992, 1993], Mumby [1982], Pasewark [1986] or Wenzel & Hochmuth [1989].

Although Habermas expresses sympathy for the possibilities of modern subjectivity, the so-called French poststructuralists take a rather pessimistic stand. They express serious doubts about the dialectic character of rationality and envision subjects to be conditioned by the mechanisms of the "all embracing" power.

Pierre Bourdieu (1979, 1980, 1981), who began his scientific career as an ethnologist in Algeria, is particularly important in this context for his sociocultural analyses of the differences in social practices and mediation as a symbolic system. His research interest is primarily in cultural and symbolic systems as the impetus in the class struggle. Instead of economic preponderance, the dominant classes call on an ideological and symbolic preponderance not only to maintain their position in the social hierarchy but to justify it. This *symbolic system* has a "symbolic power" because it is capable of construing reality in a directed manner. Bourdieu contends that this symbolic power does not lie in the symbolic system itself, but in the social relationship between those who exercise the power and those who are subject to it.

Thus, he sets out to find the social relationships in which the symbolic system is active, for example, in education, fashion, politics, language, or the media. He points out that every symbolic system is determined in two ways: by general consistencies of material production and the class oppositions that are a reflection of it, and by the specific interests of those who produce the symbolic system. Symbolic power thus functions "unconsciously," "spontaneously," and "voluntarily" as the legitimation criterion for existing social and economic power relationships and leads to a hierarchy of cultural "tastes" and "ways of life."

Therefore, Bourdieu, unlike Habermas, is extremely skeptical about the possibilities of a "power-free communication." For Bourdieu, language is not a means for achieving consensus but one of the forms in which the borders between the different classes are set. These borders are, as it were, frozen in the thought of the citizen so that, according to Bourdieu, no politically desirable course changes can be achieved via "communicative action."

TOWARD A "CULTURALISTIC" COMMUNICATION FOR DEVELOPMENT MODEL

Both the social sciences in general, and the development and communication theories, specifically, are now showing more interest in the impact and effects of aspects of the so-called "superstructure" than in previous times. This interest is generally referred to as the *ideology debate* in which one builds on Althusser's Ideological State Apparatuses concept, Poulantzas' economic-political-ideological class- and state-concept, the Gramscian study of historical social formations and his focus on hegemony, the Lukacsian problematic of revolutionary class consciousness as the key to social change, Foucault's theses on the order of discourse and power in society, the Weberian view on legitimation, and elements from semiotics and psychoanalysis.

Ideology and Culture

In the field of culture and ideology one may speak of a multiplicity in approaches and theories. Several authors have been trying to bring some order to this variety. In general, these authors concentrate more on one dimension of communication problems, namely, the relationship between ideology/culture and power. I distinguish among three trends: a structuralist-materialist, a structuralist-culturalist, and anthropological.

According to authors like Laclau and Mouffe (1985), Madrid (1983), Thernborn (1980), and Thompson (1984), who can be identified as representatives of the first trend, the task of a *materialistic theory of ideology* is twofold: to investigate the origin and change of ideologies and to devise a relational schema indicating dominance, interdependence, and subordination between ideologies. Research in the origin and change of ideologies must start with an analysis of the processes of change in the structure of a particular society in relationship to its natural environment, that is, the reproduction conditions of already present ideologies must be identified. These changes form the material foundation for the rise of new ideologies. The ideological order of power, control, and dominance present in every society has two components: maintenance of a certain discourse and the use of nondiscursive, material forms of reward and sanction. This ideological order is structured in ideological apparatuses, which can be considered clusters of discourse and material practices. Because these ideological apparatuses are the result of the class struggle, a distinction must be made between the ideological, dominating apparatuses of the ruling class and the ideological counter-apparatuses of the suppressed class.

The second trend has become well-known through studies done at the Center for Contemporary Cultural Studies in Birmingham (for a representative survey, see Clarke, Critcher, & Johnson 1979; and Hall, 1985; Hall, Hobson, Lowe, & Willis, 1980; Hall & DuGay, 1996). The attempt is made to expand the concept of culture to the ways of life of all classes and to select these *lived cultures* as the object of study. Thus, they reject, with their new definition of culture, the distinction between "high" and "low" cultures, and give descriptions from the bottom with a minimum of theoretical clarity and consistency. Emphasis is also placed on texts as the object of culture analysis. They reduce meanings to the social experiences of an individual or a collective that form the origin of each assignation of meaning. Thus, it is held that the various historical cultural contents express the communal values and worldview of class. The concepts of conscientization, experience, and collective action play an important role here.

The third, and as yet the least profiled trend, can be called the *anthropological trend* because it draws its concepts and analytical methods from cultural anthropology and ethnology. One of the first authors to translate this problem into the sphere of communication was Roland Barthes. In recent years, this trend has seen a renewal in the Anglosaxon world with the publications of Ang (1996), Carey (1988), Dahlgren (1995), Jameson (1981), Larrain (1994), Masterman (1984), Silverstone (1981, 1995), Thompson (1990, 1995), and, in particular, Jesus Martin-Barbero (1987, 1993a & b). This group proceeds from the thesis that a particular culture must be studied in its totality, that is, as a way of life with a specific meaning, value, and belief pattern that typifies that particular society or local entity. The communication media are then considered institutions by which the new meaning systems are transmitted in a ritual manner in a community. Media like television thus fulfill the role of the tellers of myths and stories. The culture of a nation is interpreted as structured around myths that can be both cosmic and national. They function on a nonintentional, symbolic level and only come to the surface at times of national crisis, rapid social change, or exterior threat.

In my opinion, the best, and until now most powerful example of such an analysis, is undertaken by the Colombian researcher, Jesus Martin-Barbero (1987, 1993a & b). He eloquently describes the process in which the narrative discourse of media adapts to the popular narrative tradition of myth and melodrama, and the way audiences learn to recognize their collective cultural identity in the media discourse. Martin-Barbero analyses this mediation process in a historical perspective and elaborates on the chemistry that takes place between the processes of media production and the daily routine of media consumption in the context of the family, the community, and the nation in Latin America.

This evolution in the scientific discussion of culture and ideology has been translated into the more general development context by a number of Latin Americans (e.g., Canclini, 1982, 1993; Escobar, 1994), among whom the Venezuelan Antonio Pasquali (1970, 1980) stands out. His view of the mass media and the national culture, and his recommendation that communication contributes to a dialogue of and between cultures, is especially relevant to our discussion. He starts from the thesis that the present world communication system is in a state of change and crisis that is being caused by economic, political, and other conflicts. The objects of the science of communication are thus not limited to being part of the cultural superstructure but are an essential component of the human potential for coexistence. Today, this is being manipulated substantially by economic, political, and cultural powers. Therefore, the science of communication bears a great intellectual responsibility: "Whether we like it or not, we are now the most critical and perhaps the most important sector of the social reflection on the way the world is developing" (Pasquali, 1980: 162, my translation). Therefore, on the basis of findings of cultural anthropology, the communication specialist must, as an operational aim, redefine the concept of *national culture*. This means a concept generic in itself, sometimes with ideological and sometimes with utopian implications, and even, at the extremes, with reactionary connotations. Within the framework of the aspirations to a greater rationality in the goals for which mass communication media must aim, the concept of *national culture* is operative for at least three reasons: First, the recognition of equal dignity for all cultures must, before anything else, follow the acceptance of the very existence of the so-called cultures that themselves have their own ratio cognoscenti in the national framework. Second, culture is a global and patrimonial concept that includes, in its essential forms, values that are abstract and ill-defined, but transferable. The alienation of a culture always proceeds from the abstract to the concrete, and, in this operation, the mass media play an essential role. Third, there is an apparent contradiction between the universalism of our time, favored in its lower and authoritarian forms as manipulated cosmopolitanism by the mass media, and the emergence of the concept of *nation*. This concept must be assumed to be positive because it allows the formerly underprivileged to reach a critical mass that makes it possible for them to act as real interlocutors. In this case, Pasquali foresees the concept of *nation* will be destined to play an important role in the formulation of the future laws of international communication.

In order to analyze the type of relationship that links the mass media and the national culture, Pasquali lists eight research variables: the input and output of communication in order to determine the degree of cultural dependency; the national regime of the structure and use of mass media; the economic regime and production relationships in mass media at the national level; the law of centrifugal acceleration of cultural pollution; the national levels of access and participation; the privileged use of mass media; the sources and forms of acculturation; and the local cultural collaborators in dependency. Although communication research has generated a number of studies on various topics, it does not seem to have developed a sufficient amount of theoretical and practical knowledge to facilitate the specific analysis of mass media/national culture relationships. Pasquali assumes that, in the future, the demand for research focused on this area will increase considerably, depending on decisions made by countries in the framework of large international organizations and within their frontiers. Therefore, he again stresses the ethical-political dimension of the problem. In the face of an increasing demand for research on new cultural and communication policies, the responsibility borne by the intellectual will increase proportionately. It will depend partly on whether attempts at cultural liberation succeed or fail, whether new policies lean toward autarchy or cosmopolitanism, and whether they can avoid extremes and be rational, moderate, and democratic.

Culture and Modes of Communication

There are different kinds of knowledge: some regularities in human behavior are explainable on the basis of culture-specific laws, others on the basis of generally valid laws. Because their epistemological status differs, these two kinds of knowledge also imply two kinds of rules (Hofstede, 1980, 1991; Kloos, 1984). In the case of *culture-specific* rules, one speaks of moral rules that have a normative character; the generally applicable laws have a more *natural-scientific* character. The laws of the forms of production, for example, cannot be changed; the laws that underlay the production relationships, however, may well be changed. Another essential feature of culture is its dynamic character:

> Culture is the dynamic synthesis, both at the consciousness level of the individual or the collectivity, of the historically conceived material or spiritual reality of a society or social group. This dynamic synthesis conditions the relationships between mankind and nature as well as between people and between social categories (institutions). Cultural manifestations are the distinct forms through which this synthesis is expressed, individually and collectively, at each stage of development of the given society or social group. (Cabral, 1980:186, my translation)

Edward Hall (1973, 1976) distinguishes among three states that together constitute processes of cultural change; a formal, an informal, and a technical state. "These states are constantly fluid, shifting one into the other—formal activity tends to become informal, informal tends toward the technical, and very often the technical will take on the trappings of a new formal system" (Hall, 1973: 90). As a classical example of these constantly shifting formal, informal, and technical states, one often refers to the concept of *time* in different cultures.

This dynamic character of a culture finds good expression in an historical analysis.

> Social change takes place more like the building of a web than the building of a chain. Many different causal strands cross and recross to form intricate designs in which each element has an independent role to play to some extent, But this does not mean that all of the strands are of equal weight; nor does it mean that the web has no center or that it lacks an overall structure. (Harris, 1987:12)

Such a study has been conducted by Edward Said (1985). His captivating overview of the way in which Asian societies and philosophies throughout the ages were perceived by the West starts from the thesis:

> That the essential aspects of modern Orientalist theory and praxis (from which present-day Orientalism derives) can be understood, not as a sudden access of objective knowledge about the Orient, but as a set of structures inherited from the past, secularized, redisposed, and re-formed by such disciplines as philology, which in turn were naturalized, modernized, and laicized substitutes for (or versions of) Christian supernaturalism. In the form of new texts and ideas, the East was accommodated to these structures. (Said, 1985:122)

To summarize the new perspective on culture previously described in the Introduction, I would like to emphasize once again that culture is not only the visible, non-natural environment of the person, but primarily his or her normative context. As culture mediates all human perceptions of nature, an understanding of these mediations is a much more important key to explaining human events than is mere knowledge of such limits. In other words, the natural world is also part of our culture, as are ideas and values.

> Since every culture is a more or less integrated system of cultural goods, realizing a more or less integrated value system, change in every culture must in the last analysis reflect change in the value system. In the framework of the dialectical interplay between subjective and objective forces within a culture, change in value system can originate in the human agents or in the cultural goods. In both, the change can be the result of the operation of immanent forces or the result of intervention by forces outside the culture. (Alisjahbana, 1974: 223)

In the patterning of their social existence, people continually make principally unconscious choices that are directed by applicable intracultural values and options. The social reality can then be seen as a reality constituted and cultivated on the basis of particular values, a reality in which the value system and the social system are completely interwoven and imbued with the activity of each other. Cultures derive an "identity" from the fact that a common worldview and ethos is active in the network of institutions or apparatuses of which they consist. This "identity" differs from culture to culture. Consequently, honor, power, love, and fear are defined and enacted through cultural forms that may differ widely from one culture to another. The task for a researcher is to reveal these distinctive structures of meaning. In other words, in the study of concrete examples of cultural identity, one must be attentive to the following aspects: (a) the characteristics and dimensions of the cultural reference framework (i.e., the worldview, the ethos, and their symbolic representation); (b) the interaction and interrelation with the environment of power and interests; and (c) the "ideological apparatuses" by which the cultural reference framework is produced and through which it is at the same time disseminated.

The relationship between culture and development has often been discussed in terms of *convergence*. Both the so-called modernization and dependency paradigms, for obviously quite opposite reasons, start from the assumption that as societies develop, they loose their separate identities and cultural differences and tend to converge toward one common type of society. This is considered to be a result of industrialization and urbanization, which are identified as the main causes of this historical movement from diversity toward conformity, toward one global village. This world is characterized by a secular culture and decline of religion; considerable geographic and social mobility; the predominance of nuclear families; a high division of labor; with growing levels of formal education, a productive economy based on industry; and so on. However, in my opinion, this reflects an abstract and idealized image of a fully industrialized modern society. In the case of the modernization paradigm it also has a Western ethnocentric bias toward the convergence theory.

Newer research findings, derived from anthropological and cultural studies, suggest that these assumptions and claims are highly questionable (see, e.g., Friedman, 1994; Hall & DuGay, 1996; Hannerz, 1987, 1992; Lull, 1995; Marcus & Fisher, 1986; Strathern, 1995; UNESCO, 1995). When discussing industrialization and modernization in the Third World, these approaches come to the conclusion that modernization does not necessarily change cultural values. Modernization and culture can walk parallel, not simply convergent, paths. This implies that cultural identity can work both in positive-liberating as well as negative-repressive ways. Cultural identity interpreted in a positive-liberating way may, among other aspects, imply a positive orientation toward historical values, norms, and institutions; the resistance to excessive external influence; the rejection of values, institutions, and forms that destroy social cohesion; and the adaptation of forms of production so that they favor the specificity of human and local social development. On the other hand, a negative-dominating interpretation of cultural identity may include the use of so-called traditional values and norms, or arguments emphasizing cultural "uniqueness" to legitimize marginalization or the existing status quo. "The 'national culture' can become a bizarre graft of selected historical incidents and distorted social values intended to justify the policies and actions of those in power," Nobel Peace Laureate and detained opposition leader of Burma, Aung San Suu Kyi (1994: 4) observes. Therefore, she continues, "the question of empowerment is central to both culture and development. It decides who has the means of imposing on a society the view of what constitutes culture and development" (see also Table 2.1).

Logic and Language

To assert that logic is culturally relative may approach blasphemy to the "scientific" mind, but the fact remains that foreign systems of reason are usually deemed illogical using the accuser's system of logic. Logic "is a cultural product, and not universal. Logic . . . is the basis of rhetoric. . . . Rhetoric, then, is not universal either, but varies from culture to culture and from time to time within a given culture" (Ishii, 1985: 98).

Considering Suzuki's study of Zen logic, Ishii (1985:99) continues. "Being is Being because Being is not Being; i.e., A is A because A is not A. Suzuki's logic is in absolute contrast with Aristolian dichotomous antimony." It follows that the logical and rhetorical framework of a culture influences the manner in which that culture perceives and employs language and communication, as well as what constitutes knowledge. This, in turn, refers to the question of "expert" and "indigenous" knowledge. Perhaps Fuglesang (1982:71) puts it best in saying, "There cannot be a formal logic which is universal. . . . So, how can there be a knowledge which is universally valid?" As such, each culture has to be analyzed on the basis of its own "logical" structure.

The reverse, that communication, language, and knowledge also impact logical frameworks and worldviews, follows. Logic and language are linked. "We overlook the simple circumstance that the universality is not a fact in reality, but only a feature in the linguistic picture we are using" (Fuglesang, 1982: 21). Rockhill (1982:15) further states, "The symbolic interpretation of gestures and words is of primary concern as they mediate human interaction and provide the lenses through which the inner experience is viewed"—in brief, symbolic interactionism. It is mistaken to imagine that one adjusts to reality essentially without the use of language and that language is merely an incidental means

Table 2.1. Two Processes at Work Simultaneously.

Cultural Identity	Self-Reliance	Basic Needs
Applied in the positive-liberating sense		
Positive orientation toward historical values, norms, institutions. Resistance to excessive external influence. Rejection of values, institutions, and forms that destroy social cohesion. Adaptation of forms of production so that they favor the specificity.	Use of local wealth and raw materials. Selective, adaptation of foreign capital, products, technology and technical assistance. Belief in one's own capabilities. Adaptation of means of production to the local environment.	Stress on the total population, not on minorities. Both material and nonmaterial needs are given priority (the former are necessary for the latter). Emancipation of each individual. Delegated participation in decisions on the distribution of disposable wealth.
Applied in the negative-dominating sense		
Use of the concept of "tradition" to legitimate marginalization. Arguing for cultural uniqueness in order to perpetuate the power of the majority.	Rejection of fundamental rights and refusal to participate, with the argument that the population is not yet "mature" or "developed" enough for them.	Stress on material consumption needs.

of solving specific problems of communication or reflection. The fact of the matter is that the real world is to a large extent unconsciously built up on the language habits of the group.

To carry linguistic relativity to its extreme, it can be held that even our most "certain" presuppositions—those of time, space, and matter—are not "real" at all. Fuglesang (1982:41) attests, "Newton did not find these concepts in reality but in language." And Kozol (1975:116) writes,

> words can be a major factor in determination of our ideologies and our desires. . . . Words that seem the most accessible, or those we have been trained to find most pleasing, are powerful forms of limitation on the kinds of things we can experience, or advocate, or even learn to long for.

Perhaps no one understood these ideas of culture and language better than Mahatma Gandhi. He adamantly used the local language and lived by and in the indigenous culture. He sought to propagate new ideals, values, and thought patterns consonant with modern times, but in terms of the traditional cultural symbolic systems.

Cultural Identity in East and West

Let me attempt to point out a few characteristics of what can be called a Western versus an Asiatic mode of communication. Such an attempt, however, cannot be undertaken without an explicit warning: As has been argued by many scholars, to bring Western and Asian culture face-to-face is not only ambitious, but it can give a very simplistic impression. With regard to the Western and Asian concept of "Self," for instance, Frank Johnson (1985) summarizes the problems inherent in attempting systematic comparisons between East and West. False antitheses and monolithic comparisons can easily slip into the cliche generalization and overstatement of the obvious. He, therefore, cautions:

> First, generalizations stressing differences between East and West gloss over the diversity within both Eastern and Western traditions themselves—over different eras, among different cultures, and as these traditions are differentially experienced by individuals. Second, such comparisons between East and West necessarily set aside civilizations and nations whose traditions have not been recorded in a manner permitting equivalent representation. (Johnson, 1985: 91-92)

These risks are particularly high in condensed versions of cross-cultural comparisons, such as this text. Therefore, both modes of communication should be perceived as ideal-typical examples of which the extremes are underlined in order to accentuate the typicalness of each mode of communication.

However, as pointed out by John Hostetler (1980:21) in his fascinating description of the Amish people (a church community whose members practice family-oriented, labor-intensive, simple living in a highly industrialized American society), this is easier said than done:

> The Amish are real people, not simply an ideal type or a theoretical construct. Like all human beings, they use signs and symbols to cope with everyday life in order to make their world more meaningful and desirable. They are engaged in a social discourse with reality, the meaning of which is revealed in the analysis of the "unconscious" structure of their religious ideology. Such an analysis takes into account the mythological, the ritual process, and the charter of the community, and thus opens doors that aid us in comprehending how the Amish view themselves as a people and how they regard their mission in the world.

Hajime Nakamura (1985) is even more critical. Although he agrees that research into the cultural contributions of various nations as seen from the viewpoint of their interrelationship is necessary, he advocates the hypothesis that

> There is no such thing as a single fundamental principle which determines the characteristic ways of thinking of a people. Various factors, related in manifold ways, each exerting its influence, enter into the ways of thinking of a people. If we deal with the question of the existential basis which brings about differences of ways of thinking, we see no way left for us to take the standpoint of pluralism. (Nakamura, 1985:37)

Nevertheless, after a comprehensive overview of all the distinct positions, he agrees that "there are some characteristic differences in the ways of thinking of East Asian nations. In the second place, with regard to all people, there is a certain logical and human connection among these characteristics" (Nakamura, 1985: 38). That is precisely the objective of this study. This research perspective is often termed "qualitative" or "interpretative" to distinguish it from the more traditional "quantitative" research methodologies. However, as Stella Ting-Toomey (1984:171) eloquently points out: "The primary difference between qualitative and quantitative research is not simply the distinction between 'qualifying' and 'quantifying' of data. Rather, the difference is rooted in the ontological or metaphorical orientations that guide each research endeavor" (see also Chapter 3).

Therefore, the following should be perceived as *ideal-typical* cases of which the extremes are underlined in order to accentuate the typicalness of each mode of communication. While outlining the Western mode of communication I had the Anglo-Saxon culture, to which I belong, in mind as the framework of reference. My appreciation of the defined Asiatic mode of communication is based on experiences in these cultures where Confucian and Buddhist influences play a major part. In each culture I have been trying to search for the *archetypes* rather than the formal and often officially propagated manifestations of a culture. More than in the West, and in a way due to Western influences, one can observe in Asia a pronounced difference between the so-called "written" and "unwritten" culture (Hsiung, 1985; Terwiel, 1984). For example, all Asian governments underwrite to so-called Universal United Nations Declarations which were issued after World War II by Western governments and were mainly based on Western ideas and philosophies. However, the reality in many of these countries is often completely different. Confucian concepts such as harmony and hierarchy are in severe contrast to the Western principles of conflict and democracy. Further, the three basic principles of Buddhism, such as "Anijjang" (everything is perpetually changing), "Dukhkang" (life is full of suffering), and "Anatta" (everything is relative; certainty does not exist), differ greatly from the static, optimistic, and "ideal-utopian" principles on which the Western way of thinking is built. John Walsh (1973:82) summarizes these differences as follows:

> One of the basic differences between Eastern and Western cultures is that the Eastern are dominated by the concept of harmony; the Western by power. In the East, it is said, knowledge is for the sake of living in better and closer harmony with nature and man; in the West, knowledge is for the sake of controlling peace and order is a prime value; in the West, achieving the things that power makes possible is considered by many as a primary goal.

Language is an instrument of communication and power. People communicate by means of language. But at the same time, language arises out of the social matrix of power relationships in a given community. Linguistic misunderstandings are not mainly due to linguistic incompetence but rather to the difference in social and cultural patterns between each communicating group or individual. One does "understand" the other, but one does not always comprehend.

In many Asian languages there is a distinction made between so-called levels of speech according to age, social status, and patterns of social interaction. One has to use other titles and forms of address when one approaches a younger or elder, a higher or lower ranked person. This kind of hierarchical language use has gradually disappeared in the West. Misunderstandings can be of a verbal and of nonverbal nature. The impact of nonverbal communication forms cannot be underestimated. According to estimates, only 35% of the social meaning in a face-to-face conversation is imparted verbally, and more than 55% in a nonverbal way (i.e., by making use of space and time, body language, etc.) (Palmer & Simmons, 1995).

There is something more involved than just the grammatical competence in the Chomskyesque meaning. Of importance are the social use and the social and cultural context in which the language appears. This broader notion of linguistic competence can be called the *communicative competence* of a language. A language cannot be separated from its social-cultural context. In different cultures the same words or concepts can have different connotative, contextual, or figurative meanings and evoke idiomatic or metaphoric expressions (Bresnanhan, Cai, & Rivers, 1994). The word fat, for instance, has a positive connotation in most Asian societies; it shows the person's well-being and wealth. In the West, however, the word is mainly interpreted in a negative way. In the West, the owl is a symbol for wisdom; in the East it is regarded as a stupid bird. O-Young Lee (1967) concludes that Asian languages have developed on the basis of auditive interpretation (listening) and emotion (pathos) and take into account the so-called "aura" of things. Because of this, Asian languages are more colorful and poetic than Indo-European languages, which are based on visual ascertainment (seeing) and rationation (logos): "A culture of the eye is intellectual, rational, theoretical and active, while a culture of the ear is emotional, sensitive, intuitive and passive" (Lee, 1967: 43).

In comparing Eastern and Western orientations to the use of language, Kim (1985: 405) postulates that the Western mode is largely a "direct, explicit, verbal realm, relying heavily on logical and rational perception, thinking, and articulation." Thunberg, Nowak, Rosengren, and Sigurd (1982: 145) apply this concept to the development professional's style, whose "manner of expression or style often seems unnecessarily complicated and abstract, and particularly bureaucratic prose tends to follow formal codes far removed from daily usage". This contrasts with the orientation of the East in which "the primary source of interpersonal understanding is the unwritten and often unspoken norms, values and ritualized mannerisms relevant to a particular interpersonal context" (Kim, 1985:405). To relate this to India as well as alternate views of communication:

According to the Indian view, the realization of truth is facilitated neither by language nor by logic and rationality. It is only intuition that will ensure the achievement of this objective. To know is to be; to know is to become aware of the artificial categorization imposed on the world by language and logic. It is only through an intuitive process that man [and woman] will be able to lift himself [or herself] out of the illusory world which, indeed, according to the Indian viewpoint, is the aim of communication. Therefore, if the Western models of communication are ratiocination-oriented models, the Indian one is intuition-oriented. (Dissanayake & Said, 1983: 30)

Another essential difference between Western and Asian society is the position of the individual and, consequently, the conception of Self. The Self is composed of both individual and group identifications. The individual and group components are complements in a "whole" Self rather than dialectical opposites. What gets stressed in each culture differs, but this does not suggest an either/or choice. Whereas Western culture is characterized by a strong individualistic self-image, in the Asian context, group consciousness plays a much bigger role (Bond, 1991, Marsella, Devos, & Hsu, 1985). Clifford Geertz (1973), for instance, in his influential essay on Bali describes how Balinese act as if persons were impersonal sets of roles, in which all individuality and emotional volatility are systematically repressed. Their notion of Self is quite different from the one described by Sigmund Freud. Freud (1951) demonstrated that one can trace out systematic interrelationships between conscious understandings of social relations, unconscious dynamics, and the ways ambiguous, flexible symbols are turned into almost deterministic patterns of cultural logic. Therefore, Westerners are I-orientated:

Their behavior is largely determined by their perception of self, a concept we define as the identity, personality or individualism of a given person as distinct from all other people. For them, the self is a unifying concept. It provides a perspective in thinking, a direction for activity, a source of motivation, a locus in decision-making and a limit to group involvement. (Stewart, 1972: 75)

Asians, on the other hand, are *We-orientated*. They get their identity from the position they hold in the group. In Geertz' study the Balinese tried to establish smooth and formal interpersonal relationships, in which the presentation of the Self is affectless and determined by the social group. A typical example is the Asian way of addressing people. A Westerner first writes his Christian name, then his surname, followed by street, town, and country. Asians do it the other way around. When one asks a

Hindu for his identity, he will give you his caste and his village as well as his name. There is a Sanskrit formula that starts with lineage, family, house, and ends with one's personal name. In this presentational formula, the empirical self comes last.

In other words, Asians are submerged, so to speak, in the group, and find themselves lost and powerless as individuals when the link with the group is taken away or does not exist:

> The predominant value is congeniality in social interactions based on relations among individuals rather than on the individual himself. A network of obligations among members of a group is the point of reference, not the self. In Oriental cultures, people's behavior is directed first to maintaining affiliation in groups and congenial social relations. Goals which could be personally rewarding to the individual are only of secondary importance. (Klopf & Park, 1982: 30)

Only after the Asian knows someone's status, age, sex, and so on (these are often the first questions that are asked of a foreigner but which are regarded as 'indiscreet' by a Westerner), will he or she be capable of communicating, of addressing the conversation partner in the 'appropriate' cultural way.

Social relations patterns, as well, are differently perceived and outwardly shown. Social stratification exists, of course, in the East as well as in the West. But where it is not accentuated in the West—moreover, in interpersonal communication one often attempts to construct a (often feigned) horizontal and equal relationship—hierarchic relations still exist and are explicitly emphasized in the East. Appearances such as clothes and etiquette play a major role. The Confucian ethic, for instance, attaches a lot of importance to tradition and etiquette. One individual is not equal to another; one is always of a higher or lower rank or status. This ranking applies to every social form or organization—family, enterprise, or school. In China, this performance of rank is called li, and it involves the ability to value the position one has to take up in each specific relationship pattern and, consequently the ability to follow the right ritual. An investigation into the way in which the Chinese Communist Party is organized and operates on the basis of Confucian principles would, in my opinion, yield many revealing views about modern-day China (see also Bond, 1991; Cheung, 1996; Spybey, 1992).

Even in more formal relations and modernistic institutions, these patterns of communication are still carried on. Yong-Bok Ko (1979) refers to Weber's three forms of administration—traditional, charismatic, and legal government—and states that Korean society, although formally a legal government, is still dominated by hierarchic and feudal conventions that the authorities justify in emotional and superstitious arguments, rather than rational ones:

> The fact that the organizational structure of political parties is based not on the from-below pattern but on the from-above pattern or, at best, on a compromise between the two exposes an inversion of value the like of which can be found in the phenomenon that the master comes first to be obeyed by the masses. As we often find in National Assembly elections, the fame of candidates, the degree of their personal acquaintance with voters, and their personal ties are more decisive than their ability. This discloses that an emotional rather than rational atmosphere prevails in politics. The fact that politicians have their own world and they are poorly equipped with elasticity so as to embrace heretics indicates that Korean politics is still not far from nepotism and factionalism. (Ko, 1979: 173)

In my opinion, this political pattern is also true in other Asiatic countries and in sectors such as commerce or industry as well. Asians feel themselves, less than Westerners, drawn by political programs; they follow charismatic leaders with whom they can identify emotionally. In business matters as well, Asians follow a hierarchic, time-consuming, and indirect pattern of communication, in which immediate friends or "group members" act as intermediaries. Don McCreary and Robert Blanchfield (1986) analyzed the patterns of discourse in negotiations between Japanese and U.S. companies. They concluded that the negotiation is complicated and dependent on several constructs unique to the homogeneous Japanese people and culture, and that three constructs are particularly crucial: *amae* (a social hierarchy of dependency relationships), *haragei* (a culturally based set of paralinguistic cues coupled with superficially misleading verbal arguments with multiple semantic readings), and the pragmatics of formal negotiation, which concerns special patterns of discourse in regard to speaking versus writing, colloquial versus formal language, responsibility spread in decision making, and translation/interpretation difficulties.

> Phatic communication, the communication and build-up of personal trust, must be included from negotiating day one. Conversation, seemingly about nothing of consequence, that is, family backgrounds, likes and dislikes, and employment history, tests the foreign negotiator's trustworthiness, how much respect and credibility is due him, and how much he is committed to a long-term outlook. (McCreary & Blanchfield, 1986: 156)

Because of this difference, less importance is attached to a number of values that, in the Western world, are considered very important, such as the equality of men and women, or democracy. On the other hand, other values and norms, such as respect for one's elder or loyalty to the group, are given a more important place in the East. Therefore, some argue that the Western concept of parliamentary democracy is incompatible with a Hindu society, whereas others claim that Marxism is more closely related to Buddhism than to Western liberal principles (Kolm, 1984). Francois Perroux (1983: 121), however, doubts the relevance of this sort of comparison and puts forward a so-called Weberian and anti-Weberian model: "At most and at best, Weber's model is a sociological construct of little real benefit even in the investigation of cultures that differ from our own. What do we gain by labelling an Oriental or African culture as 'charismatic' or 'traditional' when it stems from a living faith?" He adds that the new and another development movement in the North and the South, "If it is not to lead to the world's going up in flames, must at least adopt a line of research, a guiding principle and, basing itself on the anti-Weber model, a course of slow, patient and cumulative advance" (Perroux, 1983:12). Similar arguments are also put forward by Roland Robertson (1992) and Bryan Turner (1994), who examine the recent debate about orientalism in relation to postmodernism and the process of globalization.

The Asiatic mode of communication is indirect and implicit, the Western direct and explicit. In Asian communication processes, a lot is supposed and "implicitly said." Westerners insist on making very explicit arrangements and have almost no ear for nonverbal forms of expression. Therefore, Westerners use language in an instrumental way and emphasize herewith the exchange of ideas and thoughts. The more emotionally involved and poetical Asian is less direct. In an instrumental pattern of communication, one defends one's opinion in an assertive way. Westerners attempt to convince their listeners by way of rational, Aristotelian argumentation. The "end product," the message, is the most important part of the communication process. The communication is considered a success if the public has understood the "message." Whether or not the public agrees to the underlying viewpoint in the message is of secondary importance for a Western communicator.

Whereas Westerners start a conversation with a definite goal (i.e., they want to state or obtain something material or immaterial), for Asians the emotional exchange, the being together, the pleasure of communicating are equally important. In interpersonal communication, Asians will try to assess the feelings and state of mind of those present. They do not want to bring the harmony of the group into danger and thus will give their opinion in an indirect way. Not the product, or the message, but the process is of importance. Hence, there are also totally different perceptions with regard to work and leisure time. In the West, they are regarded as two separate aspects of life, but not so in the East. Therefore, the Asiatic mode of communication can be labeled as *defensive* and *situational*. The conversation is often abruptly stopped, or the subject changed without any obvious reason, as soon as the speaker feels that the listener does not totally agree with his point of view or that his or her feelings might have been hurt. Asians attempt to reach a *total communication*. If this is not possible they prefer no communication to the Western compromise of *partial communication*.

Whereas the Western mode of communication concentrates on the "encoding" of issues and is, as such, sender- or communicator-orientated, the Asian mode of communication attaches more attention to the "decoding" problems of messages and is, as such, receiver- or public-orientated. Whereas the Westerner actively looks "for the truth" and is convinced that this can be achieved on the basis of a logical argumentation, the Asian accepts that the "truth" will be "revealed" when he or she is ready for it, or, in other words, when enough knowledge and insight has been accumulated. The attitude is passive; data collection and argumentation—two essential elements in a Western mode of communication—are often missing. On the other hand, the action orientation of Westerners dictates their attitude with regard to nature and technology. They want to command and control these, whereas Asians try to achieve a harmonious relationship with both. Therefore, in more general terms, the vision on intuition, rationalism, and empiricism in both modes of communication is totally different. For more details, see Jandt (1995); Samovar & Porter (1995).

To summarize, an attempt to bring together the fundamental differences between the Confucian-Buddhist and Anglo-Saxon sociocultural organization and communication modes are given in Figure 2.1.

TOWARD "ANOTHER" DEVELOPMENT AND COMMUNICATION MODEL

More so than in the past, there is a search in the current development debate for the necessary content and normative components for development. Todaro (1977: 62), for instance, states that

> development must be seen as a multi-dimensional process involving major changes in social structures, popular attitudes, and national institutions as well as the acceleration of economic growth, the reduction of inequality and the eradication of absolute poverty.

Development, in its essence, must represent the entire gamut of change by which an entire social system, tuned to the diverse basic needs and desires of individuals and social groups within that system, moves away from a condition of life widely perceived as "unsatisfactory" towards a situation or condition of life regarded as materially and spiritually "better".

EAST	WEST
Socio-Cultural System (emphasis on)	
Cosmocentrical	Anthropocentric
Self is part of group	Self is central
Hierarchy/Asymmetrical	Horizontal/Symmetrical
Harmony	Power/Conflict
Passive	Active
Being	Doing
Mode of Communication (emphasis on)	
Platonic	Aristotelian
Pathos prevails	Logos prevails
Indirect	Direct
Intermediate	Face-to-face
Situational	Instrumental
Receiver-orientated	Communicator-oriented
Dialectic/Cyclic/Dialogic	Linear/Monologic
Total	Partial
Poetical/Nonverbal	Explicit/Verbal
Deductive/Accepting	Inductive/Analyzing
Affective	Assertive
Relative statements	Absolute statements
Form	Content

FIGURE 2.1. The main differences between the Asiatic (Confucian-Buddhist) and Western (Anglo-Saxon) sociocultural and communication patterns

Therefore, development for society means development of the collective personality of society. Development thus defined is a multivariate quantitative, and qualitative change and may not be immediately measurable by cardinal means.

"Another" Development

The Dag Hammarskjold Foundation established three foundations for another development: (a) another development is geared to the satisfaction of needs, beginning with the eradication of poverty; (b) another development is endogenous and self-reliant; and (c) another development is in harmony with the environment. Another development applies to all levels of all societies, not just the poor of the nonaligned world. It grew from a dissatisfaction with the "consumer society," with what is sometimes termed "overdevelopment" or even "maldevelopment," as well as the growing disillusionment with the modernization approach.

The central idea, which is pointed out by almost everyone who is searching for newer approaches toward development, is that there is no universal path to development—it must be conceived as an integral, multidimensional, and dialectic process that can differ from one society to another.

This does not mean, however, that one cannot attempt to define the general principles and priorities on which such a strategy can be based. Indeed, several authors have been trying to gather the core components for another development (see. e.g., Beck, Giddens, & Lash, 1994; Crush, 1995; De la Court, 1990; Friedmann, 1992; Goulet, 1971; Hamilton, 1990; Hulme & Turner, 1990; Itty, 1984; Kothari, 1988; Masini, 1979; Masini & Galtung, 1994; Redclift, 1987). From the search of these authors, I would cite seven criteria as essential for another development. Such development could be based on the following principles:

1. *Basic needs*: is geared to meeting human, material, and nonmaterial needs. It begins with the satisfaction of the basic needs of those, dominated and exploited, who constitute the majority of the world's inhabitants, and ensures at the same time the humanization of all human beings by the satisfaction of their needs for expression, creativity, equality, and conviviality and the ability to understand and master their own destiny.
2. *Endogeny*: stems from the heart of each society, which defines in sovereignty its values and the vision of its future. Because development is not a linear process, there can be no universal model, and only the plurality of development patterns can answer to the specificity of each situation.

3. *Self-reliance:* implies that each society relies primarily on its own strength and resources in terms of its members' energies and its natural and cultural environment. Self-reliance clearly needs to be exercised at national and international (so-called "collective self-reliance") levels, but it acquires its full meaning only if rooted at the local level, in the praxis of each community.

4. *Ecology:* rationally utilizes rationally resources of the biosphere in full awareness of the potential of local ecosystems, as well as the global and outer limits imposed on present and future generations. It implies the equitable access to resources by all as well as careful, socially relevant technologies.

5. *Sustainability:* considers the interdependency of these resources in time (short, medium, and long term) and space (local, national, transnational).

6. *Participative democracy* as the true form of democracy. It is not merely government of the people and for the people but also, and more fundamentally, "by the people" at all levels of society.

7. *Structural and sustainable changes* are required, more often than not, in social relations, in economic activities, and in their spatial distribution, as well as in the power structure, to realize the conditions of self-management and participation in decision making by all those affected by it, from the rural or urban community to the world as a whole.

These principles must be organically related because development is conceived as an integral process. The last criterion is a fundamental condition for the first five because without the demand for social change, the other priorities can be interpreted in various ways. I illustrate this by means of Roy Preiswerk's (1980) position on the problem of cultural development. From Preiswerk's cultural point of view, the "other" development concept is divided into three subconcepts: cultural identity, self-reliance, and basic needs. He holds that these three aspects can be applied both in a negative-repressing sense and in a positive-liberating one (see Table 2.1). Like Sunkel and Fuenzalida, Preiswerk sees both processes at work simultaneously.

The negative-dominating application of these principles seems to me to be situated in the modernization and dependency thought, whereas an application in the positive-liberating sense corresponds to the expectations of the third paradigm. Also Majid Tehranian (1985, 1996) elaborates on the dialectics between dominating versus liberative consequences within development and communication. He distinguish-

es among a "capitalist," "communist," and "communalist" model, out of
which, in his opinion, a fourth so-called "totalitarian" model emerges:
"All three models have also proved themselves vulnerable to a totalitarian 'solution' when their particular development strategies have failed to
produce results. The totalitarian temptation has proved to be thus a
pathology of the historical transition to the modern world" (Tehranian,
1985:4). In my opinion, Tehranian's first two "politicological" models
can, in my framework, be placed under the heading of modernization;
the third under my multiplicity paradigm. I interpret his fourth totalitarian model as an elitist application of either the dependency or modernization perspective.

The seven principles described earlier have been further elaborated by many authors. The principle of *basic needs* can, for instance, be
identified in both material and immaterial ways. Whereas the Dag
Hammerskjold Foundation pays attention to both aspects, the World
Bank is only concerned about material basic needs. "Self-esteem," "life-
sustenance," and "freedom," are, according to Vilanilam and Lent
(1979:15), the three most important principles that together constitute
another development. They attempt to identify and rank the basic needs
within another development context. "Primary needs" are, for example,
agricultural and food production; education with an emphasis on vocational and socially relevant curricula; employment for all and labor welfare with attention to occupational safety and health; freedom from fear,
ignorance and want; freedom of assembly, choice, and dissent; health
with an emphasis on public and environmental health preventive medi-
cine and rural health education; housing for all with priority on low-cost
mass housing; land reforms; reorientation of science and technology,
industrial production, and so on, for meeting the basic needs of all;
structural and administrative changes in socioeconomic relations; and
textile industry development with priority on low-cost materials and the
rural weaving industry. Examples of "secondary needs" are the development of energy sources, irrigation facilities, and flood control methods; the emphasis on self-reliant development with dependence on
indigenous materials and methods; family planning; interconnecting of
villages; international economic and technological relations; national
integration; road and transportation development; rural electrification;
rural industries; social reforms; and telecommunications development.
"Tertiary needs" are classified as cultural diversity; dignity and honor;
freedom for alternative lifestyles; freedom from affluence and alienation;
freedom from external aggression and cultural domination; freedom of
mobility; freedom of worship; mass communication development, using
both traditional and modern methods; promotion of fine arts; recognition and reward; and tourism and interregional and international travel.

The three categories contain both material and immaterial needs at distinct levels of society. One might also argue that some of the needs could be identified as clear examples of modernization. As pointed out earlier, the multiplicity paradigm builds on previous paradigms and, therefore, also adopts elements and viewpoints from these perspectives. Therefore, I agree with David Harrison's (1988:176) statement that modernization remains a key feature of development: "It occupies a major place and will continue to do so. The nature of industrialization, its accompanying features, and the degree to which they are inevitable, will remain at the center of the agenda."

However, what is new in the development discussion is the *ecological dimension*. The so-called "eco-system approach" differs at almost every point from the modernization paradigm. From an ecological perspective, a country must not compare itself with other, more developed examples for its development policy, but must proceed from its own ecology and culture. This is not to say, however, that one must revert to the romanticism of unspoiled cultures and "small is beautiful." Once again, development, in the sense of modernization, is an inherent part of every development process. Not to see or to deny this is to fall in the trap of a "simple life" fallacy, as romantic images of uncorrupted, traditional peasant societies are primarily products of Western discomfort with the consumption society. In this sense I agree with Alvin Toffler's (1985: 97) argument that "it is simply reactionary . . . to attack all economic development, all technology, all bigness, all centralization. It's simple-minded. It's romantic. It's melodramatic. It's futile". However, in my opinion, it is equally simple-minded and romantic to accuse the environmental movement at large of these shortcomings.

Also important is the notion of *self-reliance*, which is multidimensional and open to many interpretations. Johan Galtung (1980) has argued that in the English language the term *self-reliance* refers to both the concepts of independence and interdependence. In this text, self-reliance is used as the counterpole to dependency, as a sovereign and autocentric strategy for development on the basis of a community's own capabilities and needs, and the capacity of autonomous goal-setting and decision making.

The theoretical rationale for self-reliance as a more comprehensive development strategy has been summed up by Galtung in the following 13 hypotheses. Through self-reliance (a) priorities will change toward production for basic needs for those most in need; (b) mass participation is ensured; (c) local factors are utilized much better; (d) creativity is stimulated; (e) there will be more diversity of development; (f) there will be more compatibility with local conditions; (g) there will be less alienation; (h) ecological balance will be more easily attained; (i) important externalities are internalized or given to neighbors at the same level; (j) ability to withstand manipulation due to trade dependency increases; (k) the military defense capability of the country increases; and (l) as a basic approach, today's Center and Periphery are brought on a more equal footing.

In other words, self-reliance should not be seen as merely an economic policy. In my conception the political, social, cultural, and communicative aspects of the strategy should be emphasized as well; and, if consistently applied, it implies fundamental structural transformations. Moreover, problems of size, level, and degree of self-reliance have to be taken into account. Therefore, self-reliance should not be confused with "autarchy." Self-reliance, rather, is the condition for collaboration on the basis of equality, which may be striven for on the local, national, regional, and international levels.

The problem of size has long been neglected in discussions on development. Geographical factors may possibly be the reason it became a field of special concern for Caribbean scholars. These authors reject regional integration under capitalism as a viable strategy and instead attempt to develop comprehensive planning with special reference to small dependent countries. In their view it is necessary to break with capitalism and to achieve self-reliance on an economic, as well as a political and social basis. This strategy of comprehensive planning requires the convergence of domestic resource use and domestic demand. They claim that this constitutes the necessary condition for the growth of an indigenously oriented technology.

The traditional focus of interest, nevertheless, has remained national self-reliance, which basically implies a strong nation-state. Galtung argues that it is necessary to combine and distinguish among local, national, regional, and intermediate levels if one really wants to acquire a strategy based on the principle of self-reliance. Ignace Sachs (1985:29), for instance, also argues that

> self-reliance should be viewed as an inversion of market relations on two levels: first, to downscale the range of exchange relations so as to strengthen the local economy, closing more economic circuits within the regional space; and second, to stimulate unpaid work and a whole new variety of non-economic activities.

But, on the other hand, most scholars agree that an autonomous, sovereign, and independent nation-state is the essential condition for a strategy of self-reliance and sustainable development.

Therefore, the social reforms necessary for the movement from dependency to self-sufficient development raise the problems of participation, decentralization, and autonomy. In this context, the idea of selective participation has been launched, a participation that is a dissociative and associative (or delinking/linking) development strategy based on equality and sovereignty. In this regard Bjorn Hettne (1990: 179) correctly claims that

> it is an important task of alternative development theory to provide the necessary theoretical and empirical base for the strategy of selective participation with the purpose to promote self-reliance on all levels. This will require knowledge of the development process in individual countries and about the international context, a theory about which links are productive and which are counterproductive, and futuristic studies of the possible outcome of various strategies which obviously will be undertaken by the center. As the center should not be conceived of as a monolithic block, there is also a need for research about cooperation and conflict within the center and its implications for self-reliant strategies.

Toward a Public-oriented Communication Model

These developments have also affected communication research, as is reflected in the fascinating assessments and surveys by many communication scholars. Especially in Latin America, the new perspective on communication for development has been widely discussed and analyzed by people like Beltran, Bordenave, Canclini, Capriles, Martin-Barbero, Matta, Mattelart, Roncagliolo, and Somavia in journals such as *Chasqui*, *Dialogos*, *Comunicacion*, and *Comunicacion y Cultura*. It emerged as a result of the criticisms of and dissatisfaction with the research hypothesis and results of the dependency approach, and was aptly summarized in the title of the pioneering article by Luis Ramiro Beltran (1976): *conservatism, materialism, and conformism*. It goes without saying that most of these scholars were also strongly influenced by the work of Paulo Freire. Afterwards, it caught also the attention of scholars in the rest of the world.

The former hierarchical, bureaucratic, and sender-oriented communication model was replaced by a more horizontal, participative, and receiver-oriented approach. The present vision is based fundamentally on interactive, participatory, and two-way communication at all levels of society. It is more concerned with process and context, that is, *the exchange of "meanings,"* and the importance of this process, namely, the social relational patterns and social institutions that are the result of and are determined by the process. Therefore, in her analysis of dominant media criticism Joli Jensen (1990: 199-200) argues that rather than assuming that the media are invariably repressive, deforming, destructive, and evil, we can listen to those who participate in them to discover the multiple ways in which they are enjoyed and understood as well as the ways in which they are disliked and deplored. We can also seek to understand our own connection to media and society.

In other words, this "other" communication rejects the necessity of uniform, centralized, "expensive," professional, and institutionalized media, and argues for multidimensionality, horizontality, deprofessionalization, and diachronic communication exchange. A public-oriented communication model also implies more dialectic and active participation by the public. However, this is easier said than done. Therefore, as Brenda Dervin (1980:85) correctly pointed out after an in-depth overview of the literature: "One sees much mention made of the need for alternative communication strategies in general terms but very little mention made of the 'how' of that communicating."

Two Major Approaches to Participatory Communication

Today, there are two major approaches to participatory communication that everyone accepts as common sense. The first is the dialogical pedagogy of Paulo Freire (1970a, 1970b, 1973, 1983, 1994), and the second involves the ideas of access, participation, and self-management articulated in the Unesco debates of the 1970s (Berrigan, 1977, 1979; Husband, 1994; Lewis, 1993). Every communication project that calls itself *participatory* accepts these principles of democratic communication. Nonetheless, today there exists a wide variety of practical experiences and intentions. Before moving on to explore these differences it is useful to briefly review the common ground.

The Freirian argument works by a dual theoretical strategy. Freire insists that subjugated peoples must be treated as fully human subjects in any political process. This implies dialogical communication. Although inspired to some extent by Sartre's existentialism—a respect for the autonomous personhood of each human being—the more important source is a theology that demands respect for otherness—in this case that of another human being. The second strategy is a moment of utopian hope, derived from early Marx, that the human species has a destiny that is more than life as a fulfillment of material needs. Also from Marx is an insistence on collective solutions. Individual opportunity, Freire stresses, is no solution to general situations of poverty and cultural subjugation.

These ideas are deeply unpopular with elites, including elites in the Third World, but there is nonetheless widespread acceptance of

Freire's notion of dialogic communication as a normative theory of participatory communication. One problem with Freire is that his theory of dialogical communication is based on group dialogue rather than such amplifying media as radio, print, and television. Freire also gives little attention to the language or form of communication, devoting most of his discussion to the intentions of communication actions.

The second discourse about participatory communication is the Unesco language about self-management, access, and participation from the 1977 meeting in Belgrade, the former Yugoslavia. The final report of that meeting defines the terms in the following way:

- *Access* refers to the use of media for public service. It may be defined in terms of the opportunities available to the public to choose varied and relevant programs and to have a means of feedback to transmit its reactions and demands to production organizations.
- *Participation* implies a higher level of public involvement in communication systems. It includes the involvement of the public in the production process and also in the management and planning of communication systems.

  Participation may be no more than representation and consultation of the public in decision making. On the other hand, *self-management* is the most advanced form of participation. In this case, the public exercises the power of decision making within communication enterprises and is also fully involved in the formulation of communication policies and plans.

These ideas are important and widely accepted as a normative theory of alternative communication: it must involve access and participation. However, one should note some differences from Freire. The Unesco discourse includes the idea of a gradual progression. Some amount of access may be allowed, but self-management may be postponed until some time in the future. Freire's theory allows for no such compromise. One either respects the culture of the other or falls back into domination and the "banking" mode of imposed education. The Unesco discourse talks in neutral terms about "the public." Freire talked about the oppressed. Finally, the Unesco discourse puts the main focus on the institution. Participatory radio means a radio station that is self-managed by those participating in it.

A Communication Model with Active Social Participation

Participation involves the more equitable sharing of both political and economic power, which often decreases the advantage of certain groups.

Structural change involves the redistribution of power. In mass communication areas, many communication experts agree that structural change should occur first in order to establish participatory communication policies. Mowlana and Wilson (1987: 143), for instance, state:

> Communications policies are basically derivatives of the political, cultural and economic conditions and institutions under which they operate. They tend to legitimize the existing power relations in society, and therefore, they cannot be substantially changed unless there are fundamental structural changes in society that can alter these power relationships themselves.

Contreras (1980:143) supports: "To understand communications potential, one must necessarily start with a serious examination of the societal context under which communication is to operate."

Therefore, the development of another communication model has to take place in relation with overall societal emancipation processes at local, national, as well as international levels. Several authors have been trying to summarize the criteria for another communication model. Juan Somavia (1977, 1981) sums up the following components as essential:

1. *Communication is a human need:* The satisfaction of the need for communication is just as important for a society as the concern for health, nutrition, housing, education, and labor. Together with all the other social needs, communication must enable citizens to emancipate themselves completely. The right to inform and to be informed, and the right to communicate, are thus essential human rights, both individually and collectively.
2. *Communication is a delegated right:* Within its own cultural, political, economic, and historical context, each society has to be able to define independently the concrete form in which it wants to organize its social communication process. Because there are a variety of cultures, there can therefore be various organizational structures. But whatever the form in which the social communication function is embodied, priority must be given to the principles of participation and accessibility.
3. *Communication is a facet of the societal emancipation and liberation process.* The social responsibility of the media in the process of social change is very great. Indeed, after the period of formal education, the media are the most important educational and socialization agents. They are capable of informing or disinforming, exposing or concealing important facts, interpreting events positively or negatively, and so on.

4. *The communication task involves rights and obligations.* Because the media, in fact, provide a public service, they must carry it out in a framework of social and juridical responsibility that reflects the social consensus of the society. In other words, there are no rights without obligation.

The freedom and right to communicate, therefore, must be approached from a threefold perspective: first, it is necessary for the public to participate effectively in the communication field; second, there is the design of a framework in which this can take place; and, third, the media must enjoy professional autonomy, free of economic, political, or other pressure.

Fernando Reyes Matta (1979, 1981, 1986) has attempted to design just such a communication model with active social participation. He started from the following objectives:

1. Communication has a social task that is accomplished in a societal structure that determines the nature and the influence of the communication process.
2. The freedom and right to communicate must be individually and socially guaranteed and delegated to technical and professional authorities. It remains, however, a social right that ultimately pertains to the society as a whole.
3. The productive and administrative structures of the media also function on the basis of a general policy set by the society.
4. The process of local, national, and international communication takes place in a context of social responsibility in accordance with the rights and obligations drawn up in an institutional and juridical framework.
5. The receivers, as the subject of the communication process, must be allowed greater participation in and access to the media.
6. Education in communication is an absolute necessity in the educational process of each individual; this is why the authorities have the duty to entrust special agencies with this kind of training.
7. Via organized public groups and in the framework of institutionalized experiments, the receiver must be able to analyze critically and to participate in the communication process.
8. The access to and participation in the media must be organized in such a way that the receiver can participate actively and democratically in political, educative, communicative, cultural, evaluative, and other types of decision formation.

9. Communication is a dynamic process, and permanent evaluation is a necessity.
10. The installation of a supervisory commission ("media council") is necessary to enable the public groups and the communication authorities to improve the participation mechanisms and methods.

In Servaes (1987), this communication model with active social participation, designed by Reyes Matta, has been further discussed, corrected, and completed (see Figure 2.2). A three-level distinction has been added in order to point out the interrelationships among local, national, and international communication processes. By picturing both sender and receiver as representatives of a social group in a societal framework, the classic duopolarity can be dissolved and the emphasis is put on the role of an active and democratically organized public. For the same reason a number of institutionalized mechanisms that are supposed to guarantee the right to communicate in general as well as in its more specific applications (e.g., participation, access, decentralization) have been integrated.

In practice, adopting some or all of these principles, new forms of communication have been emerging. Decentralized media systems and democratic communication institutions, such as Mahaweli community radio in Sri Lanka and Radio Enriquillo in the Dominican Republic, emphasize self-management by local communities. New concepts of media professionalism bring a greater knowledge of and respect for forms of people's communication. They emphasize the recognition of and experience with new formats of journalism and broadcasting that are more consonant with the cultural identity of the community, and a greater awareness of the ways democratization of communication is taking place and can take place.

THE PARTICIPATORY MODEL

The participatory model incorporates the concepts in the emerging framework of multiplicity/another development. It stresses the importance of the cultural identity of local communities and of democratization and participation at all levels—international, national, local, and individual. It points to a strategy that is not merely inclusive of but largely emanates from the traditional "receivers." Paulo Freire (1983: 76) refers to this as the right of all people to individually and collectively speak their word: "This is not the privilege of some few men, but the right of every man. Consequently, no one can say a true word alone—nor can he say it for another, in a prescriptive act which robs others of their words."

In order to share information, knowledge, trust, commitment, and a right attitude in development projects, participation is very important in any decision-making process for development. According to the International Commission for the Study of Communication Problems, "this calls for new attitude for overcoming stereotyped thinking and to promote more understanding of diversity and plurality, with full respect for the dignity and equality of peoples living in different conditions and acting in different ways" (MacBride, 1980: 254). This model stresses reciprocal collaboration throughout all levels of participation. As a result, the focus moves from a "communicator-" to a more "receiver-centric" orientation, with the resultant emphasis on meaning sought and ascribed rather than information transmitted.

With this shift in focus, one is no longer attempting to create a need for the information one is disseminating, but one is rather disseminating information for which there is a need. Experts and development workers respond rather than dictate; they choose what is relevant to the context in which they are working. The emphasis is on information exchange rather than on persuasion as in the diffusion model.

Listening to what the others say, respecting the counterpart's attitude, and having *mutual trust* are needed. Participation supporters do not underestimate the ability of the masses to develop themselves and their environment.

> Development efforts should be anchored on faith in the people's capacity to discern what is best to be done as they seek their liberation, and how to participate actively in the task of transforming society. The people are intelligent and have centuries of experience. Draw out their strength. Listen to them. (Xavier Institute (1980:11)

According to many authors, authentic participation directly addresses power and its distribution in society. Participation "may not sit well with those who favor the status quo and thus they may be expected to resist such efforts of reallocation of more power to the people" (Lozare, 1994: 231). Therefore, development and participation are inextricably linked.

Because dialogue and face-to-face interaction is inherent in participation, the development communicator will find him or herself spending more time in the field. It will take some time to develop rapport and trust. Continued contact, meeting commitments, keeping promises, and following up between visits is important. Development of social trust precedes task trust. Both parties will need patience. It is important to note that when we treat people the way we ourselves would like to be treated, we learn to work as a team, and this brings

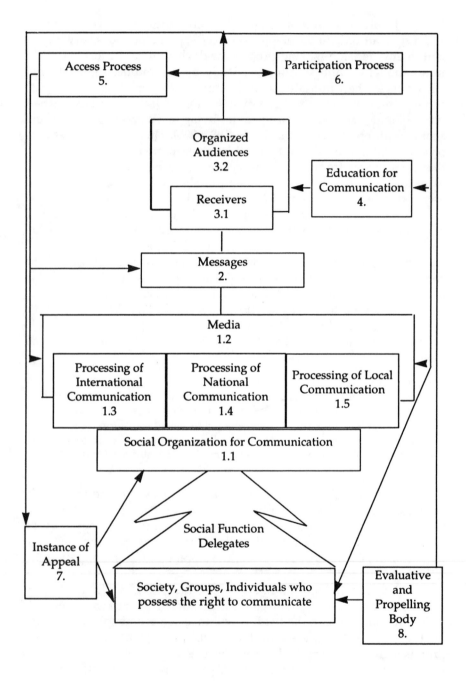

Figure 2.2. A communication model with active social participation

The elements of the model:

1.1. Social organization for communication: the coordinating and administrative policy structure in which the media function.

1.2. Media: an organized set of transmission instruments that distribute messages under the coordination of 1.1.

1.3. Processes of international communication: the interrelationship between national media and the international agencies that provide messages in accordance with national and international jurisdictions.

1.4. Processes of national communication: the mechanisms whereby the media and the receivers obtain a critical panorama of the national reality within the limits of their own nationally formulated norms.

1.5. Processes of local communication: the mechanisms whereby local media and interpersonal communication intermingle and contribute to local decision making, cultural identity, participation, and so on.

2. Messages: mainly "information" of and about events, which are received, processed, and transmitted on the basis of information for social and individual rights, previously determined at a social and global level. This information must thus provide an unfalsified, analytical treatment of the society.

3.1. Receivers: receivers of the messages, who enjoy sufficient education and adopt a critical attitude toward the message. Training should help them to become active subjects in the communication process.

3.2. Organized audiences: the receivers in their entirety. They should neither be perceived as individuals, nor as an amorphous, quantitative mass, but rather as social groups or institutions that are linked in an organizational or structural way with the society at large, such as labor unions, cultural groups, political parties, or "new social movements."

4. Education for communication: the use of educational resources at all levels of society to enable the receivers to form an opinion, to judge information, and to evaluate the role of the media as transmitters of socially interpreted events.

5. Access process: the right of the receiver to participate in the conceptualization and processing of communication and his or her potential right to use the media for further "conscientization."

6. Participation process: the mechanisms whereby an organized public obtains access to the structures where the internal planning and decision making about the media are done, as well as to organizations that deliver education for communication.

7. Instance of appeal: legal organisms established to support the right of the receivers to critical information and organized media participation.

8. Evaluative and propelling body: an institutional mechanism that has the object of guaranteeing the production of communication as a social right and obligation and of helping in its implementation.

Figure 2.2. A communication model with active social participation (con't)

about rural commitment and motivation as well. Thus, honesty, trust, and commitment from the higher ups brings honesty, trust, and commitment from the grassroots as well. This brings about true participation. And true participation brings about appropriate policies and planning for developing a country within its cultural and environmental framework.

Different "Types" of Participatory Communication Projects

In spite of the widespread acceptance of the ideas of Freire and Unesco by aid organizations and communication researchers, there is still a very wide range of projects that call themselves "participatory communication projects." There is an evident need for clarification in descriptive and normative theories of participatory media. What does it mean to be participatory? It is necessary to make further distinctions and arguments to deal with a wide variety of actually existing experiences and political intentions.

A review of the literature turns up the following ideas (Berrigan, 1979; Mata, 1990; O'Connor, 1988; O'Sullivan-Ryan & Kaplun, 1979):

1. participatory media are internally organized on democratic lines (as worker cooperatives or collectives);
2. participatory media are recognized by their opposition to cultural industries dominated by multinational corporations;
3. participatory media may be traced to the liberation of linguistic and ethnic groups following a major social transformation;
4. the strong existence of participatory media may be explained in terms of class struggle within the society;
5. participatory media may be identified as "molecular" rather than "molar" (a collectivity of individual autonomous units rather than one that is homogenized and one-dimensional);
6. participatory media (like the montage of Eisenstein and the theater of Brecht) by design requires a creative and varied reception from its audience.

Reyes Matta (1986) argues that participatory communication is first and foremost an alternative to media dominated by transnational corporations. This is the context in which any alternative must operate. To succeed is to win against the culture industries that are dominated by multinational corporations. The line of thought developed by CINCO (1987) is an outgrowth of this because it involves above all a structural analysis of communicative institutions. For the CINCO researchers a media is alternative if it has a democratic institutional structure. Here the issue is one of ownership and control that is external to the community against access and participation in the media organization.

SYNTHESIS

1. The participatory model views ordinary people as the key agents of change or participants for development, and for this reason it focuses on their aspirations and strengths. Development is meant to liberate and emancipate people and, in so doing, enable them to meet their basic needs. Local cultures are respected.

2. The participatory model sees people as the nucleus of development. Development means lifting up the spirits of a local community to take pride in its own culture, intellect, and environment. Development aims to educate and stimulate people to be active in self and communal improvements, while maintaining a balanced ecology. Authentic participation, though widely espoused in the literature, is not in everyone's interest. Due to their local concentration, participatory programs are, in fact, not easily implemented, nor are they highly predictable or readily controlled.

3. The participatory model emphasizes the local community rather than the nation state, monistic universalism rather than nationalism, spiritualism rather than secular humanism, dialogue rather than monologue, and emancipation rather than alienation.

4. In essence, participatory development involves the strengthening of democratic processes and institutions at the community level and the redistribution of power. Participation aims at redistributing the elites' power so that a community can become a full-fledged democratic one. As such, it directly threatens those whose position and/or very existence depends on power and its control over others. Reactions to such threats are sometimes overt, but most often are manifested as a less visible, yet steady and continuous resistance to change in the status quo.

3

Does it Make Sense?
Validity and Evaluation in
Communication Research

Research in the West . . . is research of social control . . . [It] tends . . . to reflect the values and reinforce the system within which it is conceived, supported, and executed . . . [It] is not marked by speculative and reflective approaches . . . consideration of alternatives, or caution and tolerance . . . but by dogma, doctrinaire statements, selective use of evidence, unsubstantiated assertions . . . arrogance and hostile intolerance. . . . The positions, firmly held by the new high priests, brook no contradictions, and evidence must not . . . get in the way of faith.
—James Halloran (1981:23-39)

All research begins with some set of assumptions that are untested but believed. Positivistic research, which comprises the mass of modern communication and development research, proceeds from the presupposition that all knowledge is based on an observable reality, and social phenomena can be studied on the basis of methodologies and techniques adopted from the natural sciences. In other words, "reality" exists apart from our interpretation of it: we can objectively perceive, understand, predict, and control it. Social scientists, enamored with the notion of a predictable universe, therefore concluded that, by applying the methods of positivistic science to the study of human affairs, it would be possible to predict and ultimately to control human social behavior. Furthermore, its methodological premises and epistemological assumptions are based almost exclusively on the Western experience and worldview, a view that holds the world as a phenomenon to be controlled, manipulated, and exploited.

Today, quantitative as well as qualitative researchers increasingly recognize the weakness of a purely objectivist position. But at the same time, Jacobson (1993: 219) argues, neither can the standard response to this recognition be seen as satisfactory:

> This response holds, basically, that if we try not to assume value-based positions then we can still say we are doing social science. This does constitute a recognition that complete objectivity is no longer possible, but it does not replace value freedom with anything of substance. The inadequacy of this response seems very likely to be the reason that participatory researchers feel that objectivism still resides in the practices of many social scientists.

In this chapter I outline the relative characteristics and merits of quantitative, qualitative, and participatory approaches to research and emphasize some of the philosophical issues on which they are based. However, I adopt Bryman's (1984; Bryman & Burgess, 1994) argument that it is not possible to establish a clear symmetry between epistemological positions and associated techniques of social research; consequently, they often become confused with each other:

> It may be that at the technical level the quantitative/qualitative distinction is a rather artificial one. . . . At the epistemological level, the distinction is less obviously artificial since the underlying tenets relate to fundamentally different views about the nature of the social sciences, which have resisted reconciliation for a very long time. (Bryman, 1984: 88)

Or, as stated by Saneh Chamarik (1993: 4): "In social science, approach and methodology are not just a matter of technique and expertise, but essentially represent an attitude of mind, that is to say, a kind of moral proposition."

Therefore, I refer again to the earlier distinction between the mechanistic diffusion versus organic participatory models. Contrary to the scientist who aims for an understanding of the world as it exists "out there," the participatory model takes as its fundamental focus the immediate world of the participants, that is, their analysis of and subsequent action in that world. However, as has been argued, both models should be regarded as opposites on a continuum.

Moreover, it should be stated at the outset that highly rigid methodology serves to limit rather than expand humanistic understanding to the detriment of both the researcher and the researched. The detachment, the reluctance to "contaminate" one's research design in the dynamic, holistic, and human social context while claiming to be working for the ultimate benefit of those studied, should be challenged, if not on a methodological, then certainly on a moral basis. Given this aloofness, many so-called quantitative, qualitative, and/or participatory researchers become largely parasitical in character and contribute little to those they research. Jumping from country to country, or village to village, many Western and local researchers alike conduct their "safari" and "airport research," collect the data, and return to the university to write it up, hopefully for publication in a prestigious journal. The subjects of the study do not learn of the results and obtain no benefit, except via a long, distorting cycle of traditional research and top-down social action.

However, the assertion is not that the entirety of empirical research or academic inquiry is of no value. The intent is not to reject science but to properly define its place within human knowledge.

Academia

Before I embark on an assessment of the different research approaches, a few words about academia—the social group with the greatest interest in the perpetuation of highly complex research practices, which mandate "correct" methodology above all else are needed. As with bureaucracies, academic institutions strive for results that paint their activities in a concise, easily visible fashion. The reasons for this include peer status as well as personal and organizational sustenance. The rule of "publish or perish" is known to all, and those who would go against the flow or approach their task in an unorthodox fashion are jeopardizing their personal careers. It is not the individual's place to question the prevalent paradigms or accepted methodologies. Consequently, many scholars continue to follow the intellectual fashions of the day. As a whole, their specialist knowledge prompts little divergence from the prevalent opinion of their social group or class (Long and Long, 1992). Linking this to reductionistic trends, Thayer (1983: 84) writes not only does it appear more scientific

> to deal with fragments; it is also a whole lot safer. If the ends of their effort are sometimes irrelevant or trivial or equivocal, it is of no great concern, for it is not the ends but the means by which they distinguish themselves.

As a result, institutions of higher education have often stayed aloof to the needs of the majority of the population.

New forms of access to and structural changes in the higher education system should be a subject of serious consideration. The search for truth succumbs to the search for funding, which is subservient to ideology. Therefore, although academia is supposed to be a "marketplace of ideas" and a forum for free discussion, it has often become part of the market. As a result, Simbulan (1985:8) charges: "Many academicians have become academic prostitutes or academic profiteers who, while trying to overcome their material impoverishments by tapping the vast sources of establishment research funds have in turn become morally impoverished." With time, the parameters under which researchers operate can constitute a social reality. They tend to see only what their terministic screens allow them to name and to do what the paradigmatic vocabulary predisposes. They see its limits as the limits of the world, not as a more-or-less arbitrary boundary between what they know and what they do not. Such trends are demeaning to the researcher as well.

Due to the widespread use and application of Western models, constructs, and methodologies, intellectuals in the so-called Third World are sadly dependent for their status and acceptance on their links with the West. Juan Bordenave (1971: 208) admonishes academics to overcome this "compulsion to perceive our own reality through foreign concepts and ideologies and learn to look at communication and adoption from a new perspective." Mimicking foreign methodologies, as well as striving for more exacting standards and tighter control, social science research is pulled farther and farther from the dynamic social context which it ostensibly strives to understand.

Rajesh Tandon (1981:17) therefore argues against a situation in which a research elite, be it foreign or local, dictates what is valid and what is not. "This whole game has been so much organized that everything else outside it is considered unscientific. Everything outside it is not knowledge." However, and once again, the assertion is not that the entirety of empirical research or academic inquiry is of no value. The intent is to properly define its place within human knowledge.

QUANTITATIVE APPROACHES TO RESEARCH

Logic and common sense tells us that such a thing as objectivity exists. It also tells us the bumblebee can fly. But by the laws of physics, the bumblebee is unable to fly. "Common sense" is just that, common sense:

Human progress has been achieved invariably at points where people were prepared to abandon the common sense approach. For
countless millennia, human beings hugged the coast and would not
put to sea because they thought they would fall over the horizon.
Similarly, common sense tells us that matter is solid, the earth is flat,
and the sun goes around the earth. (Jayaweera, 1986:41)

Social research and developmental research are claimed to be objective,
neutral, and thus scientific. In reality, however, such research often
becomes an instrument in the hands of the powerful elite to rationalize
their control of the people. Therefore, as Halloran (1981:40) claims,

it is ideology that we are now talking about, and in mass communication research, as elsewhere, there are an increasing number of ideolo-
gists who present their work as social science . . . it all depends on
what one means by ideology, and what one means by social science.

Objectivity and Subjectivity

The underlying problem of the importunate posture of "objectivity" is
that in assuming that the meanings for the conditions of subject's lives
are independent of those subjects, researchers in the human and social
studies are assuming they themselves are independent of how they see
those subjects or the phenomena they are examining.

The present discussion rejects this assumption. The idol has feet
of clay. Similar to the notion of relative logic, the assertion is that "objectivity" is nothing more than a subjectivity that a given aggregate of individuals agree on. It refers to what a number of subjects or judges experience, in short, to phenomena within the public domain. Therefore, as
Dervin (1982: 293) observes, "No human being is capable of making
absolute observations, and since it is humans that produce that thing we
call information, all information is itself constrained." And Anderson
and Meyer (1988:239) add that "the ultimate source of our knowledge is
not 'out there' pressing upon us, but it is in our own consciousness."

Hence, objectivity is nothing more than *inter-subjectivity*. For
example, to ensure coder reliability, the researcher culls out those coders
whose subjective coding is incongruent with the mean. The rejected
coders' analysis is not inter-subjective; it is not objective. Research
defines the categorical constructs, then defines and refines the instruments to measure those constructs. With time (as well as painstaking
research and adequate funding), "intelligence" becomes what the tests

measure. Science becomes the operationalization of concepts through the development of reliable measures that, in turn, serve to measure and substantiate the concepts. Reliability and internal validity are perfected. However, whether this cyclical process is related with the social reality outside the lab, with external validity, remains largely unconsidered.

The "End of Ideology" and "Value-Free" Science

Roughly corresponding with the rise of communication models and the doctrine of modernization emerged a growing sentiment of the impending "end of ideology" in the social sciences. Superstition and ideology were to yield to reason, positivism, and science. Friberg and Hettne (1985:209) relate the belief was that "controlled experiments and deductive reasoning guarantees an infinite growth of valid knowledge about the mechanisms of nature and this knowledge will lay the foundation of the technological society marked by material abundance."

This new mode of inquiry was claimed to be detached, neutral, and value free. It was "the noble and final battle of `knowledge' against `ignorance'" (Thayer, 1983: 89). The belief was that "with just a little more data, with just a few more refined techniques of inquiry, we will indeed `arrive'" (89). Not all agree. Some take a political stand and argue that "neutral" science has led to the dehumanizing and catastrophic utilization of knowledge, nuclear missiles, biological poisons, and psychological brainwashing. Others claim from a more methodological point of view that no responsible social scientist would hold that the results of social science research are comprehensive, free of value premises, or valid for all seasons.

Similar to the majority of efforts toward communication and participation in the development context, research most often derives from, and serves to perpetuate, dominant structures. Tying the notions of inter-subjectivity, ideology, and the established order together, Addo (1985:17) writes

> claims to scientific neutrality and objectivity come easily to the establishment [which] holds fast to a deep-seated common world view . . . a theoretical structure of what the world is like and ought to be like; and what it is about and ought to be about.

Power-based Research

The "dominant methodological concern is how to approach the interpretation of the modern world-system in order to make it safe for . . . the perpetuation of . . . this world-system" (Addo, 1985:20). This methodology reveals its pro-status quo bias in that it never considers the alternative of the creation of a new system but rather presents "functional" adjustments to the old. It facilitates the functioning of the existing system without ever questioning its validity, however dangerous that system may be for the future of society and man's and woman's integrity. In this way the research, although often referred to as *abstracted empiricism*, is certainly not abstracted from the society in which it operates. In sum, science, particularly at the level of social research, is laden with ideology. It serves, and is largely intended to serve, vested power structures. As such, claims of the "end of ideology" or "value-free science" do not hold true either in their premises or in their applications.

Communication is no exception. Robert White (1982:29) argues that "much of the research tradition in the field of communication—concepts, methodology, and research designs—has been in the service of authoritarian communication." Halloran (1981:22) adds that communication research

> has developed . . . essentially as a response to the requirements of a modern, industrial, urban society for empirical, quantitative, policy-related, information about its operations. . . . Research was carried out with a view to . . . achieving stated aims and objectives, often of a commercial nature.

The goal of inquiry has often been to investigate how commercial or political persuasion could be effectively used. Hence, such research is an "objective" form of intelligence gathering for social control by business firms and governments. The predominant vein of social research, resting on epistemological suppositions, strives to understand reality, with the objectives of prediction and control. However, although claiming detachment and neutrality, research functions to objectify the very "reality" it assumes to be objective. This is done in a manner congruent with and toward the benefit of the existent status quo, usually those who pay the bills. In other words, it serves more to create and perpetuate a reality than to understand one.

Methodology-Driven Research

In journals and at conferences, debate is more often about the method of investigation than the content. Halloran (1981: 23) argues that "'Scientific' is defined solely or mainly in terms of method, and . . . little or no attention is given to . . . the nature of the relevant, substantive issues and their relationship to wider sociological concerns." This overemphasis on methodology and techniques, as well as adulation of formulae and scientific-sounding terms, exemplify the common tendency to displace value from the ends to the means. A sociologist or psychologist obsessed with frameworks, jargon, and techniques resembles a carpenter who becomes so worried about keeping his or her tools clean that he or she has no time to cut the wood. Reality as experienced in the lives of people has been sacrificed to methodological rigor. Too often an emphasis on exact measurement precludes the asking of significant questions, and the result is fragmented bits of knowledge on "researchable" topics.

As the methodology becomes increasingly complex, the questions posed become ever-more trivial. The parameters of inquiry yield to increasingly sophisticated methods. It is sometimes said that modern scientists are learning so much about so little that they will eventually know everything about nothing. Therefore, many years ago Kuhn (1962: 35) had already attested that "perhaps the most striking feature of the normal research problems . . . is how little they aim to produce major novelties, conceptual or phenomenal."

With the tendency toward reductionism, the social sciences tend to compartmentalize the subject matter into separate parts, with only rare attempts at approaching the subject as a whole. This forces nature: "into the preformed and relatively inflexible box that the paradigm supplies. No part of the aim of normal science is to call forth new sorts of phenomena, indeed those that will not fit the box are often not seen at all" (Kuhn, 1962:24).

Categories, taxonomies, terms, and their relations are largely what make a given paradigm. Yet, even though this "terminology is a reflection of reality, by its very nature it is a selection of reality and therefore also functions as a deflection of reality" (Burke, 1968:44). The categorization is often derived from the literature rather than from "concepts that are necessarily real, meaningful, and appropriate from the native point of view" (Harris, 1980:32). This renders invisible the knowledge of the people involved in the real-life activity at which research is aimed. Consequently, Rockhill (1982:8) asserts skewed pictures "of people result as a consequence of a research approach which seeks to interpret human behavior using constructs which are derived from the perspective of the literature rather than from the perspective of the people being studied." She provides an excellent example in describing studies that conclude that participation is higher among the "educated." Rockhill (1982:6-10) states: "Typically people are categorically defined . . . as participants or non-participants according to whether or not they have participated in a given range of educational activities." Participation is most often defined by the researchers as "an organized educational activity." The conclusion, essentially, is that those who participate more in institutional education settings tend to participate more in institutional education settings. However, the quantum leap occurs when "non-participants are repeatedly categorized as non-learners [and] the false notion that people become educated only through educational programs is perpetuated." This is done empirically and "objectively." Rockhill (1982: 10) summarizes:

> A difficulty in quantitative research is that constructs are often selected by the researcher to name predefined variable clusters rather than derived through the effort to understand human experience from the perspective of the subject. As in the use of "non-learners," typically constructs are value laden and biased against people who do not act in ways valued by researchers who interpret data from their own, often unconscious, cultural biases.

Prevalent theories, paradigms, methodologies, and taxonomies become tantamount to human understanding; they become the goal and the reality. Adherence to widely accepted methods produce mostly one-dimensional communication research unable to cope with complex and dynamic social realities. Analysts research isolated variables, thereby removing them from the cultural context that gives them their meaning. But communication cannot be dissected and displaced to increase the convenience of observation without disrupting the process of meaning creation at the same time.

QUALITATIVE APPROACHES TO RESEARCH

Qualitative research almost mirrors quantitative research and, in this sense, discussion has already addressed qualitative approaches. However, several points require elaboration.

Subjectivity and Phenomenology

Qualitative research accepts subjectivity as given. It does not view social science as "objective" in the ordinary and simple understanding of that term, but as an active intervention in social life with claims and purposes of its own. Objectivity therefore means "seeing what an experience is for another person, not what causes it, not why it exists, not how it can be defined and classified" (Moustakas, 1974:107). As the world is constructed inter-subjectively through processes of interpretation, the premise is that "reality does not write itself on the human consciousness, but rather, that human consciousness approaches reality with certain embedded interpretations" (Anderson & Meyer, 1988: 238), and those interpretations, in turn, constitute reality. We are thus introduced to a new principle of *relativity* that holds that all observers are not led by the same physical evidence to the same picture of the universe (Rabinow & Sullivan, 1987).

As such, given the idiosyncratic nature of individuals and cultures, social reality has predominantly the character of irregularity, instead of the ordered, regular, and predictable reality assumed in empirical approaches. These implications have a profound impact on the manner in which we look at communication and the way we strive to understand and research social contexts. Further confounding this subjective, idiosyncratic irregularity is the fact of its dynamism. Christians and Carey (1981:346) assert, "To study this creative process is our first obligation, and our methodology must not reduce and dehumanize it in the very act of studying it." The emphasis should be on discovery rather than applying routinized procedures. Following the humanistic premise that people are not objects, there is no warrant for believing that the social sciences should imitate the natural sciences in form or method. The subjects of research are just that, subjects. We are not objects and cannot be objectified without losing the very humanity that is the focus of inquiry. Intellectual endeavors are needed that reach out to, rather than insulate us from popular experience. We must therefore have the courage to underwrite contextual thinking and contextual research. "Truth" lies not in objective proof, but in the experience of existence or nonexistence in the minds of men and women and their mutual affirmation. Therefore, "truth" is relative.

This brings us back to the topic of inter-subjectivity. At the risk of being "irrational" and "unscientific," it is argued that qualitative and phenomenological approaches, in their broadest sense, advocate a human approach toward understanding the human context. It is based on the human character of the subject matter. As a specifically human approach, it uses lived experience as acts on which to base its findings. Fuglesang (1984: 4) summarizes:

> If communication is difficult in today's world, it is perhaps because it is difficult to be human. Communication experts do not make it easier when they try to develop science out of something which is essentially an art.

And Ewen (1983: 223) adds:

> The impulse of our analysis ought to respect these voices in their own terms, not continually seek to distort them into faceless data. Such respect may mean our work will be *less* scientifically antiseptic, *less* arrogantly conclusive, *less* neatly tied up, *less* instrumental. Yet, being liberated from such constraints, our work will likely become *more* lyrical *more* speculative, *more* visionary, *more* intelligent and human.

Naturalistic Observation and the Participant Observer

To attempt an understanding of a human being or a social context, to the degree that is possible, we must lay aside all scientific knowledge of the average man and woman and discard all theories in order to adopt a completely new and unprejudiced attitude. The researcher must set aside pre-derelictions, what he or she already knows, because if inquiry begins with a preconceived set of interpretive templates viewpoints will be lost. Through the myopic glasses of rigid theories and constructs, other aspects that may be even more important are typically not noted because they are not looked for. This implies a re-evaluation of concepts such as "developer," "source," "expert," "neutrality," and "objectivity." In other words, the researcher immerses her- or himself in the context not to verify hypotheses, but as sources for understanding meaning. In a very real sense, the most important tool of inquiry becomes the researcher's attitude. Large egos are detrimental when the investigator considers him- or herself far above the group to be investigated and refuses implicitly or explicitly the real encounter with the subject of investigation. Anderson and Meyer (1988: 320) concur: "The 'us/them' character of ethnographic work and our own socialization as researchers—keepers of the truth—can lead to a sense of superiority about our social action as compared to those we study. Observational distancing can turn people into subjects—objects of study."

Quite the opposite of neutrality and detachment, the participant observer involves him- or herself in the natural setting in order to obtain, to the extent possible, an inside view of the social context. This involves "gaining access," but the researcher must also maintain some-what of an aloof position in order to observe. The goal is to see the other objectively and, at the same time, experience his or her difficulties sub-jectively. For the "outsider," participation is "a staged effort and obser-vation is a product of routine. At the other extreme, the insider has the 'of-course-it's-true' knowledge of the member. For the insider, participation is effortless, observation difficult" (Anderson & Meyer, 1988: 296). First among the fundamental concepts of qualitative research is the axiom that the study of human life is interpretive, Anderson and Meyer argues. It is the search for subjective understanding, rather than manipulation; the quest for prediction and control. Qualitative research has replaced prediction with emphatic understanding as its research aim so that social science can be freed from its exploitative uses and enlisted instead in the cause of freedom and justice. Contrary to quantitative inquiry, which accepts its premises and focuses on methodological rigor, qualitative study stresses the critical analysis of those suppositions to understand human understanding, thereby restoring the critical and liberating function to intellectual investigation.

In anthropology one usually distinguishes between an *emic* and an *etic* approach:

> Emic operations have as their hallmark the elevation of the native informant to the status of the ultimate judge of the adequacy of the observer's descriptions and analyses. The test of the adequacy of emic analyses is their ability to generate statements the native accepts as real, meaningful, or appropriate. In carrying out research in the emic mode, the observer attempts to acquire a knowledge of the categories and rules one must know in order to think and act as a native.... . Etic operations have as their hallmark the elevation of observers to the status of ultimate judges and concepts used in descriptions and analyses. The test of adequacy of etic accounts is simply their ability to generate scientifically productive theories about the causes of socio-cultural differences and similarities. Rather than employ concepts that are necessarily real, meaningful, and appropriate from the native point of view, the observer is free to use alien categories and rules derived from the date language of science. Frequently, etic operations involve the measurement and juxtaposition of activities and events that native informants may find inappropriate or meaningless. (Harris, 1980: 32)

In this context I would like to plead for an emic position. However, as Clifford Geertz (1973:15) warns, this is an extremely difficult approach to accomplish: "We begin with our interpretations of what our informants are up to, or think they are up to, and then systematize." Geertz therefore prefers the notions of "experience-near" and "experience-far" above the emic and etic concepts. The former are internal to a language or culture and are derived from the latter, which are posed as universal or scientific.

Critical Research

Qualitative research has often been characterized as critical research. The reverse—that critical research is often qualitative in nature—is also true, especially when that research addresses the dominant societal structures and, in particular, when the inquiry is directed toward what can be called the academic research complex. Critical research looks at the historical, societal, and dynamic context of its questions, and consequently it is not amenable to rigid methodology. Hence, there exist few similarities in approaches deemed critical research. Therefore, Halloran (1981: 26), among others, argues that "the unity of the critical approach lies in its opposition to conventional work rather than in any shared, more positive approach." Lacking in "accepted" methods, critical research is often written off as unscientific or as ideological prattle. However, just as qualitative research accepts its subjectivity, critical analysis admits its ideological premises. It can also be argued the reason critical research is deemed invalid is not because of its disparate methodology, but rather because of its more populist stance. It seeks to examine social issues of importance to the general population and not to for example, politicians and media managers. It is attacked "because it challenges the status quo and the vested interests and rejects the conventional wisdom of the service research that supports this establishment" (Halloran, 1981:33). In sum, Halloran (1981:34) asserts:

> It is now suggested that research . . . should be shifted away from such questions as "the right to communicate" to "more concrete problems." But what are these "concrete problems?" They are the same as, or similar to, the safe, "value-free" micro questions of the old-time positivists who served the system so well, whether or not they intended or understood this. All this represents a definite and not very well disguised attempt to put the clock back to the days when the function of research was to serve the system as it was—to make it more efficient rather than to question it or suggest alternatives.

Validity and Evaluation in Qualitative Research

Given this lack of methodological rigor, on what grounds should one accept the qualitative or critical argument? What makes the research worth recognition? Was the research successful? To address these questions, reference is made to the earlier assertions regarding the premises of "value-free science" and "objectivity." If we do not accept these—if we see the emperor is indeed naked—then we must accept and valuate the conclusions of all inquiry in a different light. Unlike quantitative inquiry, qualitative research does not, as a rule, seek broad generalizeability. For the qualitative researcher there is no possibility of a grand theory of social action, as theory is contextually bound. Nor does it strive for reliability in its tools of analysis. Indeed, its basis of an interpretive, and consequently idiosyncratic, social reality precludes the strict application of such tools (Herndon & Kreps, 1993).

Whereas the primarily concerns of quantitative research are reliability and construct validity, qualitative research seeks external validity, not through objectivity, but rather through subjectivity. Anderson (1988: 239) writes "The closer the analytic effort is to the lifeworld, the more direct its observation; the more it uses the concepts and language of this lifeworld, the greater the validity." Therefore, to the degree it reflects the circumstances, inquiry is valid and reliable even though it is not based on randomization, repeated and controlled observation, measurement, and statistical inference. In other words, it "is more 'objective' precisely because it can bring in more of the subjective intentionality" (White, 1984:40).

The Role and Place of the Reader, Viewer, . . . Receiver

The primary problem of validity in qualitative inquiry, then, is "of matching the researcher's conclusions and the actor's intention" (Rockhill, 1982:12) and putting those conclusions into a form that makes sense to the reader, to go "from understanding to explanation, and from explanation to understanding" (13). In light of cultural variance, indeed—the disparity of realities—this is no simple task.

Ultimately, for both quantitative and qualitative analysis, validity ultimately rests on the acceptance or rejection of the argument by the reader him or herself. Whether the statistical analysis was proper, the data clean, the surveyors well trained, and so on, innumerable attacks can be brought against any study if the reader does not care to accept the propriety of the argument. On the other hand, if the reader (or policymaker) finds the conclusions amenable, or the author trustworthy, he or she will rarely give the methods a second glance. It comes down to the skill, honesty, and ethics of the researcher.

Therefore, in the final analysis, Anderson (1988:355) writes the value of and criticism toward the qualitative study must

> be appropriate to its character as a personal encounter, documented by a careful record, which results in an interpretation of the social action which rises inductively to a coherent explanation of the scene.

To criticize this effort for its lack of objectivity, random sampling, statistical measure of validity, deductive logic, and the like is inane. Such criticism simply established the ignorance of the critic. . . . As with all research, the success of a qualitative study is dependent on reaching the knowledgeable, skeptical reader with a compelling argument. The skeptical reader will give none of these criteria away, demand an honest effort, and consider the weaknesses as well as the insights in reaching a judgement of value. That judgement of value is the bottom line of research.

PARTICIPATORY RESEARCH

If we subscribe to the notion that social research should have a beneficial impact on society, it is imperative that we pay more attention to research philosophies that can profitably handle, and indeed stimulate, social change. Therefore, participatory research, in my opinion, borrows the concept of the interpretive, inter-subjective, and human nature of social reality from qualitative research, and the inherency of an ideological stance from critical research, combines them, and goes one step further. Rather than erecting elaborate methodological facades to mask the ideological slant and purpose of inquiry, the question becomes, "Why shouldn't research have a direct, articulated social purpose?" Instead of relying on participant observation or complex techniques to gain the subjective, "insider's" perspective, it is asked, "Why shouldn't the `researched' do their own research?" Why is it "The poor have always been researched, described and interpreted by the rich and educated, never by themselves?"

In regard to the topic at hand, why is it such a great deal of research about participation has been conducted in a nonparticipatory fashion? As in the case of participatory communication, the major obstacles to participatory research are anti-participatory, often inflexible structures and ideologies. We cannot be reductionistic about holism, static about dynamism, value-free about systematic oppression, nor detached about participation. Participatory research may not be good social science in positivist terms, but it may be better than positivist social science for many development purposes.

Principles of Participatory Communication Research

That the mass of social research is largely guided by the social context in which it operates and largely does not function to serve those studied has been argued at length. Participatory research was conceived in reaction to this elitist research bias. It is ideological by intent; it is the research of involvement. It is not only research with the people—it is people's research. As such it largely rejects both the development policies of states and the "objectivity" and "universal validity claims" of many methodologies in the social sciences. Even if we momentarily assume contemporary research practices are free of ideology and do not constitute a means of oppression, the fact remains they are of little utility to the poor (DeSchutter, 1983; Fernandes & Tandon, 1981).

> We have moved beyond the whole notion of some of us leading the struggles of others. This shift . . . in the control over knowledge, production of knowledge, and the tools of production of knowledge is equally legitimate in our continued struggles towards local control and overcoming dependency. It is here that PR [participatory research] can be an important contribution . . . PR is quite the opposite of what social science research has been meant to be. It is partisan, ideologically biased and explicitly non-neutral. (Tandon, 1985:21)

The realization that most of the present professional approach to research is in fact a reproduction of our unjust society in which a few decision makers control the rest of the population has led many to move away from the classical methods and experiment with alternative approaches. In urging participatory research, we are not speaking of the involvement of groups or classes already aligned with power. These groups already have at their disposal all the mechanisms necessary to shape and inform our explanation of the world.

Therefore, a basic tenet of participatory research is that whomever does the research, the results must be shared. They must be available to the people among whom research is conducted and on whose lives it is based. Data is not kept under lock and key or behind computer access codes, and results are not cloaked in obfuscating jargon and statistical symbols.

Furthermore, and perhaps most importantly, the inquiry must be of benefit to the community and not just a means to an end set by the researcher. This benefit is contrasted with the circuitous theory-research design-data-analysis-policy-government service route that neutralizes, standardizes, dehumanizes, and ultimately functions as a means of social control: "People's voices undergo a metamorphosis into useful data, an instrument of power in the hands of another. Rather than assembling collectively for themselves, political constituencies are assembled by pollsters, collecting fragmentary data into 'public opinion'" (Ewen, 1983:222).

Again, participatory research challenges the notion that only professional researchers can generate knowledge for meaningful social reform. Like authentic participation, it believes in the knowledge and ability of ordinary people to reflect on their oppressive situation and change it. To the contrary, in many cases at the local community level, participants have proved to be more capable than "experts" because they best know their situation and have a perspective on problems and needs that no outsider can fully share. This perspective is quite divergent from the abstract concepts, hypothetical scenarios, and macrolevel strategies that occupy the minds and consume the budgets of development "experts" and planners.

Differences Between Participatory Research and Action Research

Because of this nature of involvement, participatory research is often known under the rubric of *social action* or *action research* (Argyris, Putnam & Smith, 1985; Fals Borda, 1988; Fals Borda & Rahman, 1991; Kassam & Mustafa, 1982; Whyte, 1989, 1991). In numerous respects they are similar, and participatory research is not really new. It is a novel concept only to the extent it questions the domains of the research as well as the economic and political elites.

However, there are fundamental differences between action and participatory research. Chantana and Wun Gaeo (1983: 37) write that action research

> can be non-participatory and related to top down development . . . whereas participatory research must involve the people throughout the process. Action research can be intended to preserve and strengthen the status quo, whereas participatory research . . . is intended to contribute to the enhancement of social power for the hitherto excluded people.

By way of example, in the realm of media production, Varma, Ghosal, and Hulls (1973:4) define action research as a "systematic study, incorporated into the production of media, the results of which are fed back directly and immediately to the production staff to help them to improve the effectiveness of their communication."

Conversely, participatory research assumes a bias toward the "subjects" involved in the research process rather than the professional. Participatory research is related to the processes of conscientization and empowerment. It was probably Paulo Freire who introduced the first version of this approach in his philosophy of conscientization. Rather than agendas being defined by an academic elite and programs enacted by a bureaucratic elite for the benefit of an economic or political elite, participatory research involves people gaining an understanding of their situation, confidence, and an ability to change that situation. White (1984: 28) writes this is quite divergent from

> the functionalist approach which starts with the scientist's own model of social and psychological behavior and gathers data for the purpose of prediction and control of audience behavior. The emphasis is on the awareness of the subjective meaning and organization of reality for purposes of self-determination.

Participatory research is egalitarian. Thematic investigation thus becomes a common striving toward awareness of reality and toward self-awareness. It is an educational process in which the roles of the educator and the educated are constantly reversed and the common search unites all those engaged in the endeavor. It immerses the exogenous researcher in the setting on an equal basis. Considering the necessary trust and attitudes as well as cultural differences, the task is not easy and makes unfamiliar demands on researchers/educators.

"Insiders" and "Outsiders"

Interaction fosters a pedagogical environment for all participants. The researcher, as a newcomer, contributes in that he or she requires the membership to give an account of how things are done, which fosters an atmosphere in which participants may better know themselves, question themselves, and consciously reflect on the reality of their lives and their sociocultural milieu. Through such interaction, a fresh understanding, new knowledge, and self-confidence may be gained. Furthermore, awareness, confidence, and cohesiveness are enhanced not only for group members but among and between those members and "outsiders" who may participate, thereby increasing their understanding of the context and obstacles under which the people strive. Education goes both ways. This learning process can instill confidence and, ultimately, empowerment. The intent of participatory research is not latent awareness. Relevant knowledge increases self-respect and confidence and leads both to an exploration of alternatives toward the attainment of goals and to *action*. Through this process, the givenness of the group is revealed. Based on this, one can build a superior, higher vision.

A Definition of Participatory Research (PR)

The recent popularity of participatory research and the act of labelling it as such, may imply that it is something special that requires a particular expertise, a particular strategy, or a specific methodology. Similar to participation, there has been great effort toward definitions and models of participatory research to lend an air of respectability. Also similar to participation, perhaps this is no more than an attempt to claim title or credit for an approach which, by its very nature, belongs to the people involved. As one is dealing with people within changing social relations and cultural patterns, one cannot afford to be dogmatic about methods but should keep oneself open to people. This openness comes out of a trust in people and a realization that the oppressed are capable of understanding their situation, searching for alternatives, and making their own decisions:

> Participatory research is an alternative social research approach in the context of development. It is alternative, because although business, government and the academic also undertake research with development in the end view, little thought and effort go as to how the research project can be used for the benefit of those researched. The central element of Participatory Research is participation. . . . It is an active process whereby the expected beneficiaries of research are the main actors in the entire research process, with the researcher playing a facilitator's role. (Philippine Partnership for the Development of Human Resources in Rural Areas, 1986:1).

Because there is no reality "out there" separate from human perception and, as put forth in the multiplicity paradigm, there is no universal path to development, it is maintained each community or grouping must proceed from its own plan in consideration of its own situation. In other words, to the extent the methodology is rigidly structured by the requisites of academia, participatory research is denied.

By its nature, this type of research does not incorporate the rigid controls of the physical scientist or the traditional models of social science researchers. Chantana and Wun Gaeo (1985:39) state:

> There is no magic formula for the methodology of such PR projects. . . .
> However, there are common features taking place in the process:
> (1) It consists of continuous dialogue and discussion among research participants in all stages; [and]
> (2) Knowledge must be derived from concrete situations of the people and through collaborative reflection . . . return to the people, continuously and dialectically.

Therefore, we would like to delineate participatory research as an educational process involving three interrelated parts:

1. Collective definition and investigation of a problem by a group of people struggling to deal with it. This involves the social investigation that determines the concrete condition existing within the community under study, by those embedded in the social context;
2. Group analysis of the underlying causes of their problems, which is similar to the conscientization and pedagogical processes addressed earlier, and;
3. Group action to attempt to solve the problem.

The Process of Participatory Research

Therefore, the process of participatory research is cyclical, continuous, local, and accessible. Study-reflection-action is the integrating process in this type of research. Kronenburg (1986: 255) gives the following characteristics of participatory research:

> [It] rests on the assumption that human beings have an innate ability to create knowledge. It rejects the notion that knowledge production is a monopoly of "professionals"; [It] is seen as an educational process for the participants . . . as well as the researcher; It involves the identification of community needs, augmented awareness about obstacles to need fulfillment, an analysis of the causes of the problems and the formulation and implementation of relevant solutions; The researcher is consciously committed to the cause of the community involved in the research. This challenges the traditional principle of scientific neutrality and rejects the position of the scientist as a social engineer. Dialogue provides for a framework which guards against manipulative scientific interference and serves as a means of control by the community.

Evaluation and Validity in Participatory Research

Given a continuous cycle of study-reflection-action, participatory research inherently involves formative evaluation. Indeed, the terms *participatory research* and participatory evaluation are often used synonymously. Actors are often exercising themselves in participatory evaluation by the whole group.

Congruent with the objectives of participatory research, the purpose of evaluation is to benefit the participants themselves. It does not function to test the efficiency of an exogenous program, formulate diffusion tactics or marketing strategies for expansion to a broader level, gather hard data for publication, justify the implementing body, or collect dust on a ministry shelf. In brief, it is an ongoing process as opposed to an end product of a report for funding structures.

Whether participatory research succeeds or fails is secondary to the interaction and communication processes of participating groups. The success of the research is no longer seen in publications in "reputed" journals but in what happens during the process of research. Bogaert, Bhagat, and Bam (1981:181) add that

> participatory evaluation generates a lot of qualitative data which is rich in experiences of the participants. It may be . . . quantitative data is sacrificed in the process. However, what is lost in statistics is more than made up by the enhanced richness of data.

The Integration of Different Methodologies

The implication is not that quantitative or qualitative methods or exogenous collaboration in participatory evaluation are forbidden. Writing of research participants, D'Abreo (1981:108) states:

> While they, as agents of their own programme, can understand it better and be more involved in it, the outside evaluator may bring greater objectivity and insights from other programmes that might be of great use to them. However, the main agents of evaluation, even when conducted with the help of an outside agency or individual, are they themselves.

Turning to the question of validity, Tandon (1981:22) suggests, on a methodological level, "getting into a debate about reliability and validity of PR is irrelevant because it is quite the opposite shift in understanding what this research is." Its focus is on authenticity as opposed to validity. However, referring to generalizeability and validity in relation to qualitative research, it can be argued that validity in its less esoteric sense is participatory research's hallmark. "If ordinary people define the problem of research themselves, they will ensure its relevance" (Tandon, 1981: 24), and their involvement "will provide the 'demand-pull' necessary to ensure accuracy of focus" (Farrington, 1988: 271).

Finally, indigenous knowledge, the basis of participatory research, is inherently valid. This is not to say conditions are not changing or that this knowledge cannot benefit from adaptation. The argument is that, in most cases, this knowledge is the most valid place from which to begin.

A Word of Caution

Participatory research can all to easily be utilized as yet another tool of manipulation by vested interests. Charges are correct that it is often a means of political indoctrination by the right and the left alike. Often organizers are attacked for manipulating people's minds and managing their actions toward their own ends.

Although the approach strives toward empowerment, challenges existing structures, and is consequently ideological, rigidly prescribed ideologies must be avoided. In addition, the knowledge and perspective gained may well empower exploitative economic and authoritarian interests instead of local groups. Far from helping the process of liberation, if the researcher is not careful, he or she may only enable the traditional policymakers and vested interests to present their goods in a more attractive package without changing their substance.

Even the best intentioned researcher/activist can inadvertently enhance dependency rather than empowerment. If he or she enters communities with ready-made tools for analyzing reality and solving problems, the result will likely be that as far as those tools are successful, dependency will simply be moved from one tyrant to another (Salmen, 1987).

In other words, overzealous researchers can easily attempt to compensate for an initial apathy by assuming the role of an advocate rather than a facilitator. "What looks like progress is all too often a return to the dependent client relationship" (Kennedy, 1984:86). This approach is no better than more traditional researchers with hypotheses and constructs to validate, or the diffusionist with an innovation for every ill.

SYNTHESIS

1. Most contemporary research is based on positivistic assumptions, that we can objectively know the social world "out there." It is argued that objectivity is nothing more than inter-subjectivity, principles, and parameters that people agree to agree on. The danger occurs when one group assumes its constructs and methods are universally valid.

2. Qualitative and quantitative research are largely polar in orientation. The qualitative approach accepts, indeed advocates, subjectivity as a valid avenue of understanding. The emphasis is on how people perceive, understand, and construct reality rather than how they mechanistically react to manipulative stimuli.

3. As such, qualitative research is a human approach to the understanding of a human world. The researcher strives to see the naturalistic environment of those he or she is studying from their perspective. This forbids rigid, preformulated constructs and hypotheses.

4. What makes the qualitative study of value is not its construct validity or reliability, but its external validity. This validity arises from its foundations in human perception rather than rigorous methodology. In the final analysis, the relevance of any research rests on the reader's quite subjective acceptance or rejection of the argument advanced.

5. Combining aspects of qualitative and critical research, participatory research asks why shouldn't the researched do their own research. A further question is why is the mass of research on participation done in a nonparticipatory manner?

6. Like all research, participatory research is ideological. It is biased in the sense that research should be guided by, available to, and of direct benefit to the researched rather than privileged information for a manipulative elite. It further believes research is not, nor should be, the domain of a powerful few with the "proper" tools.

7. Participatory research is similar but not equal to social action research. It is research of involvement, not detachment. It includes all parties in a process of mutual and increasing awareness and confidence. It is research of conscientization and empowerment.

8. As has been argued for participation, and similar to qualitative approaches, there can be no strict methodology for participatory research. However, it must actively and authentically involve participants throughout the process, and the general flow is from study to reflection to action.

9. Evaluation is inherent in participatory research. However, it is formative rather than summative evaluation. Its purpose is not for journal publication, ego boosting, or to solicit further funding, but rather to monitor and reflect on the process as it unfolds. Furthermore, people's involvement in the research assures the validity of the inquiry, their validity.

4

From Theory to Policy

The struggle for democracy is the centerpiece for the struggle for liberation. Yet it is also clear that democracy has different meanings for different peoples throughout the world. For some, it is synonymous with capitalism, the propagation of acquisitiveness and greed, the barbaric practices of colonialism, and conceptually opposed to socialism. For others, it is a process of achieving equality of social justice for all peoples through popular sovereignty.
—Paulo Freire (1993: XI)

A review of the three paradigms of communication for development reveals a number of shifts in scientific thinking:

1. from a more positivistic, quantitative, and comparative approach to a normative, qualitative, and structural approach;
2. from a universal, formally descriptive model to a more substantial, change-oriented, and less predictable model;
3. from a Euro- or ethnocentric view to an indigenistic view and then to a contextual and polycentric view;
4. from endogenism to exogenism and then to globalism;
5. from an economic interest to more universal and interdisciplinary interests;

6. from a primarily national frame of reference to an international perspective and then to combined levels of analysis;
7. from segmentary to holistic approaches and then to more problem-oriented approaches; and
8. from an integrative and reformist strategy to revolutionary options and then to an integral vision and revolutionary and evolutionary change.

As has been argued earlier, paradigms in the social sciences tend to build on one another rather than break fundamentally with previous theories. Returning to Rosengren's cross tabulation (Figure 1.1), how much and in what ways can communication contribute to the process of development?

The basic idea in the *modernization paradigm* is that mass media and mass communication stimulate and diffuse values and institutions that are favorable to achievement, mobility, innovation, and consumption. Therefore, most of the communication approaches toward modernization can be placed under the heading of idealism in Rosengren's typology. The *dependency and communication paradigm* contains both materialist and idealist elements because it points both to technological and economic dependence on the Center and to cultural and ideological penetration by Western values and thought patterns. However, as its basic argument starts from an explicit economic assumption, that is, the state of underdevelopment in the Periphery is determined by the development of the Center, I find the materialist elements to be dominant. In the *multiplicity paradigm*, the four aspects of the typology are there. As it is an emergent paradigm I consider it too early to explicitly point out a dominating element in it.

Shifts in Scientific Thinking

These shifts can be observed among individual scientists as well as in particular research projects and publications. Some of the well-known protagonists of a particular paradigm may have adhered to their original standpoint; others may have adopted new notions and gradually changed their views. Moreover, the problem of the internal consistency of particular viewpoints and research results can be evaluated from this perspective.

The evolutionary perspective in which these paradigms have to be evaluated is, in the case of the dependency paradigm, well described by Chilcote and Johnson (1983:17):

Dependency analysis served two purposes. On the one hand, it offered an alternative explanation to the sterile and dogmatic Stalinist analysis emanating from the pro-Soviet communist parties in the period after World War II. On the other hand, it undermined the hegemony of modernization theory in the field of developmental studies. Attention to dependency theory raised new questions, placed old issues in new perspective; and while the concept led to no unified theory, it allowed for reformulation of analysis on imperialism and class struggle. Attention to modes of production analysis opened the way to in-depth research on modes and relations of production and understanding of concrete situations rather than unsubstantiated theory and abstract analysis.

Some of the spokespersons for the modernization and communication paradigm have long remained active in the communication research field. Their original optimism and enthusiasm, as shown in their early works published in the 1950s and 1960s, has since been questioned and become more moderate. This change is best explained by the late Wilbur Schramm

It [research on modernization and development, JS] started, therefore, in a climate of optimism and almost missionary zeal, then took a toboggan slide from the heights nearly to the depths. The Western model did not work as its proponents had expected. . . . Many scholars come out of the development experience with less than medals of honor. (Schramm, 1982: VIII)

Nevertheless, some of the advocates of the modernization approach stuck to their original views on communication and development. This can be illustrated most clearly in Daniel Lerner's case. Although his theory and research design has been severely criticized, he has never changed the basic assumptions on which it was built. He only gradually broadened his frame of reference and shifted from an originally national to a more global analysis (see, e.g., Lerner, 1977, 1978; Lerner & Schramm, 1967). Others also introduced or adopted some new notions without changing the core of their thinking. This occurred, in my opinion, to Schramm and Ruggles (1967), Schramm and Lerner (1976), and Ithiel de Sola Pool (1983).

Sometimes adjustments are made in very subtle ways. In their interesting, intercultural comparative analysis of the television drama *Dallas*, Liebes and Katz (1986) still hold to original diffusionist concepts. For instance, they conclude that "more 'modern' groups are less involved in the programme, knowing the mechanisms of distancing and discount, while the more traditional groups are more 'involved'" (168). Even Everett Rogers, although criticizing the early perspective for being too linear and manipulative from "above" (1976a; Rogers & Schoemaker, 1973) and introducing more contextual factors in a so-called network analysis (1976b, 1986; Rogers & Kincaid, 1981), has, in my opinion, not been able to go beyond this "dominant" paradigm (for more critical accounts of Rogers' approach, see Barton & Rogers, 1981; Choudhary & Prasad, 1986; McAnany, 1980).

However, it would be misleading to state that there have not been any major changes in conceptions of the role of communication in the modernization paradigm. For example, one just has to compare the two books edited by Lerner and Schramm (1967, 1976). The articles written by Dube, Oshima, and Inaytallah are of particular interest in this context.

Changes in Asian Communication Theories and Policies

Two books, both published by the Singapore-based Asian Mass Communication Documentation and Information Center (AMIC), with an interval of one decade between them, nicely portray the changes that have taken place in the development of both theory and policy formulation in Asia.

The first, edited by Peter Habermann and Guy de Fontgalland (1978), observed that

> the difficulties for the adoption of a viable development communication policy are caused very much by the fact that the planning of such a policy has to take into account that there is a horizontal and a vertical level which requires simultaneous approaches. The horizontal and vertical level consists of diversified institutions such as governmental developments, semi-governmental agencies (Rural extension Service etc.), independent development organizations, and private media, which are all active in communication in one way or the other. The coordination of these institutions, e.g. the problem of assigning them to communicative tasks they are able to perform best becomes thus a major item of a meaningful development communication policy. The vertical level is defined by the need for a mutual information flow between the population base and the decision-making bodies. On this level even more institutions are involved because of the local and supra-local administrations which of course are active in handing out directives and in feeding back reports to the government. Coordination of development communication becomes a more difficult task on this level because with the exception of the governmental extensions no institution is really prepared until now to pick up the information from the grass root levels and feeding them back meaningfully to the administration. (173)

However, the second book by Neville Jayaweera and Sarath Amunugama argued that

> (a) the pursuit of the modernization model, as recommended by the modernization and diffusion theorists and policymakers, was neither practicable nor desirable; (b) Third World societies should aim instead to satisfy the "basic needs" of their people; (c) fundamental reforms in the structures of international trade and monetary institutions were a necessary condition of development; (d) likewise, fundamental structural reforms within Third World societies themselves, such as land reform, opportunities for political participation, decentralization etc., were a prerequisite for development; (e) reliance on foreign aid and capital intensive technology must give way to self-reliance and appropriate technology, and that the bias for industry must give way to a greater commitment to agriculture; and (f) development is unthinkable except within a framework of culture. (1987: xvii)

The Need for New Approaches

In spite of the described reorientations and my earlier observation that the modernization and dependency paradigms have lost their attractiveness among academics, this definitely does not mean that they have vanished as theories. On the contrary, sometimes support comes out of unexpected places.

I illustrate this by briefly discussing two reports that attempted to assess the role and place of communication and culture in a global perspective: the report by the International Commission for the Study of Communication Problems, chaired by the late Lenin and Nobel Peace Prizes winner, Sean MacBride (1980), and the report of the World Commission on Culture and Development, chaired by former UN-Secretary-General Javier Perez De Cuellar (1995).

It goes without saying that other more general attempts could also be named: the report by the Independent Commission on International Development Issues, chaired by the former West-German Prime Minister Willy Brandt (1980); the report by the Commission on Global Governance (1985), chaired by the former Tanzanian President Julius Nyerere; the report by the World Commission on Environment and Development (1987), chaired by Norway's Prime Minister Brundtland; as well as the agenda for development of the past UN-Secretary-General Boutros Boutros-Ghali (1995).

The Brandt Report has often been recommended for advocating an "alternative" development model. Hence, it has been criticized by some western institutions for being too progressive. However, in my opinion, the basic idea in the report is the principle of interdependence. By recommending a Massive Resource Transfer as the solution to world poverty, it uses modernization indicators to guide political and economic policy and, in fact, propagates a strategy of mutual interest. Therefore, in a special issue of the journal *Encounter*, Minogue (1980:19-20) concludes rather ironically:

> Fundamentally, the Commission proposes to solve the world's problems by the creation of a Global Welfare State—and its report appears at just the moment when Welfare States of the North are in a state of collapse. The economic arguments, which are Keynes crossed at times with Machiavelli, derive from the 1930s and consist largely in the suggestion that we shall all get prosperous by giving lots of money to the South and then earning it back in exchange for what we produce.

The so-called Brundlandt Report was among the first to emphasize the crucial role of the ecological issue for development. Explicit in most of the report is the fact that change can only come about as a result of political action. The report draws attention to what it calls a "standard agenda" of environmental concern which it wants to call into question. This agenda commits a number of errors of bias or omission which the Commission seeks to correct. First, it is usually the effects of environmental problems that are addressed in public documents. Second, environmental issues are usually separated from development issues and frequently pigeon-holed under "conservation." Third, the Commission complains that critical issues such as acid rain or pollution are usually discussed in isolation, as if solutions to these problems can be found in discrete areas of policy. Fourth, the Commission criticizes what it sees as a narrow view of environmental policy, which regulates the environment to a secondary status—it is "added on" to other, more important development issues. However, as Michael Redclift (1987: 14) observes,

> it remains unlikely that the developed countries (or even the developing ones) will put into action the measures advocated by the Brundtland Commission. It is the argument of this book that they cannot do so without involving themselves in very radical structural reform, not only of methodologies for costing forest losses or soil erosion, but of the international economic system itself.

Similar comments have been made by De la Court (1990) and Martin Holdgate (1996).

The MacBride Report

Undoubtedly the work that has had the greatest influence on the international communication scene is the publication of *Many Voices, One World. Communication and Society. Today and Tomorrow* (1980) by the so-called *MacBride Commission*. The 19th General Conference of Unesco, held in Nairobi from October 26 to November 30, 1976, authorized the Director-General to appoint an international commission to study the problems of communication in the modern world. The commission's mandate was defined in four points:

> (a) To study the current situation in the field of communication and information and to identify problems which call for fresh action at the national level and a concerted, overall approach at the international level. The analysis of the state of communication in the world today, and particularly of information problems as a whole, should take account of the diversity of socio-economic conditions and levels and types of development; (b) to pay particular attention to problems relating to the free and balanced flow of information in the world, as well as the specific needs of developing countries, in accordance with the decisions of the General Conference; (c) to analyze communication problems, in their different aspects, within the perspective of the establishment of a new international economic order and of the measures to be taken to foster the institution of a "new world information order"; (d) to define the role which communication might play in making public opinion aware of the major problems besetting the world, in sensitizing it to these problems and helping gradually to solve them by concerted action at the national and international levels.

The commission's interim report was presented to the 20th General Unesco Conference, held in Paris in November 1978. Though it was regarded as a compromised text by most academic observers, at the same time it was severely criticized by a number of Western member states for being too critical in its analysis of the (Western) principles of press freedom and free flow of information. Therefore, the final report, which had to be ready for the 21st General Conference in Belgrade (September 23-October 28, 1980), was an even greater compromise. "One can only imagine the long hours spent in drafting inoffensive wording," wrote an American scholar who reviewed it for the *Journalism Quarterly* journal in 1981.

Apart from the foreword and annexes, the report is divided into five chapters: Communication and Society (pp. 3-46), Communication Today (pp. 47-136), Problems and Issues of Common Concern (pp. 137-

202), The Institutional and Professional Framework (pp. 203-252), and Communication Tomorrow (pp. 252-278). This is not the place for a summary of the report, as an abridged version has been published by Unesco. Let me only point out the major issues of relevance for the communication policy and planning field.

The commission's conclusions and recommendations were generally consistent with earlier resolutions and the main direction of Unesco's programs on communication. The report made a strong case for treating communication as a crucial societal resource and, therefore, incorporating it into overall development policymaking and planning processes at national and international levels:

> Development strategies should incorporate communication policies as an integral part in the diagnosis of needs and in the design and implementation of selected priorities. In this respect communication should be considered a major development source, a vehicle to ensure real political participation in decision-making, a central information base for defining policy options, and an instrument for creating awareness of national priorities. (MacBride, 1980: 258)

The various recommendations in this area clearly imply that national planning should aim at greater independence and self-reliance by paying more attention to communication policy formulation and resource allocation. Similarly, the international development assistance program for communication should be expanded and better coordinated across nations. All communication planning processes should be participatory, involving all the constituencies affected by communication development:

> Communication policies should (a) serve to marshal national resources; (b) strengthen the coordination of existing or planned infrastructures; (c) facilitate rational choices with regard to means; (d) help to satisfy the needs of the most disadvantaged and to eliminate the most flagrant imbalances; (e) enable all countries and all cultures to play more of a leading role on the international scene. (MacBride, 1980: 207)

The commission also called for reducing commercialism in communication and increasing access to scientific and technical information. A substantial part of the commission's recommendations dealt with sensitive matters—the democratization of communication, and the integrity, responsibility, and protection of journalists. The report emphasized the media's role in promoting oppressed people's struggles for freedom, independence, access to information, and the right of expression:

Communication can be an instrument of power, a revolutionary weapon, a commercial product, or a means of education; it can serve the ends of either liberation or of oppression of either the growth of the individual personality or of drilling human beings into uniformity. Each society must choose the best way to approach the task facing all of us and to find the means to overcome the material, social and political constraints that impede progress. (MacBride, 1980: 253)

While welcoming the MacBride report as "the first international document that provides a really global view on the world's communication problems" (Hamelink, 1980), most commentators generally felt that the report, for obvious political reasons, looked more like a hodge-podge than a consistent academic exercise (see, e.g., Aguirre-Bianchi & Hedebro, 1980; Gerbner, Mowlana, & Nordenstreng, 1993; Keune, 1984; McPhail, 1987; Nordenstreng & Schiller, 1993; Servaes, 1987; Ugboajah, 1985). Such comments have even been raised by some of the commission's members themselves (see, Abel, 1979, 1985; Lubis, 1986; Somavia, 1980). Someone ironically observed that the title of the report—*Many Voices, One World*—was also reflected inside the report itself. The major reason for this is that the report is a kind of political compromise in which the views of the Third World, as well as the opinions of the West and former Communist World, had to be represented. Therefore it was a mission impossible. This has led to a number of contradictory policy guidelines. Although phrases like "democratization of communication" and "the right to communicate" are scattered throughout the report, its main policy recommendations are more consistent with the political aims of the dependency paradigm, rather than being in line with the multiplicity paradigm.

The Report of the World Commission on Culture and Development

The more recent Report of the World Commission on Culture and Development, chaired by Javier Pérez de Cuéllar, argues that development divorced from its human or cultural context is growth without a soul. This means that culture cannot ultimately be reduced to a subsidiary position as a mere promoter of economic growth. It goes on to argue that "governments cannot determine a people's culture: indeed, they are partly determined by it" (Pérez De Cuéllar, 1995:15). The basic principle should be

the fostering of respect for all cultures whose values are tolerant of others. Respect goes beyond tolerance and implies a positive attitude to other people and a rejoicing in their culture. Social peace is necessary for human development: in turn it requires that differences between cultures be regarded not as something alien and unacceptable or hateful, but as experiments in ways of living together that contain valuable lessons and information for all. (Pérez De Cuéllar, 1995:25)

More is at stake here than attitudes. It is also a question of power. Policymakers cannot legislate respect, nor can they coerce people to behave respectfully. But they can enshrine cultural freedom as one of the pillars on which the state is founded. *Cultural freedom* is rather special. It differs from other forms of freedom in a number of ways. First, most freedoms refer to the individual. Cultural freedom, in contrast, is a collective freedom. It is the condition for individual freedom to flourish. Second, cultural freedom, properly interpreted, is a guarantee of freedom as a whole. It protects not only the collectivity but the rights of every individual within it. Third, cultural freedom, by protecting alternative ways of living, encourages creativity, experimentation, and diversity, the very essentials of human development. Finally, freedom is central to culture and, in particular, the freedom to decide what we have reason to value and what lives we have reason to seek. "One of the most basic needs is to be left free to define our own basic needs" (Pérez De Cuéllar, 1995: 26).

However, this need is being threatened by a combination of global pressures and global neglect. Therefore, the report advocates a search for a global ethics that involves culture. The Commission suggests that the following principal ideas should form the core of a *new global ethics:* (a) human rights and responsibilities; (b) democracy and the elements of civil society; (c) the protection of minorities; (d) commitment to peaceful conflict resolution and fair negotiation; and (e) equity within and between generations. The report observes that many elements of a global ethics are now absent from global governance. Therefore, the Commission has defined several areas of policy and action for governments, international organizations, private voluntary associations, profit-seeking firms, trade unions, families, and individuals, culminating in an International Agenda. Its purpose is to mobilize the energies of people everywhere in recognition of the new cultural challenges of today. It is selective and illustrative, not comprehensive.

Consequences for the Formulation of Communication Policies

These shifts in the scientific domain are also apparent in policy and policymaking. One often claims that policy, in practice as in theory, is based on a number of assumptions, usually provided and supported by social-scientific research. These serve as a guide for policymakers in various social sectors to justify their policy.

In communication sciences we usually refer to *Four Theories of the Press* (Siebert, Peterson, & Schramm, 1956) for an interpretation of this issue. These authors started from the assumption that "the press always takes on the coloration of the social and political structures within which it operates. Especially it reflects the system of social control whereby the relations of individuals and institutions are adjusted" (1-2). Referring to special political science models, these authors discerned four normative press theories: authoritarian, Soviet-communist, liberal, and social responsibility.

Since then, these four press (or better media) theories have been regularly discussed and modified (cf., e.g., Gordon & Merrill, 1988; Hachten, 1981; Jakubowicz, 1993; McQuail, 1983).

Merrill (1974; Merrill & Lowenstein, 1979) deserves particular mention in this context. Merrill and Lowenstein's thesis is that Siebert et al.'s classic models are based, on the one hand, on a too restricted (Western) description of concepts like "freedom," "democracy," and so on, which allow little or no generalizations, and that, on the other hand, reality often does not comply to the principles defined in philosophical terms.

Therefore, Lowenstein and Merrill propose a double, but integrated, distinction with both an economic and a philosophical base. The previously mentioned thesis, which was Siebert et al.'s starting point, was never questioned because, as with the former, these authors also think that

> media systems are, of course, closely related to the kinds of governments in which they operate; they are, in essence, reflective and supportive of the governmental philosophy. When viewed in this way, it is possible to say that all press systems are enslaved—tied to their respective governmental philosophies and forced to operate within certain national ideological parameters. (Merrill, 1979: 153)

But instead of the philosophical, they prefer a more economic approach because "the source of support will, in almost every case, indicate important operational characteristics of the press" (Merrill, 1979: 164). Thus, they implicitly accept the Marxist thesis that the economic basis defines and determines the ideological and sociocultural superstructure.

Next they bring in a distinction on both the economic (social would have been a better term) and the philosophical base. Within the dominant ownership structures they discern three forms: (a) private media (ownership by individuals or nongovernmental corporations; supported primarily by advertising or subscriptions); (b) media owned by different parties (ownership by competitive political parties; subsidized by party or party members); and (c) media owned by the government (owned by government or dominant government party; subsidized primarily by government funds or government-collected license fees).

This economic basis could be expanded threefold. First, by also taking the indirect and long-term control mechanisms and structures into account. Therefore it is too simplistic—but as it often happens—to judge the so-called democratic nature of a country only by the presence or absence of direct censorship. (see, e.g., the annual reports by the Zurich-based International Press Institute). Second, ownership and control structures can be of a local, national, international, or transnational nature, and should therefore be studied at these distinct levels, either separately or in an integrated fashion. Third, the splitting up into a private, public, and mixed sector on the one hand, and a distinction between control and/or property structures within the production versus distribution sector on the other hand, seem to allow a more useful classification.

Therefore, not only the obvious political-economic structures but the direct and indirect control mechanisms and structures should be taken into account. After an extensive survey of press censoring and controlling mechanisms all over the world, Curry and Dassin conclude,

> No political or social system exists with a totally free flow of information. Control over information and ideas is inherent in the very nature of human society—the human desire to conform; the natural coloring of events by the observers' preconceptions; the necessary bureaucratic pressures and interests involved in journalistic work; the monopoly of bureaucrats over information; and the needs of politicians and officials to ensure their own legitimacy with and penetration of their societies. These forces limit and structure the content of the mass media everywhere far more than do laws and explicit practices of directing and censoring the mass media. (1982: 283)

In this context Rowat (1981:315) also points out how subtlely this is often done:

> Modern governments make a genuine effort to inform the public about their administrative programmes and activities. As a result, the general public are not fully aware that much information is purposely withheld, or that the information released is slanted in favour of the government and its bureaucracy.

Referring to the philosophical starting points of a certain press system, Lowenstein and Merrill set out from a five-fold typology: (a) an authoritarian philosophy ("government licensing and censorship to stifle criticism and thereby maintain the ruling elite"); (b) a social-authoritarian philosophy ("a government and government-party ownership to harness the press for national economic and philosophical goals"); (c) a liberal philosophy ("absence of governmental controls—except for minimal libel and obscenity laws—assuring a free marketplace of ideas and operation of the self-righting process"); Merrill and Lowenstein prefer the concept "libertarian" to the more customary "liberal." In American economic thinking the term "libertarian" is associated with Smith, the term "liberal" with Keynes. In European thinking, however, the former term has a rather "anarchistic" connotation. Therefore, I prefer to use the term "liberal"); (d) a social-liberal philosophy ("minimal governmental controls to unclog channels of communication and assure the operational spirit of the libertarian philosophy"); and (e) a social-centralistic philosophy ("government or public ownership of the limited channels of communication to assure the operational spirit of the libertarian philosophy") (Merrill & Lowenstein, 1979:164).

With Lowenstein and Merrill the authoritarian and the liberal models are given the same definition as in the original typology. The social-authoritarian model stands for the communist one, which is eventually to be completed in these developing countries with a central and authoritarian media policy. Because the social responsibility model is rejected as being ambiguous, it is split up into a social-liberal and a social-centralistic version. Both models are built on liberal ideas "but each recognizes that modern society and modern technology have in some ways restricted the marketplace of ideas and that societal interference is necessary to unclog these choked channels" (Merrill & Lowenstein, 1979:165). Whereas the social-liberal model puts the responsibility for regulating and adopting the course of the system in the hands of the media systems themselves, in the social-centralistic model the external participation of public institutes or the government is not improbable. The fundamental difference between the social-centralistic and the social-authoritarian vision is that the first assumes a multitude of opinions and communication channels competing with each other, whereas the authoritarian vision wants to subject the media to the established power. Both, however, still start from a sender-oriented perspective in which the receiver of communication messages is not regarded as an active participant in the communication process.

Communication Freedoms in Cultural Settings

In my opinion, although this latter typology offers more possibilities for the reality of policymaking than the classic but still accepted classification of 1956, I would like to introduce a third dimension that I find of major importance to the earlier discussion; that is, a more *culturalist-anthropological dimension*. If there are ever to be principles that not only "claim" but entail a "universal appeal and validity," a more culturalist-anthropological understanding of communication principles is of crucial importance. Let me illustrate this by briefly describing the way communication principles have been regarded in distinct cultural settings.

The concepts *freedom of information* and *free flow of information* are of a relatively recent date. However, the ideas on which they are based are very old. In fact, they go back to the old Western principles of "freedom of opinion," "freedom of expression," and "freedom of the press." For centuries, these principles have been at the base of the Western way of thinking. They, among other things, were explicitly referred to in the American Constitution of 1776 and during the French Revolution. Article 12 of the *American Bill of Rights* states that "the freedom of the press is one of the great bulwarks of liberty and can never be restrained but by despotic government." In the French *Les Droits de l'Homme et du Citoyen* of 1789, it is stated that "the free expression of ideas and opinions is one of the most precious human rights; every citizen should be able to speak, write, and print freely; this freedom can only be restricted in those cases determined by law" (my translation, JS). Although the freedoms of word and expression have always been subject to fundamental restrictions, they nevertheless are part of the European and American ways of thinking, which led to freedom of printing and a free press (for an historic survey, see Barendt, 1985; Galtung, 1994; Hook, 1987; or Smith, 1981).

Nevertheless, the practical application of these liberties soon escaped the national level and the need for international agreements was felt. This shift can partly be explained as a result of changing power factors, and partly through culturally defined interpretation problems. Moreover, for international agreements and declarations, their nonbinding character is a crucial factor. Ricoeur (1986:11) therefore states,

> two shortcomings thus appear: that of law without force, as Pascal would have said, and that of law that is open to conflicting interpretations. The latter mainly concern the relation between asserting that economic, cultural and social rights are individual rights and asserting that these rights have their origins in the social policies of states. These two shortcomings are interrelated.

The following are examples of both shortcomings. The interpretation of communication principles, the MacBride Report, or the New International Information Order, is linked to powershifts on the political and/or economic level, as well as to the questioning of their universal validity. Wilcox (1975: 101), for example, writes, all too often, there is the tendency in the United States and Europe to think of Africa as a single, monolithic country, with an unstable, authoritarian government. In such a setting, press freedom is written off as an impossibility. Such superficial impressions of course are far from the truth. The social, political and press institutions at work in every country are as diverse as the geography and peoples of Africa.

Additionally, in most cultures, there is a difference between the rules of the written and unwritten culture (Hsiung, 1985; Terwiel, 1984; Turner, 1994). Although many (non-Western) governments, in their official declarations and documents, underwrite the Universal Declarations issued by the United Nations, which for a number of historical reasons are mainly based on Western ideas, in reality they do not pay much attention to their implementation. This is often due to reasons that have to do with power and culture. Consider, for instance, the discussion on the freedom of expression. According to Article 19 of the United Nations' Universal Declaration of Human Rights, "Everyone has the right to freedom of opinion and expression; this right includes freedom to hold opinions without interference and to seek, receive, and impart information and ideas through any media and regardless of frontiers." Section 39 of the Constitution of the Kingdom of Thailand also stipulates similar content: "An individual has the freedom to express his viewpoints through speech, writing, publishing, advertising and other means of communications." Given that Thailand once again has a so-called democratic rule, such freedoms are among those the Thai should be able to enjoy equally. However, in practice, it is a different story for the Thai media and the public at large (Siriyuvasak, 1997).

Moreover, in Asia, a number of values and norms, which the West considers very important, such as equality of men and women or democracy, are considered less important in reality. Other values, like respect for the elderly or loyalty to the group, on the other hand, are in the East considered much more important than in the West. This also counts for the interpretation of concepts such as cultural and press freedom in, for instance, the Western versus former Communist world (see Goldfarb, 1982; Zassoursky, 1997). Therefore, in 1981, the Universal Declaration of Human Rights was amplified with a Universal Islamic Declaration of Human Rights. The drafters argued that the United Nations' declaration was too much of a compromise between liberal humanism and Marxist humanism. In October 1986 the African Charter of Human Rights also came into operation.

The Public's Rights and Responsibilities

In the domain of the freedom of expression and the freedom of the press, one can observe a double evolution in the post-war period. Whereas originally the active right of the so-called sender-communicator to supply information without externally imposed restrictions was emphasized, today the passive as well as active right of the receiver to be informed and to inform gets more attention.

Therefore, the principle of the right to communicate was introduced as it contains both the passive and active right of the receiver to inform and be informed. This principle first appeared in 1969 in an article by Jean D'Arcy, the then-director of the UN information bureau in New York. D'Arcy (1969:14) wrote that "the time will come when the Universal Declaration of Human Rights will have to encompass a more extensive right than man's right to inform, first laid down twenty-one years ago in Article 19. This is the right of man to communicate." Not until 1974 was this principle introduced in Unesco. Both individual and social rights and duties are included in this right to communicate. This right will, in my opinion, become basic for the future search for a public- or user-oriented view on communication issues (see also, among others, Fischer, 1982; Fischer & Harms, 1983; Harms, Richstad, & Kie, 1977; Jorgenson, 1981).

At the same time, there is another and related shift taking place in the discussions on communication rights and responsibilities; that is, a shift from the so-called maintenance duty of the government toward the media to an emphasis on the government's duty to take care of and to create the conditions and infrastructure in which the freedom of communication can be realized and stimulated as a fundamental social right. The Belgian jurist Dirk Voorhoof (1985:11) sums up both evolutions (see Figure 4.1).

The New International Information Order

Both shifts in the definition of communication freedom principles and the role of the government can be briefly illustrated by the discussion on the concept for a New International Information Order (NIIO). As in the case of the principles just discussed there is no clear unified definition of the NIIO concept: "There is no model for the new, more just order in the field of mass communication, no instructions to be followed, and there is no unified, valid definition of it either" (Bunzlova, 1986: 23). In other words, it is a concept that covers different meanings (Roach, 1986). Nevertheless, most authors who have tried to define the content of the NIIO concept (see, e.g., Becker, Hedebro, & Paldan, 1986; Hamelink, 1994b; Nordenstreng, & Schiller, 1993; Yadava, 1984) discern two funda-

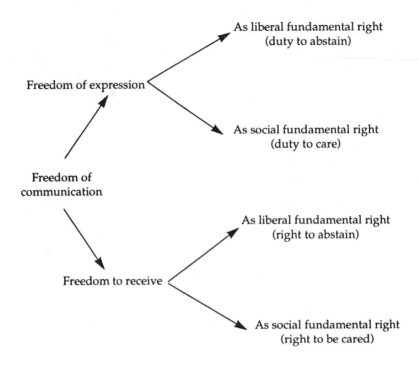

Figure 4.1. The dimensions of the communication freedoms

mental fields of tension: tension between freedom and sovereignty, the tension between private and government or public initiatives.

Whereas the West emphasizes the individual liberal freedom of the private initiative, the group of *Non-Aligned Countries* in particular claims the right of self-determination and national sovereignty in a global context. Thus they plead for a direct link between the New International Economic Order (NIEO) and the NIIO. They argue every nation should be able to dispose of its own information resources, elements, and channels (see also Nwosu, 1985; Pavlic & Hamelink, 1984).

The former Soviet-Russian or communist interpretation, though closely related to the position of the Non-Aligned Countries, nevertheless diverged from it with regard to two essential issues. First, the link between the NIEO and the NIIO is not considered fundamental and consequently does not gets priority; second, they hardly pay any attention to the structural forms of dependency and concentrate more on the ideological aspects and, therefore, on the content of the communication processes (Kolosov & Tsepov, 1984; Nordenstreng, 1984).

In my opinion there is also a possible fourth interpretation that starts from a bottom-up perspective in which the receiver is the starting point. Robert White (1985:53-54) summarizes this perspective in the following six points:

> (a) The communications media should serve the interests of all the public, not just the interests of the economically and politically powerful, whether the powerful be individuals, corporations or countries; (b) communication is not a process of handing down in didactic fashion the knowledge of an elite, but rather a fostering of horizontal interchange and a mutual fashioning of culture among equals; (c) more decentralized communication systems are needed, allowing broader access to, participation in and use of these systems; (d) communication is a human right and communication systems should allow greater participation in their creation and administration; (e) if the right to communication is basic, then education to use this right should be an integral part of all education; (f) the authoritarian models of communication need to be questioned and radically reformulated.

In line with this perspective, in 1994 a provisional version of the *People's Communication Charter* was proposed (see Hamelink, 1994). Also, the statements adopted by organizations such as the World Association for Christian Communication or the so-called MacBride Roundtables accepted the same principles (see WACC, 1991).

The Policy Options of the Three Paradigms

The principle of *free flow of information* can be considered the communication policy application of the modernization paradigm. After a fascistic and authoritarian period of war, it took little effort in 1945 for the free West, led by the United States, to have this principle accepted as a universal value within the United Nations. This principle of freedom was initially interpreted in a rather individualistic and liberal manner and formed the basis of the so-called *free press theory* that still determines the international communication policy of many Western government and communication transnationals, as well as of the Third World elites oriented to the West. It took considerable time before this extreme liberal vision would be provided with a more social explanation, particularly in the so-called social responsibility or social-liberal theory. The major difference between the free press and *social-responsibility theory is* related to the question of whether the freedom of information principle can or should only be guaranteed by private competition, or also by public authorities and institutionalized groups of media workers and media consumers. In everyday life one observes that publishers, both in western and Third World countries, advocate extreme liberal interpretations of this principle. Governments, on the other hand, tend to take more ambivalent and varied positions, which are more in line with the latter interpretations of the free flow principle. Therefore, Balle (1985) observes differences between Western European and U.S. governmental policies. Whereas the former attempt to regulate the market, the United States is, at least theoretically, in favor of total liberalization and deregulation policies.

With the development of the dependency viewpoint, this free and unhindered flow of information, grafted into the free-flow doctrine, was challenged. From the Third World arguments were put forth for a *free and balanced flow of information, a* principle that was backed particularly by the Non-Aligned Nations in the debate on the New International Information Order. At the same time, it was contended that this free and balanced flow could be better guaranteed and organized by governments than by private enterprises. These viewpoints are explicitly formulated in the so-called *development media theory* (Hachten, 1981; McQuail, 1983) and are also implicitly there in the just-mentioned social-authoritarian and social-centralistic philosophies.

This position was strongly contested by the defenders of a free press, who charged that it could lead to governmental censure and curbs on the press. And, indeed, in reality this did often appear to be the case. In Latin America, the mother continent of the dependency paradigm, the process of capitalistic state intervention brought authoritarian, generally military governments into power that tried to centralize decision making and opinion formation. These governments control the production and distribution of communication and use the media for their own legitimation purposes. Participation and politization of the population is countered with every possible means. Similar situations occur in other developing countries, for instance, in countries known to be prominent proponents of the demands of the Non-Aligned Nations, like India, Malaysia, Mexico, Nicaragua, Ghana, Guyana, and Tanzania (see, e.g., Boafo, 1989; Casmir, 1991; Fox ,1988; Hoover, Venturelli, & Wagner, 1993; Kivikuru ,1990).

These countries have a *contradictory communication policy.* Abroad, they support a free and balanced flow of information, while they do as much as they can to keep it under control within their own borders. The same applies, moreover, for many Western nations. The U.S. government, for example, supports free export of American communication products but tries as much as possible to stop the import of such products from abroad by protectionist measures. Even Ithiel de Sola Pool (1983), one of the fierce propagandists of free-flow principles, had to admit that "in rhetoric, the United States government favors diversity of voices and seeks to break up communications monopolies. The reality, however, is more ambiguous" (241). For general evaluations of Western government communication policies one can also refer to Mansell's (1984) analysis of the Canadian communication policies; Wigand, Snipley, and Shipley's (1984) comparative analysis of the transborder data flow in 22 nations; or the internal inconsistencies in software versus hardware policies (Schiller, 1981, 1984). In this respect, Jeremy Tunstall concludes: "One basic dilemma democratic governments almost make a virtue of having no coherent media policy (this lack shows how free their media must be), but a policy about communications hardware is acceptable" (Tunstall, 1984:310).

In general, the governments of these countries hold rather contradictory views with regard to external versus internal communication policy principles. They support the demands for an expansion of the free and balanced flow between and among countries, but not within the borders of their individual nations. Therefore, the policy options of the two paradigms have one fundamental trait in common: they are *elitist* in the sense that they only want to increase the power of their respective elites and certainly do not strive to achieve universal social development. Whereas the modernization paradigm legitimates the interests of Western political and economic interest groups and their "bridgeheads" in the Third World, the dependency theory meets the economic and political needs of those Third World elites who want to play an autonomous role. Whereas the first group thus strives for international integration, the second group wants to turn back the international dependency relationship by means of a radical and dissociative policy. In both cases, however, little is done to alter the internal power relationships and dependency structures.

I therefore distinguish between an international or external-national and intra-national or domestic policy level (see Figure 4.2). "Underlying this double polarization there is a relationship of domination that is expressed at both levels: between nations in the context of the international system and between classes within each country" (Dagnino, 1980: 298). It is in this context that Jayaweera's (1986) critical comments on Hamelink's (1983) thesis of dissociation have to be interpreted:

One misses in Hamelink's formulation of remedial measures two important elements. One is an appreciation of the systemic character of the culture problematic and of its organic relationship to the problem of international capitalism. And the other is an appreciation of the complexities and parameters that constrain decision making in the "Realpolitik" of the Third World. (33)

Similar comments can be raised with regard to Asante and Kim's (1984) association strategy. First, they only concentrate on the extern-national dimension of the problematique, and second, they start from the "idealistic" assumption "that the elites of those societies reorient their priorities" (147).

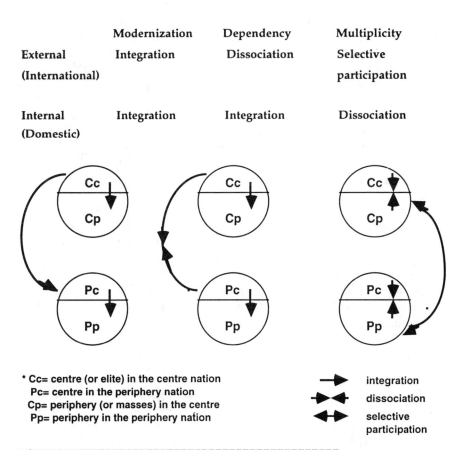

	Modernization	Dependency	Multiplicity
External (International)	Integration	Dissociation	Selective participation
Internal (Domestic)	Integration	Integration	Dissociation

* Cc= centre (or elite) in the centre nation
  Pc= centre in the periphery nation
  Cp= periphery (or masses) in the centre
  Pp= periphery in the periphery nation

→ integration
►◄ dissociation
◄► selective participation

Figure 4.2. Policy options of the three paradigms

The Right to Communicate

The right to communication is offered as a translation of the communication policy of the multiplicity paradigm. This principle, as a fundamental human right, clearly indicates that another communication model necessitates democratization and thus a redistribution of power at all levels. The point of departure is not an elitist position, but development from the grass-roots (Lee, 1995). Even the MacBride Report suggests that the right to communicate "promises to advance the democratization of communication on all levels—international, national, local, individual" (MacBride, 1980: 171).

Fundamental here is the other vision of the role of the authorities in processes of social change. Unlike the confidence in and respect for the role of the state, which is characteristic of the modernization and dependency paradigms, the multiplicity paradigm has a rather reserved attitude toward the authorities. Policies therefore should be built on the more selective participation strategies of dissociation and association.

The points of difference between the two options and the ideal-typical political consequences following from them are set side-by-side in Table 4.1, which makes a political division between a dominant and a pluralistic model (adapted from McQuail, 1983: 68). Along with this political distinction goes an implicit distinction between two models of the process in which the top of society is related, by way of mass communication, to the various groups at the bottom. This *dominance model* could stand for the "elitist" aims of both the modernization and dependency paradigms, whereas the *pluralist model* is more suitable for the "basic" needs of the third perspective. The assumptions underlying both models are clearly opposite and, according to Merrill's (1974) typology, belong to the authoritarian and the libertarian orientation, respectively.

These two models have fundamentally different policy and planning implications. It makes a great difference whether policy priorities and planning projects are designed and worked out from the perspective of the top or the grass-roots. This is illustrated in Table 4.2 (adapted from Tehranian, 1979:123), which places the two positions next to each other for a number of development and communication objectives.

SYNTHESIS

1. The paradigm shifts can be observed among individual scientists as well as in particular research projects and publications. Some of the protagonists of a particular paradigm adhered to their original standpoint; others adopted new notions and gradually changed their views. Also, the problem of the internal consistency of particular viewpoints and research results was evaluated from this perspective.

TABLE 4.1. A Comparison between a Dominance and a Pluralism Model.

	Dominance Top to Bottom	Pluralism Bottom to top
Societal source	Ruling class or dominant elite	Competing political, sociocultural interest groups
Media	Under concentrated ownership and of uniform type	Many and independent of each other
Structure	Hierarchical, bureaucratic	Horizontal, egalitarian
Production	Standardized, routinized, controlled, synchronic	Creative, free, original, free, diachronic
Content and ideology	Selective and coherent, decided from "above"	Diverse and competing views, decided from "below"
Audience	Dependent, passive organized on large scale	Fragmented, selective, reactive and active
Effects	Strong and confirmative of established social order	Numerous, without consistency or predictability of direction

TABLE 4.2. Development and Communication Objectives Viewed from a Top Versus Bottom Perspective.

Top perspective	Bottom perspective
National power and security	Individual choice and freedom
Social mobilization	Social mobility
National identity, integration and unity	Subnational (ethnic or group interest) identity and solidarity
Economic growth (rise in national income)	Income distribution and social justice
Political socialization	Political participation
Property and business rights	Public and consumer rights
Educational and professional advance	Educational and professional opportunities
Information control	Information access
Majority rule (where there is electoral democracy)	Minority rights
Central control and direction	Regional and local autonomy
Cultural and artistic direction (sometimes censorship)	Cultural and artistic creativity (sometimes subversive)
Ideological and cultural control	Intellectual and artistic freedom
Mass-media centered (one way communication)	Multiple communication use (media and interpersonal communication)
Emphasis on solutions	Emphasis on questions and problems
Product oriented	Process oriented

2. In spite of these reorientations and shifts, it does not mean that older paradigms have "vanished" as theories. On the contrary, sometimes support comes out of unexpected places. This has been illustrated by discussing two reports that attempted to assess the role and place of communication and culture in a global perspective: the report by the International Commission for the Study of Communication Problems, chaired by Sean MacBride (1980), and the report of the World Commission on Culture and Development, chaired by the former UN Secretary-General Javier Perez De Cuellar (1995).

3. These shifts in the scientific domain are also apparent in policy and planning. Policy and planning are based on a number of assumptions, usually provided and supported by social-scientific research. These assumptions serve as a guide for policymakers in various social sectors to justify their policy.

4. In the domain of the freedom of expression and the freedom of press, one can observe a double evolution in the post-war period. Whereas originally the active right of the so-called sender-communicator to supply information without externally imposed restrictions was emphasized, today the passive as well as active right of the receiver to be informed and to inform gets more attention. Therefore, the principle of the right to communicate was introduced as it contains both the passive and active right of the receiver to inform and be informed.

5. These shifts in the definition of communication freedom principles and the role of the government were briefly illustrated by the discussion on the concept for a New International Information Order (NIIO).

6. It was concluded that many countries have a contradictory communication policy with regard to external versus internal communication policy principles. Abroad, they support a free and balanced flow of information, while they do as much as they can to keep it under control within their own borders. They support the demands for an expansion of the free and balanced flow between and among countries, but not within the borders of their individual nations. Therefore, the policy options of the two paradigms have one fundamental trait in common: they are elitist in the sense that they only want to increase the power of their respective elites and certainly do not strive to achieve universal social development. Whereas the modernization paradigm legitimates the interests of Western political and economic interest groups and their "bridgeheads" in the Third World, the dependency theory meets the economic and political needs of those Third World elites who want to play an autonomous role. Whereas the first group thus strives for international integration, the second group wants to turn back the international dependency relationship by means of a radical and dissociative policy. In both cases, however, little is done to alter the internal power relationships and dependency structures.

Part II
. . . To Policy and Planningmaking

5

Communication Policy and Planning for Social Change

National communication policy is a generic term for the struggle against cultural and social domination in all its forms, old and new, exercised from within or outside the nation. Consequently, communications-cultural planning cannot be formulated by experts and delivered to the rest of the population as a legislative gift. Specialists and administrators may provide leadership in the initial stage of understanding; but for the effort to begin to approach a level of widespread development of critical consciousness, the fullest participation of the local community is indispensable. Anything less will make the likelihood of diversion and atrophy inevitable.
—Herbert Schiller (1976: 96)

Previously I argued that in contrast to the more economically and politically oriented policy options in the modernization and dependency paradigms, the central idea in the multiplicity paradigm is that there is no universal development model, and that development is an integral, multidimensional, and dialectic process that can differ from society to society. This implies that the development problem is a relative one and that no one nation or community can contend that it is "developed" in every respect. Therefore, I believe that the scope and degree of inter(in)dependency must be studied in relation to more content-related qualitative aspects of the development or social change problem.

As discussed earlier, the basic principles of "another" development imply an orientation toward basic needs, ecology, self-reliance, endogeny, sustainability, participatory democracy, and structural transformations. In other words, each society or community must attempt to delineate its own sustainable strategy to development, based on its own ecology and culture. Therefore, it should not attempt to blindly imitate programs and strategies of other countries with a totally different historical and cultural background.

HISTORY AND CONCEPTS

Before addressing in some detail the issues of policy and planningmaking for social change, some general information on the history and definition of these subjects seem to be necessary.

The "Role" of Policy and Planning for Social Change

Policymakers and planners face important choices not only about the communication problems they address and the solutions they propose in their plans, but about the way in which planning will be organized and carried out:

> Obvious variations in historical and socio-cultural backgrounds, standards of living, education, orientation towards the outside world and in existing systems of communication, indicate that for each of the communities different linkages with the modern communication systems should be sought. The national communication system to be developed should be socio-culturally based. Only in this way would it be possible to avoid violent psychological or social upheavals stemming from the introduction of new technologies, including the most recent communication technology via satellite. (Susanto,Alfian, Santoso, Suwardi, 1981:72)

Different kinds of problems and situations may call for different solutions. Again, also in this case, there is no universal approach that can be used in all circumstances. Therefore, as in theory, one propagates either a combination of policy and planning approaches, or the creation of a *hybrid approach* drawing on several theories. Thus, as argued by John Middleton (1985:33), "there is no 'role' for communication in development, but rather many roles."

However, despite these fundamental and important disclaimers, most policy and planning-makers still feel the need for a general conceptual and operational framework. One of the reasons for this is that policy and planning is both a theoretical and an applied discipline: "A process of conducting research on, or analysis of, a fundamental social problem in order to provide policymakers with pragmatic, action-oriented recommendations for alleviating the problem" (Majchrzak, 1984:12). In this definition, one may notice two elements that are also crucial to the theoretical underpinnings of the multiplicity paradigm, that is, the attention for substantial social problems and for the application and action-orientedness of research recommendations.

Majchrzak (1984) divides the overall policy research field into four disciplines on the basis of its focus and applicability (see Table 5.1). Within this typology I focus particularly on the third and fourth type of fundamental policy research.

Definitions of Communication Policy and Planning

Although the origin of the communication policy and planning field cannot be pinpointed with any accuracy, one may state that it is a very recent history that is largely a matter of growing consciousness. That is why Alan Hancock (1981: 16) claims

> the history of communication policies and planning . . . is one of gradual, sometimes barely perceptible, moves towards integration: towards the perception of coherent systems in communication . . . .
> It is implicit in such documents as the reports of Unesco research meetings on mass communication, which often pick up with considerable accuracy the mood of a particular time.

Table 5.1. A Typology of Policy Research.

| | | Focus | |
		Technical	Fundamental
Applicability	Low	Analysis of policy	Analysis of fundamental policy research
	High	Technical research	Policy and planning research

One of the earliest discussions of the concept of *communication policies,* though in its embryonic form, was during a meeting of experts on "Information Media and Society," held in Montreal in June 1969, and hosted by the Canadian Unesco Commission. Two of the adopted recommendations read:

> (i) More comprehensive, system-oriented research into mass communication is needed at all levels and in all areas. This includes the analysis of media organization, ownership and financial support, the decision-making processes in media production, the codes of professional ethics, the actual value systems of communicators, and their perception of their role in society. The ways in which such factors impinge upon the creative process involved in media production are of particular interest. It may also be useful to inquire into whether it would be advisable to bring about change, where indicated, in production and information structures to allow for a wider participation into management and decision-making processes on the part of the professional working elements of media units. The special contexts of the developing countries deserve special attention. (j) In addition to the actual process of mass communication, there is need for research into the goals of mass communication systems and their possible future goals. Such "goal research" might help to clarify policies and objectives in relation to any given society, suggest to policymakers and practitioners new bases for mass media performance, and stimulate more comprehensive theories with regard to mass communication in general. (quoted in Hancock, 1981: 16-17).

Two years later, the "Proposal for an International Program of Communication Research," elaborated by a consultants' committee meeting in Paris in September 1971, made the concept of communication policies more concrete:

> If something is socially significant it should be self-evident that we need to know something about it. More questions arise: Who governs and controls the media? Whose interests do they serve? What resources do they use? What is the nature of their products? What needs are being met and what are not met? These are just some of the general questions that should be central within any program of communication research.... In short, we need the knowledge that only research can provide before we can develop adequate communication policies. Ideally, such policies should be based on "total" knowledge (i.e., on the operation of the media in the wider social-economic-political setting), and on "public" needs rather than on "partial" knowledge and "private" needs as is so often the case at present. (UNESCO, 1971)

As a result, the first "official" description of communication policies was outlined during a meeting of experts on Communication Policies and Planning, held in Paris in July 1972. It states:

> Communication policies are sets of principles and norms established to guide the behavior of communication systems. Their orientation is fundamental and long range, although they may have operational implications of shortrange significance. They are shaped in the context of society's general approach to communication. Emanating from political ideologies, the social and economic conditions of the country and the values on which they are based, they strive to relate these to the real needs and prospective opportunities of "communication". Communication policies exist in every society, though they may frequently be latent and disjointed, rather than clearly and harmonized. What is proposed, therefore, is not something radically new, but rather an explicit statement and deliberately prospective formulation of practices already established in society. (UNESCO, 1972)

At this meeting the implications for planning were also discussed:

> Beyond policies is strategic planning, which determines the alternative ways to achieve long-range goals and sets the frame of reference for shorter-range operational planning. Strategic planning translates into quantified targets and systematic approaches the general objectives of communication policies.

In my opinion, a more operative and accurate definition has been provided by Cees Hamelink (1980: 26):

> A systematic, organic and specific set of principles of organization, action, control, evaluation and re-orientation, intended to direct the public planning of systems and social communication processes, within a specific political framework and according to a model of economic and social development.

In this definition the relation to planning is direct and functional. Most definitions of planning claim that it is both a theoretical and applied discipline as in Dror's (1973: 323) definition of planning: "Planning is the process of preparing a set of decisions for action in the future, directed at achieving goals by preferable means." In the communication policy and planning field one often refers to definitions provided by John Middleton: "Planning is the application of theory to reality in order to decide what to do, when and how" (1980:19), or "planning is the conscious effort to adapt a system to its environment in order to achieve system goals" (Middleton & Wedemeyer, 1985: 41). These definitions point out that planning has to be conceived as a *continuous process* and as an activity that can be executed at different levels. Furthermore, the final decision most often is made by other than those involved in the policy and planning process; for instance, by the so-called political, economic, or sociocultural powerholders. Moreover, these definitions emphasize the need for evaluation and modification. Planning thus implies an integrated and "holistic" package of realistic recommendations, based on normative and value-loaden objectives, with an emphasis on future action/implementation. Because of this interrelatedness of policy and planning Hancock calls them "siamese twins". Although policies may exist and be discussed without planning, planning cannot be expected to take place without (often implicit) policies.

Therefore, workable definitions of communication planning can be the following: "The preparation of both long-range and short-range plans (i.e., strategic and operational) for the efficient and equitable use of communication resources, in the context of a particular society's goals, means and priorities, and subject to its prevailing forms of social and political organization" (Hancock, 1981:12); or "Communication planning is the creation, allocation and/or use of communication resources to achieve socially valued communication goals, in the context of a particular social image or images" (Middleton & Wedemeyer, 1985: 21). (For more details, see also Bordenave & DeCarvalho, 1978; Hancock, 1992; Mody, 1991; Rahim & Middleton, 1977; Woodcock, 1986).

TOWARD A FRAMEWORK FOR COMMUNICATION POLICY AND PLANNING

Referring to the modified version of Sunkel and Fuenzalida's (1980) model to analyze relationships among processes of integration, disintegration, and reintegration at the various levels of a specific societal system, and to Matta's (1981) communication model with active social participation, and building on the work of Hancock (1981, 1992), Hill (1993), Korten (1986), Mowlana (1997), Rahim, Lamberton, & Wedemeyer, (1978), Tri (1984), Tuazan (1983), and Villegas, Braid et al., (1986), I have attempted to develop a conceptual and operational framework for communication policy and planning for development and social change (see Figure 5.1).

I have been trying to grasp the complexity of the problematique in a structural-dynamic way by integrating at least four basic elements

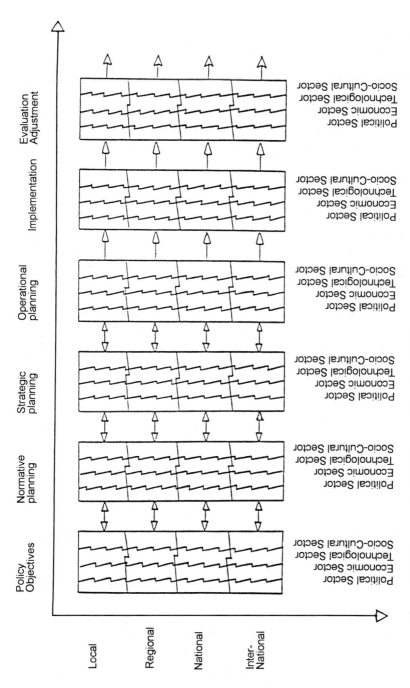

Figure 5.1. A conceptual and operational model for communication policy and planning

into this model: (a) *content related variables,* which can be of an external or internal nature (objectives, goals, and functions of the communication policy, etc.); (b) interrelated *factors* (economic, political, technological, etc., sectors) and *actors* (institutions, public groups, etc.); (c) a distinction at the *level of analysis* (international, national, local, etc.); and (d) the *process of policy and planning* (policy formulation, planning, implementation, evaluation, etc.). A 'realistic' and coherent policy model can only be formulated if one succeeds in explaining the interrelationships among the various interactive, horizontal, and vertical components of the system.

Levels of Analysis

Policymakers and planners have to solve problems at distinct levels. There are not only contradictions at the international level, between the metropolis and the dependent countries for instance, but at the national level the clash between the interests of the state and "organized communicators" (e.g., media owners) on the one hand, and between the government and the population at large is evident.

Here I mainly focus on the latter, that is, *intra-national* contradiction. This option is only a strategic one as I share the vision of people like Alger (1984), Baumgartner (1984), Chesneaux (1983), Forester (1989), Friedman (1988, 1992), Garcia-Zamor (1985), Robertson (1992), and Wignaraja (1993) that it is necessary to combine and integrate local, national, regional, international, and intermediate levels if one really wants to acquire a strategy based on the multiplicity paradigm. There is a second reason for this option. I would claim that, contrary to analyses at the extra-national or international levels, culturalistic issues have been studied far less at intra-national levels.

Our perspective and approach on the so-called *nation-state,* however, has to be different from that of the modernization scholars, who also adopted it as their level of analysis: "The nation states were often the units of analysis in the traditional international relations framework, rather than communities, cultures, or regions in their anthropological, cultural, and historical contexts" (Mowlana, 1997:16). In this latter conception, principles of decentralization and participation on the one hand, and the involvement in action and change on the other, have become essential:

> The new conception holds that it is not enough to provide participation in the system, even if this can be made less formal and more substantial; the aim is also to create a just society. Participation is necessary but not sufficient for this to happen. What is needed is self-government, a decentralized order through which the masses are empowered. This would not be decentralization in the sense of a territorial

revolution of functions and resources to lower levels but decentralization in which the people are the center. (Kothari, 1986:182)

Smith (1985) agrees to this statement and adds:

> It is important to reject a romantic view of decentralization. It is not an absolute good in its own right. Decentralized administration and local government may be used for a variety of ends, just as central government can be. How decentralization is evaluated should depend on the purpose for which it is employed. Centralization may be a preferable strategy if it leads to territorial justice or the redistribution of wealth. (191)

In this sense, centralization does not necessarily have to be in conflict with the principle of decentralization. *Centralization* can have two different meanings: first, it can be used to reinforce national unity; second, it can refer to an increase of the power over local activities. In the first sense, centralization is not necessarily in conflict with the principle of decentralization: central organisms can be a synthesis of regional and local services. Centralization is thought to free the population from certain responsibilities such as the maintenance of law and order, the water supply, the health system, transport, and education. Institutions were established in order to provide these services collectively. But the degree of centralization must be controlled: when all decision-making domains disappear, the individual is left powerless and passive. This is related to the second meaning of the concept. Thus, there is great complexity in the interrelationship between centralization and decentralization, and each so-called decentralization project must be carefully examined.

It is within this context that the complexity and flexibility of the relationships between local and national initiatives and projects has to be studied:

> If the grass roots organizations were linked across space and sustained each other through exchanging ideas, they could contribute to the eventual emergence not just of a new consciousness but a new kind of state structure. Within such a state structure decentralization of power and mass participation in economic/social decision making could become a real possibility. In the short run grass roots experiments and people's movements could act as sources of countervailing power to the mechanisms of inequality and repressive control. In the long run when structural changes at the macro level could occur, such organizations would form the institutional basis of developing a collectivist consciousness and unleashing the creative potential of the people for sustainable development. (Wignaraja, 1986:36)

The mass media, in the context of national development, were generally used to support development initiatives through the dissemination of messages that encouraged the public to support development-oriented projects. Although development strategies in developing countries diverge widely, the usual pattern for broadcasting and the press has been predominantly the same: informing the population about projects, illustrating the advantages of these projects, and recommending that they be supported. A typical example of such a strategy is situated in the area of family planning, in which communication means such as posters, pamphlets, radio, and television attempt to persuade the public to accept birth control methods (Sadik, 1991). Similar strategies are used on campaigns regarding health and nutrition, agricultural projects, and education (for overviews and cases, see Casmir, 1991; Contreras, 1993; Dhillon & Philip, 1991; Goonasekera, 1990; Hornik, 1988; McKee, 1992; Moemeka, 1994).

The participation idea does not deny the need for these media functions. The need for information is real, but the supporters of community media argue that this is still a limited view of communication for development—one that is vertical or one-way communication—and that active involvement in the process of the communication itself will accelerate development. Research has already shown that, although the public can obtain information from impersonal sources like radio and television, this information has relatively little effect on behavioral changes. And development envisions precisely such change. Similar research has led to the conclusion that more is learned from interpersonal contacts and the mass communication techniques that are based on them. At the lowest level, before people can discuss and resolve problems, they must be informed of the facts; information that the media provide nationally as well as regionally and locally. At the same time, the public, if the media are sufficiently accessible, can make its information needs known (see Canini, 1994; Mayo & Chieuw, 1993; Moore, 1986; Oepen, 1995; O'Sullivan-Ryan, 1979; Wang & Dissanayake, 1984).

Therefore, the point of departure of regional and local communication must be the *community*. It is at the local community level that the problems of living conditions are discussed, and interactions with other communities are elicited. The most developed form of participation is self-management. This principle implies the right to participation in the planning and production of media content. However, not everyone wants to or must be involved in its practical implementation. More important is that participation in the decision making regarding the subjects treated in the messages and the selection procedures is made transparent. One of the fundamental hindrances to the decision to adopt the participation strategy is that it threatens existing hierarchies.

Nevertheless, participation does not imply that there is no longer a role for development specialists, planners, and institutional leaders. It only means that the viewpoint of the local public groups is considered before the resources for development projects are allocated and distributed and that suggestions for changes in the policy are taken into consideration (for more details, see Berrigan, 1979; Boeren, 1994; Gran, 1983; Morehouse, 1989; Ramana, 1982; Ramirez, 1990; Ross & Usher, 1986; Servaes, Jaconson, & White, 1996; White, Nair, & Ascroft, 1994).

A Normative Starting Point

As long as the goal of development is not clearly articulated, policy and planning objectives, both at micro and macro levels, will be unclear as well. Therefore, the value system on which the economic, political, social, and cultural activities of a community or society operate are very essential:

> The point here is not to emphasize which values ought to be adopted at the expense of others, but rather, to recognize that stability and equilibrium of any living system is directly connected to the process of value orientation and value maintenance as factors of homestasis warding off decay, disorganization, and disintegration. (Mowlana, 1997:9)

Therefore, to better understand the complexity and dialectics of the distinct aspects related to communication policy and planning, the meaning and philosophy of development and social change must be assessed in a coherent and integrated way.

Actors and Factors

From a structural and static perspective one can distinguish between actors and factors that influence policy and planning. Actors can be defined as public or interest groups that, by both direct and/or indirect means, try to push through their explicitly or implicitly agreed on program. Factors, on the other hand, determine the contours within which the actors can operate. Factors are time and space bound and differ from society to society. Some are of a conjunctural nature, others of a more structural nature. I attempt to categorize a number of potential actors and factors per sector in Table 5.2. This structural policy model partly builds on Mowlana's multidimensional and integrative approach to communication utility (Mowlana, 1997:170), in which he makes a distinction

Table 5.2. A Structural Policy Model.

	Factors	Actors	Needs	Policy Objectives
Political Sector	*Structural:* Bureaucratization Excolonial political structures Political Systems Supernational cooperation Local sociocultural systems *Conjunctural:* Federalization Decentralization Revolutionary movements Opposition movements	Political parties Pressure groups Parliament Government Ecological movement Grassroots Lobbies	National Unity Political support Integrated development policies Integration of minorities Participation in policy Decentralized decision making	National identity Support for national and local policies Integration of minorities Participatory democracy Decentralization
Economical Sector	*Structural:* Resources Geography The end of growth Economic Dependency *Conjunctural:* Economic crisis Privatization Deregulation Labor-Capital Relationships	Transnationals National corporations Labor Unions Farmer Unions Cooperatives Bureaucracy	Sufficient resources Qualified personnel Technical information Management and consumption Local production Primary material needs Structural reforms	Economical self-reliance South-to-South Cooperation Basic needs Ecological production Changes in consumption patterns

Table 5.2. A Structural Policy Model (con't).

		Factors	Actors	Needs	Policy Objectives
Sociocultural Sector		*Structural:* Social Injustice Cultural Patterns Mode of Communication Ethnic Religious, etc. Composition of population Way of living *Conjunctural:* Linguistic problems Liberalizing the sociocultural sector Consumption Patterns Apathy	Cultural organizations Educated and noneducated Schooling system Religious groupings Minority groups Young and elderly Media	Preservation of cultural heritage Abolishment of illiteracy Family Planning Local cultural initiatives Right to communicate Education for all	Cultural identity Social integration Free education for all Information campaigns Promotion of local cultural production
Technological Sector		*Structural:* Vision Technology Progresss Technical Infrastructure S Status of research *Conjunctural:* Professional know-how Financial, legal constraints Interest from public	Ministry of science technology Research institutes Universities Planning boards Industrial planning commissions Software and hardware producers	Technological autonomy Technology transfers Intermediary technologies	Technological self-reliance Appropriate technology and research Preventing brain drain

between a "communication infrastructural axis" and an "individual-system level axis"; on Hancock's (1992) evolutionary framework for policy and planning; and on McQuail and Siune's (1986) typology of actors.

The drafting of policy objectives must be attuned to the needs and expectations of the various public groups, and it must also take account of the resources available and the capabilities of the country. Therefore, I specify a number of *policy objectives and needs per* sector in which the communication policy must be applied:

1. In the first place, the identification of existing needs and requirements is necessary for the formulation of policy objectives. Thus, regarding the *political sector*, most scholars point to an obvious lack of cohesion in most developing countries. The lack of contact between the authorities and the public at large means that the latter cannot or will not identify itself with the nation or community, although such identification is the first condition for development.

A situation in which there is no flow of information and consultation between the ruling minority and the population not only causes alienation in that population with respect to its own community, but the legitimacy of this minority is threatened. This is one of the reasons that development planning often generates inadequate appreciation among the population and sometimes even negative attitudes. This lack of cohesion is often also maintained and simultaneously aggravated by the excessive bureaucratization and corruptive practices of governmental services. On the national level, one of the primary objectives has therefore often been the creation of a sense of national identity. Parker (1977), for instance, defines this as a condition in which the various segments of the society interact by means of a two-way communication system. This interaction or two-way communication must also manifest itself regionally and locally through horizontal communication. Vertical communication, however, can also be of use, especially when it is conceived as a flow of information and consultation in both directions among the national, regional, and local segments of the society.

Legitimacy and political credibility can be fostered by the establishment of what is called *participatory democracy*, the building in of actual participation from the public. This is only possible when the communication system is decentralized. The control over communication and information may not be monopolized by one or a few segments of the society. Unfortunately, most of the time structural aspects stand in the way of the ideal of democracy. In most developing countries, the first stone for bridging the gap between the ruling elite and the masses has still to be laid. For the establishment of participatory democracy, therefore, dialogue must be made possible between the authorities and the public—nationally, regionally, and locally. In the political sector, this can be done through political parties, pressure groups, civil action groups, environmental movements, and the like. Thus, political credibility as well as the social and cultural identity of the population and an awareness and support of development goals are needed.

2. Economists define development principally in terms of economic growth—the increase of real output per capita. Although I consider sustainable economic development as only one (although fundamental) of the elements of development, the striving for prosperity and a more just distribution of jobs and income remains an important element in any kind of development. In the *economic sector*, therefore, communication policy has a major task. By means of an appropriate policy, one can make groups of the population receptive to changing circumstances and generate positive attitudes toward sustainable socioeconomic change.

Also important for a *self-reliant development* is that the communication policy sets out to inform the population of its own resources and available means and shows the importance of its own food production and self-supply. The communication media must also reflect a production and consumption pattern that occurs with the development strategy and thus counteracts foreign commercial and consumption influences. Through horizontal regional and local communication, regional and local initiatives can be promoted. Here, too, account must be taken of the presence of the necessary resources and restrictions of the environment such as physical and geographical barriers, legal regulations (rights and demands of organizations and associations, commercial unions, and so on), the possibilities of economic growth present or available human and material resources, and financial restrictions.

3. Continuing processes of "cultural synchronization," "cultural homogenization," or "cultural globalization," and the enthusiastic adoption of an internationally distributed set of values, conceptions, and life styles that is elevated by the elites of the periphery to a model for society as a whole, threaten the diversity and identity of local cultures (Ritzer, 1996). In addition, in most developing countries, and primarily in the rural regions, there is a lack of formal education and basic literacy, and a lack of knowledge of hygiene, nutrition, family planning, and agricultural production that hinders the general development of these communities. Illiteracy and insufficient formal education limit the ability to profit from information (e.g., reading newspapers) and also have a negative influence on the adaption to and acceptance of social change. A lack of cultural information also results in alienation of the population from its traditional cultural values and thus from its own *cultural identity*. This results in the relatively low cultural level and social status of less privileged groups. Educational planning is, therefore, an important and rele-

vant portion of communication planning. Hence, Criticos (1989), Camre, Giese et al. (1982), Kaplun (1992) and McAnany and Mayo (1980), among others, see educational planning as fundamentally associated with processes of social mobilization and structural change. In a similar fashion, Seriki (1982) emphasizes the relationship between the training and education of engineers and technological policy and planning (using the case of telephony in Nigeria). He concludes that "experience has shown that the greatest impediment to technological development in developing countries has been the problem of coordinated policy decisions both in the field of technological education and in the actual implementation of technological policies" (203).

As far as specific cultural objectives are concerned, communication policy can comprise the following: the elevation of the cultural level and social status of less privileged groups of the public (nationally, regionally, and locally), the support of traditional cultural products, and the promotion of a greater awareness of the national and/or local culture. In the formulation of objectives not only must they play a role but the spatial and the temporal environment imposes limitations that are primarily structural and must be taken into account. Existing cultural values, distorted by (post-)colonial and multinational influences, are facts that will not disappear but rather contribute to new emerging values. Also, the composition of the population can lead to significant problems: often one must deal with major religious or ethnic differences and divergent linguistic groups.

The levels of literacy can also diverge strongly in function within the different population groups. The social demand for education cannot be ignored, and this is influenced not only by the sociocultural profile of the population but by factors such as income levels and distribution, the private costs of education, nonformal educational opportunities, the labor market, cultural and religious norms, and political options with an impact on social expectations and local receptivity for education. Important selections must be made and functional decisions must be taken with regard to dilemmas such as the options for local versus national needs; local initiatives versus vertical collaboration on the national, regional, and local levels; and education as active intervention in formal education versus the construction of specific, independent, multimedia services.

4. *Communication technology* has a direct impact on economic development and political organization. Three points should be stated from the outset. First, there is the predominant impact of transnational corporations over technology transfer. In virtually all the Third World countries, the advantages of technology transfer primarily benefit the transnational industries (the suppliers) and the transnational banks (the financiers).

These corporations account for approximately 80% to 90% of the technology transferred to developing countries, and most of the Third World countries depend on transnationals for their own technical development capacity. Therefore, according to Hamelink (1984: 79), *technology transfer* is characterized by the following dimensions: (a) the strong oligopology in the production of this technology which makes the acquiring parties dependent on very few suppliers; (b) the transfer of obsolete technology, which in itself may not always be disadvantageous, given national objectives, but which demands a rather sophisticated assessment procedure; (c) the lack of specialized expertise for the integration of the technology and the generation of innovation; and (d) the common practice of delivery of relatively cheap systems which offers decreasing hardware prices together with large and profitable software contracts.

Second, technology is called into existence by a particular set of historical circumstances that shape and define the technology. One must understand that set of historical circumstances if one is to comprehend the effective relationship between technology and society: "Technology does not cause society. Nor does society cause technology. Rather, technology is developed in society, in the complex interplay of social forces that are at the same time both cause and effect" (Slack, 1984: XV). Therefore, contrary to popular belief, technology is not politically neutral and value free; technology definitely determines the sociocultural structure and communication patterns of a given society. The major problem, therefore, is not technical:

> The problem, and indeed the solution, is not simply technical. Even if reliable and easily maintained low-cost technology could be introduced into the Third World, which is still not a proven solution, the appropriateness or value of the technology still depends on the value and appropriateness of the information being processed and transmitted. Information is a very peculiar resource, whose value is determined not by its quantity, but by its quality, timeliness and relevance. Information, then, which does not have an explicit use value ceases to be a resource and becomes a cost, a commodity which is in turn added to the expense of mining those few bits of information that are pertinent to some need. (Mitchell, 1978:91)

In the international field, accelerating technological developments suggests that opportunities for the expression of cultural differentness can be ensured. In reality, these developments appear to be the very instrument for the destruction of this differentness and for its replacement with a uniform, Western-dominated technological model. According to Goulet (1977) there are three basic values in Western technology. First,

Western technology shows little respect for myth, symbol, or the power of the mysterious. Every phenomenon has to be broken down into component parts, tested, and verified. Second, the technology is based on the cult of efficiency. The central considerations are productivity, cost-benefit ratio, and the bottom line. Third, the technology dominates and manipulates nature rather than being in harmony with it. Problem solving is the goal; hence, reality is reduced to those dimensions that can be studied as problems needing solutions. The values implicit in Western technology may therefore come into conflict with the preexisting values of the Third World.

Therefore, in general I would like to state that media policy, on the technological level and oriented to the elimination of the dependency relations with multinational firms and to the meeting of the needs of the population, must primarily be able to decide autonomously about the nature of the media technology (this is related to the ability to obtain and process information about media technology). Such a policy must then achieve a combination between the autonomous position cited earlier and the opportunities for development of the country's own technical indigenous knowledge necessary for the production process of the media. Thus, the policy must enable the production and reproduction of media technology and media content by the developing country itself.

The Dialectics of Structural Dynamics

From a dynamic perspective one can distinguish among five overlapping phases in the policy process: formulation of policy, strategic or long-term planning, operational or short-term planning, implementation of the policy and planning, and evaluation of it. Each level and phase of analysis of the policy process is determined by the dialectical intercourse of structural and dynamic components (see Figure 5.2).

1. The formulation of the policy options on the central level must be a synthesis of the objectives envisaged by the sectoral policies. We could summarize them as the satisfaction of basic needs regarding information, the creation of a cultural identity, the reappreciation of authentic cultural values, democratization by social participation, and the integration of development projects. The condition for an adequate information policy is that, in the formulation of these objectives, account is taken of the determinants of the environment (i.e., factors such as the principles of the national political system, the social institutions, factors of the national economic policy, ecological restrictions) and also of the active participation of the various public groups, identifiable by sector (or the so-called actors). In this phase there must be consultation between the

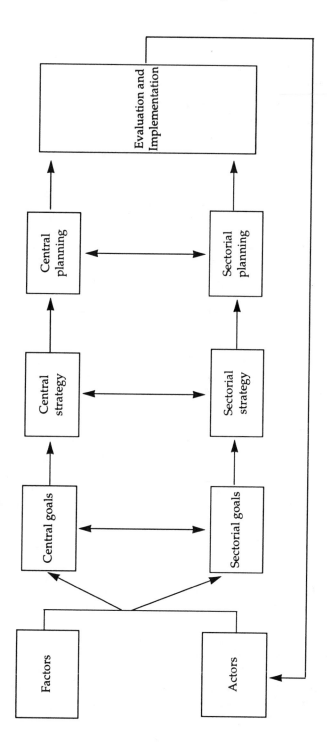

Figure 5.2. A dynamic policy model

sectoral planning and the central planning; only by dialogue can the central policy options be a synthesis of the sectoral policy objectives. On this level, central communication planning functions as the coordinator of a limited number of smaller, sectoral organisms.

2. In the second phase of the process, a central long- and short-term strategy must be defined. This is based on the desirable and practicable sectoral proposals and is, therefore, not only a synthesis but a *compromise*, for a system cannot give total satisfaction to everyone. The principal policy task in this phase is the translation of the central objectives into strategic options, starting on a sectoral scale. The need for consultation between sectoral organisms with each other and between them and the central planning organism applies as well. In my opinion, these sectoral strategies must be based on the following fundamental principles: orientation to the basic needs of the population for communication and information; endogeny and self-reliance, thus relying primarily on the local strength and selective participation in external operations. The synthesization of proposals on the central level is primarily a question of an optimal technical and political balance and, thus, a critical harmonization.

3. The third stage a policy process must proceed through is that of its *concretization into executable plans or options for action*. In the first place, a general framework must be developed by the collaboration of sectoral organisms and the central level. Operational programs must then be produced, which are most often technical. The critical moment of this phase is when an optimal and realistic translation of theory into reality is made. Two principles are at the basis of this: *decentralization and participation*, a programming and execution of action plans in sectoral organisms in which as high a degree as possible of active participation must be achieved. At the same time, the decentralized sectoral organisms must work out plans for each sector on the national, regional, and local levels, while always being seen as social organizations, that is, as being characterized by the active input of representative participants from the general public.

4. Finally, alongside the creation of mechanisms that should make active participation possible, an evaluation procedure based on research must be created so that correction and adaptation can be made within the system. Also, the institutional aspect of planning and execution of the policy needs some explanation. Alongside the establishment of central, national, and decentralized sectoral organisms, the media must be structured in a meaningful way. This concerns specific regulations concerning the concrete organization, management, and status of the media. This is an open and cyclical process, as shown in Figure 5.2.

Policy and Planning Issues

"Another" policy model not only necessitates "another" structure and dynamics but "other" policy principles. As has been argued throughout this book, the study of communication for development problems in general, and especially those related to the multiplicity paradigm in particular, are much more normative than other scientific approaches or previous development paradigms. This can be illustrated by discussing a number of problem fields and principles in policy and planning.

I would like to identify five interrelated policy and planning issues that can be considered as guidelines in formulating communication policies and plans: (a) the overall development strategy, of which communication policies and planning should form a part; (b) the definition of the goals and functions of the communications system; (c) the availability and the form of adaption of resources; (d) the design of the institutional structure, concrete organization, and content of the communication system; and (e) the rules and mechanisms by which the internal and external functioning of he system can be controlled.

1. The first issue is the need for an integrated development policy and strategy. Because communication technology is often introduced without specification of the objectives to be achieved, a priority would be the precise definition of a country's or community's communication needs.

There are at least five dimensions of development strategy on which Third World countries can make significant *policy choices:* (a) individualistic versus collectivistic development needs, (b) human-intensive versus capital-intensive development plans, (c) long-term infrastructure versus short-run projects development, (d) national versus regional or local development, and (e) urban versus rural development. In each of these dimensions the choice is not an either/or dichotomy but rather a matter of how to strike a balance.

For instance, as Betz, McGowan, and Wigand (1984:14) argued, "Appropriate technological analysis would indicate that there is a place for the most advanced twenty-first century technologies in most countries. There is a place for modern capital-intensive production. There also is a place for labor-intensive activities." Unfortunately, as has been pointed out by Hancock (1984) after an overview of some case studies on communication technology transfer, in reality there is little interest among decision makers and manufacturers in the promotion of indigenous technologies and little desire to investigate alternative approaches. If one wants to create an endogenous, self-reliant technology, Hancock argues, this must be supported politically with a commitment born of conviction rather than pragmatism. As long as this is not the case, one may say that technologies in general, and information technology—which is essentially a "convergence technology"—in particular, will reinforce existing social structures rather than transform them.

2. The specific communication goals and functions for development must, by definition, be consistent with the previously described general development choices. Technologies that are currently offered to Third World countries have to be carefully analyzed and matched against stated developmental objectives and communication needs. One of the consequences of the fact that most Third World countries have jumped from oral to electronic media, skipping the intermediate stages of literacy and the printed word, is that broadcasting organizations are highly centralized at a national level and know little about their audiences. Therefore, they treat them as undifferentiated. The fact that a large proportion of the programs must be imported, combined with the cultural-leveling effects of mass media, may threaten the traditional and autonomous forms of self-expression and impoverish the cultural life of people. If a government intends to encourage local initiative and wants to enrich cultural identity, it has to make this concrete by, for instance, providing sufficient citizen access to local communication systems to serve as effective feedback to the government concerning its development goals and plans.

3. Before translating the function of a communication system into a concrete organization, technical infrastructure, and content, it is necessary to analyze both the availability and the form of adaptation of resources. It is important to consider resources in terms of three categories, namely as (a) resources that are an integral part of the national context, (b) resources already imported and adaptable to local needs, and (c) foreign resources that must still be imported. These resources can be of a natural, human, or organizational nature. Within each category one should search for the integrative, disintegrative, and reintegrative dimensions and consequences.

Each society already has natural, human, and organizational resources of its own such as traditional social values and institutions. Later I focus on the case of Thailand with its long tradition of likay folk opera. In some cases these traditional forms can be successfully combined with modern media. Through stories and songs on radio and TV programs, the traditional Thai culture can, for instance, be propagated and renewed.

When one has to import foreign technology, which is not available inside the country, a major criterion should be whether this technology can contribute to autonomous and sustainable development. Because communication policymakers have often concentrated on the procurement of hardware only, careful analysis and projection should be made regarding the secondary impact of communication technology, in terms of the distribution of political, economic, and cultural benefits. The danger of technology transfer is precisely that technological models are adapted to the social structures of the technology exporters, and thus primarily are a product of an institutional structure designed for the maximization of profit and advantage (even though some social needs are not met or some regions are not serviced) rather than for the maximization of the national development effects of the technology. As argued earlier, the importation of North American radio and television technology in many countries has also brought about the transfer of the organizational model of western broadcasting: commercial or corporate structures, bureaucratic procedures, staff hierarchies, and institutional objectives. In addition, foreign technologies bring with them not only an alien production method but external cultural elements and consumption patterns. For these reasons, Tanzania (with the exception of its island Zanzibar) has long resisted the pressures to introduce television. The Tanzanian government did not feel that the country was ready for television, primarily because only an urban elite could make use of it. Moreover, there would be an almost total dependence on imports of foreign software as well as hardware. Tanzania opted instead to introduce a video system (Tanzania Year 16) which served primarily rural areas. This video equipment is used for horizontal communication between ujamaa villages and between the villages and government. It is a relatively inexpensive medium through which an important contribution can be made to social development and political consciousness. It is at the same time an important beginning in the development of an indigenous communication infrastructure. By using a minimum of imported technology, there is less danger of a dependent media system (Kivikuru, 1990; Ng'Wanakilala, 1981).

Hancock (1984) argues that successful technology transfer cannot occur unless a certain level of capability has already been built up in the recipient. If this is not the case, the partnership will be unequal, and the transfer will be mechanical and imitative. He concludes that commercial transfers are of little use: no real transfer is involved, and the recipient is at a total disadvantage. Moreover, looking at domestic technologies, he observes that indigenous forms do badly at first, when they are compared with imported models, and as a result they need a good deal of committed and resolute policy support if they are to have the chance to survive, to become entrenched and competitive.

In other words, there is a clear lack of control over technical knowledge and infrastructure, as well as over the software and the hardware. This control is, however, an absolute condition for the dismantling of the international standardization brought about by the large-scale production and dissemination of information technology by Western firms. Indeed, as documented by many authors, imported technology has often turned out to be inadequate for meeting the basic needs of the importing nation, as is the case with capital-intensive technology in countries with high unemployment. This condition is aggravated because imported technology often neglects the application and development of local knowledge and local resources. It is primarily the end-product of the technological process that is transferred, not the knowledge itself (Mignot-Lefebvre, 1994).

A communication technology must be planned in such a way that it supports sustainable development rather than to the implantation of alien technologies. The "appropriateness" of any technology chosen for application in the process of development should therefore depend on its contribution toward general development goals. Thus, it is often more efficient to import knowledge than to create undesirable technological dependence, even though the transfer of the end-product of the technology might be functional (Jouet and Coudray, 1991).

4. The fourth issue deals with the kind of *institutional structure* that should be established. The structure and content of a communication system will have to be designed in relation to crucial functions and available resources. On the one hand, one observes both in developed and developing countries the resistance of existing institutions to change. On the other hand, the importation of an institutions model and the technology inevitably brings with it a set of assumptions, including norms, unwritten rules, styles of production, values, professional codes and expectations, and beliefs and attitudes. Careful attention has to be given to the institutional context within which the technology is applied. Future studies will need to address whether present infrastructural arrangements are sufficiently solid to monitor and control the applications. However, there is no single prescription that can be given for devising workable institutional structures. It is seldom possible to implement an ideal structure out of nothing. Almost always one has to plan within an already existing institutional system:

> It is seldom possible to implement an ideal structure de novo. Almost always it is necessary to work within a pre-existing institutional structure, making whatever adaptations, innovations, and reorganizations are possible. Previously existing institutions usually have a good deal of inertia, making change difficult. The specific national goals, the national geography, the existing technology, and the talents of the people involved all need to be taken into account. (Parker, 1977:66)

For example an important problem is advertising. The principle of media with no form of advertising seems, apart from its desirability, utopian in most developing countries. A commercial orientation of the communication system is, indeed, open to serious criticism, for commercial media are usually oriented to profit and thus are selective in their orientation to public groups, and they generally have a prejudicial effect on consumption patterns and cultural values. They can hinder local production, and the low investment-high profit principle is often reflected in relatively low professional standards. As advertising is not only a technical issue, but even more an issue of social-psychology, transnational politics and economics, and ultimately a cultural issue (of "rising expectations," consumer dreams and materialism), it should be examined and discussed carefully by policymakers and planners.

However, in spite of the obvious negative effects of advertising, the advertising industry could be included in the communication system in a *functional* manner. Therefore, "the answer is not so much 'yes' or 'no' but that it depends on how commercialization is implemented and regulated. Whatever balance is sought between public service and private gain is a delicate adjustment, strongly inclined to shift" (Adkins, 1985:55). If one is able to establish a workable *control system,* advertisements can promote the products of national enterprises and thus foster national production and local culture. They can reflect an adapted consumption pattern and the country's own cultural values. At the same time, they can contribute to the economic base of the media, although total dependence on advertising income must be avoided. The point of departure must be that advertising is subject to the educational and cultural objectives of the media. Advertising policy is thus an important task in a development strategy that is based on basic needs and self-reliance. Stipulations and restrictions must be formulated for advertising access to the various mass media and the way in which the advertising is conducted. These basic limitations on advertising could be the following: the advertisements must be primarily for national companies instead of for transnational or foreign firms; financing of the media must be provided that guarantees independence from advertising income or minimizes dependency; special regulations must be enacted regarding certain product categories such as tobacco, alcohol, medical, and pharmaceutical products; maximum transmission time in broadcasting or space in the press for advertising must be established; and there must be supervision of the international advertising industry, which disseminates mostly advertisements of products of transnational firms and has a great impact on the process of cultural globalization.

5. The final issue to be considered is *control of the process and structure of the communication technology transfer.* Such control mechanisms can be internal

as well as external: internal regulation determines whether the functions that are defined for the communication system are indeed met, and external regulation includes a variety of international agreements that have an impact on the national communication system such as the transfer of communication technology, telecommunication tariffs, or frequency allocations. Regulations and mechanisms for sanctions can be voluntarily imposed by those directly responsible for communication processes; for example, through journalistic professional codes and media councils. Another possibility is for the state to legislate norms and check on their implementation. Finally, the audience itself can organize in consumer unions and take action. Codes of conduct will have to be developed to regulate the activities of both governments and private corporations.

To return to the earlier example of advertising, advertising control mechanisms can rest on two basic methods: legislation and self-censorship by the advertising industry. The points of departure for such a system can be determined in a national advertising ethics in which the responsibility rests on the advertisers themselves, and the supervision of the adherence to the rules devolves on, for instance, groups of the public, perhaps organized in consumer associations. A central organism would be able to impose sanctions by, for example, prohibiting further advertising, bringing legal suits, or imposing fines. In my opinion the basic points that must be included in an advertising code are the following: advertisements should not conflict with the objectives of the development policy; they should not conflict with the law and must be honest; they must be created with a sense of responsibility to the consumer; and advertising should not violate the principle of advertising as a service to the public and the agreed on development goals.

This policy and planning model has also implications for the practice of the policy and research process. Many policymakers and researchers, however, who support these principles, seem to forget that such an engagement must be materialized as well. Forms of rational-comprehensive or allocative planning, which have been executed by technocrats and bureaucrats at distinct levels for many years, do not fit the demands of another communication policy and planning, especially the applied methodology, the choice of the place and the context of research, and the place and role of the policymaker and researcher. These differ fundamentally from conventional models.

SYNTHESIS

1. Policymakers and planners face important choices not only about the communication problems they address and the solutions they propose

in their plans, but about the way in which planning will be organized and carried out. Different kinds of problems and situations may call for different solutions. Therefore, there is no universal approach that can be used in all circumstances. As in theory, either a combination of policy and planning approaches, or the creation of a hybrid approach drawing on several theories is propagated.

2. However, despite these fundamental and important disclaimers, most policymakers and planners still feel the need for a general conceptual and operational framework. One of the reasons for this is that policy and planning is not only a theoretical but, at the same time, an applied discipline.

3. The complexity of the problematique has been dealt with in a structural-dynamic way by integrating four basic elements: (a) content-related variables that can be of an external or internal nature (objectives, goals and functions of the communication policy, etc.); (b) interrelated factors (economic, political, technological, etc., sectors) and actors (institutions, public groups, etc.); (c) a distinction at the level of analysis (international, national, local, etc.); and (d) the process of policy and planning (policy formulation, planning, implementation, evaluation, etc.). The formulation of a "realistic" and coherent policy model can only succeed if it explains the interrelationships among the various interactive, horizontal, and vertical components of the system.

4. From a structural and static perspective one can distinguish between actors and factors that influence policy and planning. Actors are public or interest groups which, by both direct and/or indirect means, try to push through their explicitly or implicitly agreed-on program. Factors, on the other hand, determine the contours within which the actors can operate. Factors are time and space bound and differ from society to society. Some are of a conjunctural nature, others of a more structural nature.

5. From a dynamic perspective one can distinguish among five overlapping phases in the policy process: the formulation of policy, the strategic or long-term planning, the operational or short-term planning, the implementation of the policy and planning, and the evaluation of it. Each level and phase of analysis of the policy process is determined by the dialectical intercourse of structural and dynamic components.

6

Technology Transfer for Whom and for What? (The Case of Thailand)

Any meaningful technological growth needs a cultural basis upon which modern science and technology can be effectively implanted, not imposed and forced upon as has been the case up to now. The fact is that every human society naturally has its own tradition of science as understood in a broad cultural sense of accumulation of knowledge about nature, at least to satisfy minimum needs for survival. In a large sense, then, traditional communities can be said to possess a measure of self-reliance, autonomy, and cultural identity. It may be problematic as to if and how a better quality of life could be further promoted in traditional context. But at the very least, it forms a rational basis of people's existence, which certainly is not entirely unscientific. The peasantry themselves are quite susceptible to technological innovations introduced from outside, whenever proved appropriate and relevant to their needs. The only problematique to be solved is the question of access and opportunity for modern and traditional societies to meet and merge into even more advanced and humanistic science truly in the service of mankind.
—Saneh Chamarik (1993: 104-105)

Until July 1997 there was much talk of Thailand being on the verge of becoming a newly industrialized country (NIC). After a recession in

1985-1986, the Thai economy was said to be growing at an unprecedented rate, and businessman and government officials expected the Thai economy to remain buoyant into the next millennium. At first glance, former Prime Minister Chatichai Choonhavan's much-proclaimed policy of turning the battlefields of Indochina into a marketplace proved successful. The aim seemed to be to sell to anyone who can buy. On closer inspection, however, the question may be to sell or to sell-out? Thailand enjoys the proud achievement of having never been a colony. However, in view of today's economic crisis and the devaluation of the currency, I fear that it is rapidly resembling one because an export-oriented economy that offers all kinds of facilities to transnationals has a fundamental impact on the structure of dependency of a country. This observation refers to a study by the Thailand Development Research Institute (TDRI). The TDRI (1994) found that, despite the increased level of industrialization, income distribution had not improved. It found that in 1975-1976 the income share of the top 20% of the population was 49.26% of the national income. This figure increased to 51.47% in 1980-1981, 55.63% in 1985-86, and 56.48% in 1990-91. The rich were getting richer. At the same time, the income of the lowest 20% of the population accounted for only 6.05% of national income in 1975-76. This fell to 5.41% in 1980-81, 4.55% in 1985-86, and 4.05% in 1990-91. The poor were getting poorer. Whereas the income gap between the poor and the rich in 1988 was at a ratio of 1:12, in 1995 it increased to 1:20 (Kiatiprajuk, 1995: 7). In other words, economic growth does not necessarily bring about equal income distribution, especially in a still very hierarchically organized society as the Thai continues to be.

The Thai government seems to be very reluctant to define autonomously technological goals and design policies to employ alternative channels for enhancing their technological capability. The basic question which they try to avoid answering is: How do we adapt external technology to internal conditions in order to avoid hasty applications that may disrupt highly valued societal norms and cultural values?

After briefly exploring the relationship between technology and society and presenting three views on technology transfer, I focus on some policy issues to be faced in technology transfer. By way of conclusion I briefly discuss a problem that is at the heart of technology transfer in Thailand, that is the educational system and the research on science and technology.

Technology and Culture

To technology is attributed a direct impact on the economic development, the political organization, and the sociocultural value system of a society.

However, as explained earlier, technology is called into existence by a particular set of historical circumstances that shape and define that technology. One must understand that set of historical circumstances if one is to comprehend the effective relationship between technology and society. Therefore, I do not believe in the idea that Western technology can be borrowed without taking in Western culture at the same time. In my opinion, science and technology are much more than the mere instruments they were expected to be; they cannot be just borrowed or bought. Thai policymakers seem to assume that technical and economic progress is simply a means to an end and that it hardly affects the culture in which it occurs. It seems to me as if they believe that they can achieve Western-style progress and at the same time retain their culture and their morals or, at the least, most of the essential parts of them.

In the international field, accelerating technological developments suggest that opportunities for the expression of cultural differences can be ensured. In reality, however, these developments appear to be the instrument precisely for the destruction of these differences and for its replacement by a uniform, Western-dominated technological model. As already discussed in the previous chapter, there are at least three implicit basic values in Western technology. First, Western technology shows little respect for myth, symbol, or the power of the mysterious. Every phenomenon has to be broken down into component parts, tested, and verified. Second, the technology is based on the cult of efficiency. The central considerations are productivity, cost-benefit ratio, and the bottom line. Third, technology dominates and manipulates nature rather than being in harmony with it. Problem solving is the goal; hence, reality is reduced to those dimensions that can be studied as problems needing solutions. The values implicit in Western technologies may therefore come into conflict with the preexisting values of the Third World. In their interesting analysis of computerization in Southeast Asia, two researchers at the East-West Center in Honolulu, Syed Rahim and Anthony Pennings (1987: 141), note:

> the metaphorical concept structuring computer rhetoric seems to be coherent with some basic values of the mainstream Western industrial culture. We can easily associate the computer advertising concept with such value concepts as individualism, rationality, freedom of communication, sociability, salubrity, innovativeness and material progress. It is also interesting to note that the representation of the computer values is strikingly similar to the representation of certain values in the American popular media, for instance, in the Superman movies.

Furthermore, science and technology penetrate other subsystems of society as well. They are a whole system of explanation that not only affects science and technology alone, but seemingly unconnected areas like positive law and a modern government and bureaucracy in which traditional ascriptions, hierarchies, and authorities are replaced by objective standards and decision making. Referring to its historically rooted adaptable culture, most Thai scholars, in my opinion, underestimate this overwhelming and comprehensive aspect of modern Western science and technology. I would like to argue that technology is not politically neutral and value free. Therefore, technology definitely determines the sociocultural structure and communication patterns of a given society. This also implies that technology may not be equated with mere technical equipment, but that it should refer to knowledge in all its varied applications. Technology produces, innovates, and maintains industrial products as well as industrial production methods, basic as well as luxurious commodities, and creates material as well as immaterial results (for more details, see, e.g., Matthews & Nagata, 1986).

The Transnational Technology Transfer

Another fundamental point is the predominant impact and role of transnational corporations in the production and distribution of technology. In virtually all Third World countries, it is primarily the transnational suppliers and financiers that benefit from the advantages of technology transfer. Most of the Third World countries depend on transnationals for their own technical development capacity. These transnational corporations spend not only billions of dollars in advertising products, services, and corporate images in a highly competitive market, but, as Rahim and Pennings (1987) observe, they have successfully used cultural values and symbols to promote their products. For instance, the famous IBM campaign in Southeast Asia, entitled "The Fruits of Our Labour," showed a fresh looking red tomato that covered two pages of the two-and-a-half page advertisement. In the Chinese culture red symbolizes success and prosperity, and the round shape of the tomato signifies unity and wholeness.

In the Thai case, even Phisit Pakkasem (1988: 218), of the National Economic and Social Development Board, warns against the hidden costs related to technology transfers and their appropriateness for Thailand. Technology transfer remains limited to the telecommunications sector. The production and research of high technology is concentrated in Western countries. They only offer training facilities to Third World countries that opt for their products.

Three Different Views of Technology Transfer

The problem of technology transfer can be looked at from three different perspectives. The first viewpoint builds on the modernization paradigm and integration model. It maintains that technology produced in the West is appropriate to the needs of developing countries and that the most efficient and adequate mechanism for transferring this technology is commercially, through transnational corporations. The rationale for this strategy is based on the proposition that (a) commercial technology transfer through transnationals offers all necessary combinations of technology components within a complete system of technology development and transfer, and (b) technology transfer needed to establish any new productive facility is a complicated process, requiring special knowledge and skills for each stage of its development. Moreover, this viewpoint claims that the alleged success of transnationals in transferring technology is due not only to their mastery of the whole "technology package," but to the fact that this package is closely integrated with management, marketing, and financing skills. As a consequence one can argue that any attempt to separate elements of technology transfer will either fail or result in considerably larger "costs."

The second point of view, growing out of the dependency school, can be said to be the opposite of the first position. It completely rejects the premises of the integration model. It states that because the social and economic structures and problems of developing countries are different, technology available in the West is not appropriate for Third World societies. All the developing countries that accepted technology imports with private capital investment are today more technologically dependent on the outside world than ever because they never developed their own indigenous scientific and technological capabilities. The only way to break out of this existing technological dependence, this viewpoint advocates, is to drastically limit imports of privately owned and controlled technology and to turn to inward-organizing broad technology import-substitution programs. Rather than copy advanced technologies these programs should involve the design of "appropriate" technologies and the fostering of technological cooperation and exchange among all developing countries, or, in other words, establish a so-called South-to-South cooperation.

The third position, which I advocate, tries to strike the right balance between the two strategies just described. It states that developing countries need an appropriate mix of technologies and not just appropriate "home-made" technologies. Such a mix may include modern foreign-produced and traditional indigenous technology—it may blend the "latest and the best" with "primitive technology." Appropriateness is not measured in terms of the dimensions of that technology, but as a function of the relationship between technology and development. Transnational companies are invited to participate provided certain conditions are fulfilled. One such condition is that transnational technology transfer be directed and controlled by the host countries in order to contribute to the creation of domestic scientific and technological capability. Another condition should be that these transnational technology imports not be considered the exclusive or the most important channel of transfer. A real policy problem for Third World nations will be the need to strike a balance between self-reliance and strategic imports. Thus, local industry, in order to remain competitive, may require the importation of advanced technology. The assessment process must be guided by the goal of autonomous development. Furthermore, assessment must be based on a nuanced view of technology; that is, one must differentiate between the various kinds of technologies (i.e., technologies used in production, consumption, and distribution) and the impact that these technologies are likely to have. One must ask: Who will benefit most from the importation of these technologies?

Consequences for Policymaking

Observing the real process of technology transfer, two related considerations become obvious: on the one hand, the technological and other objectives of transnationals (and Western governments) differ considerably from the sometimes explicit, but mostly implicit, national objectives of developing countries; and on the other hand, many Third World nations continue to regard the transnationals as the major channel of international technological transfer. Vincent Lowe (1987) and Rahim and Pennings (1987), for instance, point out that none of the ASEAN countries have yet adopted a coherent and comprehensive policy in the field of information technology and that "very little systematic research on the social and cultural problems of computerization has been carried out in the Asean region. [Moreover,] there is very little public discussion about it" (Rahim & Pennings, 1987: 162). These authors indicate that this may be due to (a) the rather recent explosive development of the field; (b) the uncertainty as to where in public administration the responsibility for technological matters reside; (c) the degree of technical complexity that demands a very specialized expertise; and (d) in several countries the dominant climate of privatization and deregulation does not favor public policymaking. Moreover, Third World countries are increasingly affected by the modernization recipe of economic growth by either donor countries or donor agencies (such as the World Bank, the IMF, or—in the Southeast Asian context—the Asian Development Bank), which implies the retreat of the state in favor of various forms of privatization. Finally, there appears to be a general concern about missing the so-called "information revolution," and as a consequence the majority of policy decisions relate to the spending of public funds on the acquisition of the latest generation of computers and new technology in general. Most of the Third World governments fear remaining "backward," and therefore often overlook the specific socioeconomic and sociocultural contexts in which technology transfer has to be considered.

Critical assessments of the Thai development process, or its successive development plans reach similar conclusions (for more details, see, e.g., Prasith-Rathsint, 1987; Phongpaichit & Baker, 1996; Warr, 1993). Moreover, measures suggested by the government committee overseeing the implementation of the Sixth National Economic and Social Development Plan are in line with the earlier observations. One of the proposed measures explicitly refers to the problem of technology transfer. It states that "foreign companies will be encouraged [sic] to transfer technology to Thais" (The Nation, 1989: 13). I doubt whether mere "encouragement" will be sufficient to implement this policy objective.

Alan Hancock (1984) argues that successful technology transfer cannot occur unless a certain level of capability has already been built up in the recipient. If this is not the case, the partnership will be unequal, and the transfer will be mechanical and imitative. He concludes that commercial transfers are of little use: no real transfer is involved, and the recipient is totally disadvantaged. Thailand is no exception. For instance, at a seminar on "Japanese Investments in Thailand" at Thammasat University, Prathueng Srirodbang, Deputy Director-General of the Department of Internal Trade, stated that most of the contracts of Thai-Japanese businesses, primarily in high-tech production and for temporary construction work, are found to restrict profits for the Thai side to very small amounts. Loopholes in business laws concerning foreign investments are being exploited by Japanese entrepreneurs who export virtually all benefits garnered in Thailand, according to experts (Limprungpatanakit, 1989: 15).

Moreover, looking at domestic technologies, Hancock observes that indigenous forms do badly at first, when they are compared with imported models, and as a result they need a good deal of committed and resolute policy support if they are to have the chance to survive, to become entrenched and competitive.

Who Is In Charge?

The regulation and control of the process and structure of technology transfer is a very important issue that has not received proper consideration from Thai policymakers. Such control mechanisms can be internal as well as external.

According to most Thai experts there are many weak points in Thai law concerning foreign investment and ownership. The Civil and Commercial Code on the establishment of limited companies has provided no protection for Thailand. Therefore, the Juridical Council has proposed sweeping revisions of laws and the lawmaking process to cope with the country's social, economic, and political development. Amorn Chandara-Somboon, Secretary-General of the Juridical Council, argued that Thailand faces increasingly complicated legal problems caused by obsolete laws that are impediments to national development (The Nation, 1989: 13).

External regulation includes a variety of international agreements that have an impact nationally, such as telecommunication tariffs, frequency allocations, or intellectual property protection agreements. In this regard, the copyright controversy presents an interesting case. It is not only of special importance to current Thai politics but it led to dissolution of the House in May 1988. Moreover, the 1989 US decision to remove some Thai export products from import duty exemptions—granted to developing countries under the U.S. Generalized System of Preferences (GSP)—in retaliation for Thailand's position on the copyright of computer software and pharmaceutical patents, is an interesting case with which to study the relationship between internal and external regulations. Because, according to the U.S. Ministry of Commerce, Thailand has committed itself to enforce intellectual property laws, this decision was reconsidered in November 1994. Since then Thailand has been put on a watch list.

Education and Research in Technology

Education and research in technology are generally considered of fundamental importance for a self-reliant development objective. However, in Thailand everyone concerned seems to be convinced that education may become a future stall to national development. "Self-reliance requires that the country has its own well-educated scientists and engineers and depends as little as possible on developed countries, except for the transfer of the latest scientific and technological advances," argued the French scientist Jean Faullimmel (1987: 4), who worked at Chulalongkorn University in Bangkok.

Thailand lags behind other regional nations with regard to technology education and research. The number of high school graduates is only 30% of the population in Thailand, compared with 94% in South Korea, 91% in Taiwan, 53% in Malaysia, 71% in Singapore, and 68% in the Philippines. In Korea and Taiwan the number of vocational school and university graduates each year averaged 17.4 and 8.5% of all school-goers, whereas the figure for Thailand is limited to only 3.6%. Moreover, most reports indicate that the country lacks qualified technology teachers and researchers because the universities instead focused on the skills needed by the bureaucracy. "Many studied public administration. Rather few studied engineering" (Phongpaichit & Baker, 1996: 108).

During the Asia-Pacific Forum on Telecommunications, held in December 1988 at the Asian Institute of Technology, it was once again emphasized that telecommunications development in Asia is severely hindered by the lack of high-level telecommunications planners and executives with knowledge of computer-based technologies (The Nation, 1988: 19). The bottleneck of poor education and research will in the long term result in the shortage of a skilled labor force. For certain professions such as engineers, this is already the case. According to estimates by the Office of the Board of Investment (BoI), Thailand needs about 5,000 engineers a year, whereas in 1989 there were only 3,000 engineering graduates (The Nation, 1989: 27). The shortage of qualified manpower results from the lack of accurate planning. Although Korea and Taiwan have undergone four significant stages in their industrial development—namely, simple assembly, fabrication, design improvement, and engineering design—within the past two decades to become a NIC, Thailand, which started at the same time, has just entered the second stage.

At one of the many seminars that focused on Thailand's road to becoming a NIC, Professor Sippanandha Ketudat, chairman of Thailand Research Fund's policy committee, said that Thailand only allocates about 0.5% of its gross domestic product for science and technology development, whereas other Asian countries like Taiwan or Korea spend an average 3% of their GDP for R&D activities. In order to develop one's own technology one has to focus on improvement of the educational system. In this respect Thailand is also far behind its other Asian partners, not only quantitatively but also qualitatively (Sukin, 1994).

Apart from infrastructural, budget, and bureaucratic (so-called redtape) reasons, one should also look at the following "problems" for an explanation of the Thai culture: low salaries, nepotism, the patronage system, and an educational system which favors submission and discourages critical thinking are not the best incentives for scholarly performance and, consequently, lead to low morality and quality (Hallinger, 1994).

SYNTHESIS

1. The discussion on the transfer of technology forms part of a complex social problem. Discussions and most of the research on this subject, apart from several rare exceptions, do not go far beyond their own sector-based domain. These "gaps" in research urgently need to be filled in. Therefore, a critical evaluation of the particular relationships between technologies and society is needed in order to formulate policies and strategies for technology transfer.

2. Compared to the other ASEAN countries and contrary to all the Thai government's rhetoric, Thailand, together with Indonesia, is a latecomer in the technology field. It concentrates on consumer electronics and components and can only attract these kinds of operations because of its ability to offer lower labor costs than the other NICs in the region. Much will depend on how the international structure of the electronics industry evolves during the next 10-15 years. If the transnational electronics corporations in the United States, Japan, and Western Europe move toward a high level of automation in components and consumer electronics manufacturing, the ASEAN countries will be forced to redirect their efforts toward faster product diversification and seek new markets within and outside the region.

3. The problem of technology transfer can be looked at from three different perspectives. The first viewpoint builds on the modernization paradigm and integration model. It maintains that technology produced in the West is appropriate to the needs of developing countries and that the most efficient and adequate mechanism for transferring this technology is commercially, through transnational corporations. The second point of view, growing out of the dependency school, can be said to be the antithesis of the first position. The only way to break out of the existing technological dependence, this viewpoint advocates, is to drastically limit imports of privately owned and controlled technology and to turn to inward-organizing broad technology import-substitution programs. The third position states that developing countries need an appropriate mix of technologies and not just appropriate "homemade" technologies. Such a mix may include modern foreign-produced and traditional indigenous technology, it may blend the "latest and the best" with "primitive technology." Appropriateness is not measured in terms of the dimensions of that technology, but as a function of the relationship between technology and development.

4. There is no simple formula for resurrecting appropriate indigenous technology. However, the capacity to cooperate and communicate is decisive in creating a climate for indigenous technological innovations. This demands political will and self-confidence:

> Careful choice and adaptation of technology as well as research and development for indigenous technology shared among Third World countries can foster a spirit of cooperation, self-reliance, and autonomy. The less developed countries can thereby reduce their dependence on advanced states and begin to solve the basic problems of poverty. In the words of Julius Nyerere, technology can then be made to serve human need, not human greed. (Stover, 1984:78)

7

Participatory Strategies for Policymaking and Research

The true development of human beings involves much more than mere economic growth. At its heart there must be a sense of empowerment and inner fulfillment. This alone will ensure that human and cultural values remain paramount in a world where political leadership is often synonymous with tyranny and the rule of a narrow elite. People's participation in social and political transformation is the central issue of our time. This can only be achieved through the establishment of societies which place human worth above power, and liberation above control.
—Aung San Suu Kyi (1994: 4)

Traditional positivist-functionalist approaches still implicitly start from the assumptions that all knowledge is based on an observable reality and that social phenomena can be studied on the basis of methodologies and techniques adopted from the natural sciences (see Chapter 3). However, as Anthony Giddens (1979) eloquently points out, the social sciences differ from the natural sciences in at least four respects: with regard to the study domain the social sciences are, contrary to the natural sciences, in a subject-subject relationship; they deal with a preinterpreted world in which the meanings developed by the active subjects form part of the production of that world; the construction of a theory of society therefore necessitates a double hermeneutics; and, finally the logical status of generalizations in the social sciences differs from natural scientific generalizations. Therefore, in my opinion, the social sciences are hermeneunistic and nomological in nature and need to be approached from a critical perspective (see also Fay, 1987).

First I briefly present a framework that attempts to incorporate participatory strategies for policymaking and research; and second, by way of warning, I mention a number of obstacles that condition or sometimes even obstruct the successful implementation of a participatory approach.

TOWARD A FRAMEWORK FOR PARTICIPATORY POLICYMAKING AND RESEARCH

The classic materialist-idealist distinction between political-economy and interpretative approaches has become outdated. Therefore, I advocate the relative autonomy of a *cultural analysis*. In general, one can distinguish between two basic types of cultural critique. The first is of a philosophical nature, posing as an epistemological critique of analytical reason, of the Enlightenment faith in pure reason, and of the social progress that rationality is supposed to engender. This type of critique attempts to demystify power and ideology. The second approach uses more empirical and therefore more conventional social science techniques to analyze social institutions, cultural forms, and the modes of discourse in social life.

Research Perspective

So far, most of the research on participatory and user-oriented communication has dealt with small-scale and isolated initiatives. Certainly, this kind of research is of value, for instance, as a space to experiment with new patterns and processes of societal communication. However, more important and less performed are analyses of large-scale, social liberation movements in First, Second, Third, and Fourth World environments, like the Latin American peasant movement, nationalist movements such as the Nicaraguan or Philippine revolution, or the ecological movement in Western Europe.

What I have in mind is a text that takes as its subject not a concentrated group of people in a community affected in one way or another by politico-economic forces, but the *system itself*—the political and economic processes, encompassing different space and time constraints. This kind of analysis, which builds on the ideas of Archer (1988), Canclini (1993), Foucault (1977, 1980), Geertz (1983), Giddens (1984, 1991), Martin-Barbero (1993), Marcus and Fisher (1986), Sanderson (1995), and Thompson (1995) should also involve the relative power-linked articulation and conflict over ideologies, worldviews, moral codes, and the locally bounded conditions of knowledge and competence. Although all social research presumes a hermeneutic moment, often it remains latent because researcher and research inhabit a common cultural milieu. Moreover, it is in the study of the unintended consequences of action and the creation of meaning that some of the most distinctive tasks of the social sciences in general, and communication studies in particular, are to be found. At least two types of unintended influences can be distinguished: first, the unconscious ones, and second, influences conditioned by the context in which the different forms of social action take place.

Without disqualifying and underestimating the significance of other research contributions, I advocate a research design that starts from a more dialectic and multicentered perception of power factors in the context of communication for social change. In other words, I advocate a framework that also takes into account counter-power or empowerment from a bottom-up or grassroots perspective. In general, three problem areas can be discerned: (a) the mutual dependency between the macrolevel of the society or a given structure and the microlevel of the social actions involved; (b) the position and the autonomy of organized subjects; and (c) the relationship of domination, dependency, and subordination versus liberation, selective participation, and emancipation of power and interest contra positions.

The main actors in this new perspective are *social movements* with a concern for the multiple public issues just described. Therefore, instead of one central, objective, and mainly economic "conflict," several segmented, subjective, and "postmaterialistic" issues can be identified. Instead of one central collective actor (the proletariat or exploited class), several different, sometimes opposing collective actors can be identified (see also Beck, 1986; Ekins, 1992; Escobar & Alvares, 1992; Esteva, 1987; Eyerman & Jamison, 1991; Gunder & Fuentes, 1988; Wignaraja, 1993).

This research project must center around two problem areas. First, it must determine what actors or interest groups and what factors or structural constraints exercise influence from above. These influences can transform, reinforce, or weaken each other. What is required is a much more precise analysis of influence patterns that function from top down by means of power in the broad sense. With this, the role of the state also becomes more central. According to James Midgley (1986:VII):

It is naive to argue that state involvement in social development is superfluous and that local communities in the Third World can solve the serious problems of poverty and deprivation wholly through their own efforts. But it is equally naive to assume that a cosy relationship between the centralized, bureaucratic state and the local community will emerge and that political elites, professionals and administrators will readily agree to the devolution of their authority to ordinary people. While community participation is a desirable goal, the extensive involvement of the state in social development complicates the issue and requires further analysis.

The second problem area is the grass-roots reaction to this influence. Research must be focused on the rational objectives of target groups and social movements. The difference from traditional anthropological research should be that the choice of the symbolic order for the research is determined by key concepts such as *reproduction* and *identity*. It is not the more-or-less by chance differences in rational objectives that are interesting, but the systematic tendencies and therefore, the generalizable differences. This implies that the choice of the place and the context of research cannot be random but must be based on macrostructural insights. However, there always exists a danger that the research area will be selected on the basis of practical reasons rather than theoretical considerations (Bagguley, 1992).

Participatory Strategies

This policy and research model, which builds on the multiplicity paradigm, starts from more dialectic mobilization and conscientization strategies. Social resistance and conscientization is developed from the bottom-up via interpersonal communication or media channels. This theme immediately brings to mind the conscientization method developed by Paulo Freire (1970a & b, 1973, 1974, 1983, 1994) in Brazil. Because Freire himself clearly states that the "third world" is also found in industrialized societies (what is involved here is not a geographical but a relational and structural categorization), the "exemplarisch lernen" method (imitative learning) of Oskar Negt (1971), which originated in Western workers' situations, can be mentioned as an important addition.

As we explained previously, Freire's conscientization method is oriented toward bringing the individual to critical reflection about his or her own living conditions whereby he or she breaks through the "culture of silence" and actively participates in an historical process. The right to participation and emancipation regarding social, cultural, and historical reality is a fundamental right for everyone. The basis of the conscientization method forms the philosophical and sociocritical notion that individuals must be able to achieve their essential goal—being a subject—and that the social structures, social relationships, and interpersonal relationships that interfere with it must be changed. The absence of any form of a guideline for political organization for those who are conscienticized is partially resolved by Negt. In his method, he tries to bring the marginal people in the society to see their individual need as a collective need that can only be satisfied in the context of organized groups (for a critical assessment of these methods, see, e.g., Kidd & Kumar, 1981; Mackie, 1981; McLaren, 1995; McLaren & Lankshear, 1994; McLaren & Leonard, 1993; Thomas, 1993).

In the literature, this approach is often described as participatory action or *participatory research*. Eurich (1980), the Farmers Assistance Board (1985), Gran (1983), Huizer (1983, 1989), Kassam and Mustafa (1982), Kronenburg (1986), Seguier (1976), and Tobias (1982), among others, have attempted to identify the major characteristics of participatory research. Kronenburg (1986: 255-256) summarizes them as follows:

(a) Participatory research rests on the assumption that human beings have an innate ability to create knowledge. It rejects the notion that knowledge production is a monopoly of "professionals";

(b) Participatory research is seen as an educational process for the participants in the research program as well as for the researcher. It involves the identification of community needs, augmented awareness about obstacles to need fulfillment, an analysis of the causes of the problems and the formulation and implementation of relevant solutions;

(c) The researcher is consciously committed to the cause of the community involved in the research. This challenges the traditional principle of scientific neutrality and rejects the position of the scientist as a social engineer;

(d) Research is based on a dialectical process of dialogue between the researcher and the community. Dialogue provides for a framework that guards against manipulative scientific interference and serves as a means of control by the community over the direction of the research process;

(e) Participatory research is a problem-solving approach. The objective is to uncover the causes of community problems and mobilize the creative human potential to solve social problems by transforming the conditions underlying the problems;

(f) The major asset of participatory research is its potential for the creation of knowledge. Close cooperation between researcher and community forms a condition enabling all participants to analyze the social environment and formulate adequate plans of action.

In other words, this participatory approach calls for upward, transactive, open, and radical forms of planning that encompass both grass-roots collective actions (i.e., planning in the small) and large-scale processes (i.e., planning in the large). This kind of planning and research is centrally conceived with human growth, and learning processes through mobilization. The basic aim is to involve the people under study cooperatively in the planning and research process, with the planner or researcher as a facilitator and animator (see Table 7.1).

Therefore, one could call the conventional strategies "diffusion-mechanistic" models, as the human being is considered just a "thing," whereas participatory strategies are more "organic," spiritually oriented, and "human"; they believe in the humanness, the importance of people (see Table 7.2). Both models should be regarded as opposite positions on a continuum.

Empowering Research

This research can be performed on small-scale, large-scale as well as integrated levels. As Emile McAnany has commented in Wang and Dissanayake (1984: XVII):

> The challenge of the next decade is to examine the indigenous and the modern systems to see how each may contribute to the integration that is called for in a nation's development without sacrificing either basic cultural values or the advancement of human needs.

In all cases one needs to break through artificial boundaries of distinct media and communication systems, in search of those elements that constitute the ideological order of power/empowerment and domination/emancipation, which is the historical outcome of (class) struggle:

> At all these levels, the objective of research/action should be the demystification of "technology" and science; the necessary relationship between theories and practice; the decentralization of control and communication; the democratization of communications institutions and practices; mass mobilization for organization and action; and the paramount significance of communications for peace. (Smythe & Van Dinh, 1983:127)

The main target of this new approach are social groups or movements with a concern for public issues like ecology, social justice, peace, educa-

Pity	Sympathy	Empathy
Characterized by a concern or regret for one considered to be inferior and by a condescending or paternalistic attitude. It implies a disposition to help, but little emotional sharing of the distress.	A feeling of sorrow for the distress of another, but connotes spontaneous emotion rather than a considered attitude. Primarily on his or her terms, so the relationship tends to be one sided.	A conscious involvement with a person's situation, in the sense of vicarious identification. Implies a willingness to take the time to learn and understand how the other person perceives the situation.
Serves as a "go-between" controlling the information flow between communities and government decision makers. A minimum amount of involvement and identification with either party. Creates a dependent situation in which people being represented feel "absolutely weak."	Acts on behalf of the community they represent. "Issue" or "program" oriented and do not think in terms of an ongoing process. The resolution of an issue or the initiation of a program are ends in themselves. Community lets advocate do all the work, and gets angry if there are no results.	Primary concern is to create an attitude change within the community. Believes that the community will eventually develop a sense of collective power that, when exercised in a responsible manner, will provoke a response from government officials. Community will act on its own behalf.

BROKER   ADVOCATE   ANIMATOR

INVOLVEMENT
RESULTS
INDEPENDENCE

−   +

Figure 7.1. Attitudes, roles, and the development communication worker
Based on Kennedy (1984, 1988)

Table 7.1. Two Ideal-typical Models for Policymaking and Research.

Mechanistic Model	Organic Model
Overall Objectives	
Motive for Cooperation:	
People need to be helped	People are able to help
Charity	Themselves. Empowerment.
Assumption about target group:	
People lack abilities and resources to develop themselves. They are helpless.	People do have abilities to develop themselves. These can be mobilized.
Attitude toward problems:	
Problem solving.	Problem posing.
Attitude toward participation:	
Means to achieve ends.	A never-ending process.
Objective of policymakers or researchers:	
Implementation of project objectives	Striving toward a common vision and understanding of self-development.
Learning relationship:	
Teacher-student; know-all versus know-nothing. Paternalistic.	Everybody is teacher and student at the same time; everybody has something of interest to share. Empathic.
Valuation of knowledge:	
Western knowledge is superior.	Traditional knowledge is equally relevant.
Agent of change:	
Policymaker or researcher.	People themselves.
People seen as:	
Targets, objects.	Subjects, actors.
"Leadership" position:	
Project leader.	Coordinator, animator, facilitator.
Selection of "leaders":	
Appointed by higher authority.	Preferable selected by people themselves.
"Leadership" qualifications:	
Decision making, management, authoritative.	Cooperation, delegation, receptive, adaptability to new circumstances.
Relationship with people and colleagues:	
Expert-counterpart; authority centered.	Shared leadership; shared responsibility.

Table 7.1. Two Ideal-typical Models for Policymaking and Research (cont'd).

Policy and Planning

Design criteria:

Productivity and economic growth	Needs and criteria for well-being formulated by people themselves.

Organizational structure:

Hierarchical, vertical	Horizontal, two-way.

Type of work:

Technical-economic.	Educational-organizational.

Approach to work:

Executing tasks	Listening to people. Facilitating.

Organization of work:

Formal, static.	Informal, dynamic.

Mode of communication:

Monologue, consultation.	Dialogue.

Communication Projects

Type of media used:

Mainly mass media.	Mixed and integrated media use; also interpersonal communication.

Direction of ideas and information:

Top-down, one-way.	Bottom-up, two-way.

Implementation and Evaluation

Planning format:

Blue-print.	Open-ended.
Project approach.	Process approach.

Change seen as:

Improvements.	Transformation.

Time perspective:

Short term.	Long term.

Effect of absence of leader:

Project activities slow down	Development process continues.

Initiative for evaluation:

By funding agency or higher authority.	Usually initiated by people themselves.

Type of solutions:

Symptom curing; evolutionary change.	Aimed at elimination of root causes; structural change.

tion, human rights, civic action, and so on. These types of social group-ings transcend the notion of political parties or interest groups as tradi-tionally understood and conceived. The guiding principle of these groups is to proceed from a bottom-up perspective, rather than from the top downward as is the case in the classic power structure which disre-gards the views of the masses and is therefore elite-oriented. The most effective forms of mobilization of these social groups and movements are rooted in popular cultural and ideological expressions in both inter-personal and mass communication. Their greatest ontological challenge is the political rationality of traditional knowledge or, as Orlando Fals Borda (1985: 2) calls it: "The rediscovery of forms of wisdom which have become obscured or discarded by Cartesian methods and Kantian empirical presuppositions." In other words, the goal of these social movements is political in the old sense of the word.

OBSTACLES TO PARTICIPATION

Participation is currently popular, and one can hardly argue against the concept, broadly conceived. However, even though it is widely shared theoretically, it is difficult to promote in practice, as most scholars admit, in fact, that participation in communication hardly exists, except in a very limited way in a number of small localized experiments. In translat-ing broad policies to specific practices, obstacles arise: "The danger for development practice is that we will mistake the consensus of academics for the prevailing situation of the real world and the existing obstacles to social change. It is clear that proclaiming development to be a widely participatory process of social change . . . to bring about both social and material advancement . . . for the majority of the people through gaining greater control over their environment" (as did Rogers, 1976a:133) would be readily accepted by many academics. Yet when such efforts are implemented they are complicated by real-world realities and sharp political conflicts.

The inherency of conflict, and the propensity to avoid it, is but one example of a *barrier to participation*. Another is that participative endeavors are not in the interest of those seeking high visibility. Their demands for detailed, up-front planning, coupled with rigorous adher-ence to fast-paced implementation schedules and preplanned specifica-tions ensures that the real decisions will remain with professional tech-nicians and government bureaucrats.

In an organization's excitement and zeal to demonstrate quanti-tative results from new projects, the tendency is to promote rapid expan-sion of highly structured program models that emphasize quantitative targets and quick evaluation, reflecting a "compulsion for measurement." The thrust is results over process, ends over means. Efficiency is the watchword, and participation is not likely to be efficient.

Change and Agencies

Frustrated with the participatory approach, a social marketing specialist states "participation was just not consistent with the organizational realities of development where you have fairly narrow time frames, you've got to get projects off the ground" (McKee, 1994: 26). McKee also states funding agencies introduce their own bias in this respect. Their concerns are budgets and "reports on progress. They are rewarded according to the size of their portfolios and are often looking for a 'blueprint' to follow, not a complicated community process that may take years to be realized (40)."

Hence, even when people authentically participate and are thus committed to an idea, and they can often mobilize an astonishing variety of resources to realize it, it is certainly not the most expedient or easily assessable route from this "quick and visible results" perspective because it takes time, money, and effort to consult the people. Therefore one could say that building roads and dams and breeding high-yielding crops is child's play compared with the difficulties of working with people.

Such highly publicized, tightly structured, and deeply institutionalized projects also serve to "give the appearance that social development is underway, thereby throwing a smoke-screen over the deeper causes of poverty" (Fuglesang, 1984:46). Nyoni (1987:53) adds that

> most development agencies are centers of power which try to help others change. But they do not themselves change. They aim at creating awareness among the people yet they are not themselves aware of their negative impact on those they claim to serve. They claim to help people change their situation through participation, democracy and self-help and yet they themselves are non-participatory, non-democratic and dependant on outside help for their survival.

Participation and Power

Neither is genuine participation congruent with the concerns of those who would maintain a facade of social harmony, order, bureaucratic and economic efficiency, or political continuity. Participation can lead to developments that are of an unpredictable nature. However, to embark on a conscious policy of participative or democratic decision making is consciously to sacrifice the ability to make fast and stable decisions. Conversely, policies implemented in the name of order and efficiency are often more akin to repression.

Authentic participation directly addresses power and its distribution in society. It touches the very core of power relationships. Consequently, it may not sit well with those who favor the status quo, and they may be expected to resist such efforts to reallocate more power to the people. In other words, it is not in the interest of dominant classes, both at national and international levels, to implement policies and plans that would substantially improve the conditions of the lower classes or masses. In a certain way every center needs its periphery!

Just as the multiplicity paradigm argues for structural change, it also asserts that the route to individual and social development is precisely the route to increased participation. Development and participation are inextricably linked. Participation involves the more equitable sharing of both political and economic power, which often decreases the advantage of certain groups. On the political front, when participation is likely to encourage such changes, it is probable that it will be viewed as a potential threat to those who stand to loose some of their power. For instance, Bordenave (1994:8) writes

> it is difficult to imagine a participative society in which the means of production are owned by a few persons who have the capital and who reserve important decisions exclusively for themselves. The organization of the economy, then, is the crucial difference between a non-participative society and a participative one. However, the major resistance to participation is most often not such overt, cataclysmic actions. Rather, the main obstacle is the much less visible, yet insidious and continuous reluctance to organizational change.

Governments and Bureaucracies

Even though development advocates encourage change and discourage maintenance of the status quo, believing that only when change takes place will there be progress and improvements, criticism of peoples' traditionalism, under-education, and recalcitrance are often lamented as major obstacles to change. However, far less attention is given to the reverse—institutional or bureaucratic intransigence. In describing efforts to promote participation at the local level, Blair (1981:80) relates:

The programs were seeking the benefits of structural change for the poor while trying to avoid substantial change for the status quo. For participatory institutions to make decisions that can improve the lives of the participants, they must have political power. "Empowerment" at the bottom, however, was the one thing that those in charge were unwilling to give.

Governments have historically been timid toward direct or participatory democracy. In framing the U.S. constitution, for instance, many of America's founders feared the political influence of undereducated people, and participation was therefore deliberately restricted through the establishment of a representative system and an electoral college, in order to establish government by those thought best able to contribute. This representative democracy is not to be confused with direct democracy or popular participation, which more directly realizes the conditions of self-management and participation in decision making by all those affected by it (Held, 1987, 1993). The premise here is that control over an action should rest with the people who will bear the major force of its consequences, not with their mouthpieces, nor their representatives. However, this direct participation is often not feasible, efficient, or, at broader levels, even possible. Silberman (1979:100) states "bureaucrats and planners tend to look with disfavor on participation, particularly when it involves their own domain . . . participation could reduce their own social status." Furthermore, change may be resisted even in institutions that publicly acknowledge the need for alternative communication for development and take pride in their progressive stance.

Participation and Hierarchies

The elites go to great lengths to maintain their positions of power and what those positions bring to them. What those positions of power often bring is more power and material wealth. The purpose is not only maintenance, but expansion. For some, it is advantageous to conserve a particular social arrangement that allows for their own development as a group or, in a stricter sociological sense, as a class. During the British occupation of India, Lord Macaulay maintained one of the goals was to create "a class of persons, Indian in blood and color, but English in taste, in opinions, in morals, and in intellect [who would] be interpreters between us and the millions we govern" (quoted in Narula & Pearce, 1986: 65). Terms such as "morals," "intellect," and "govern" are open to interpretation, of course, but an argument could be made this class continues not as interpreters but as governors.

It is argued that the primary objective of any bureaucracy or organization, much like all living organisms, is its own sustenance, perpetuation, and possible expansion. The Peace Corps/Vista adage—to work oneself out of a job—is contrary to the individual and collective aspirations of government personnel. Describing efforts to "streamline" the government sector of the Comillia project, Khan (1976:73) states "the prospect of fewer government `workers' did not at all please the departments. Instinctively they hated decentralization, delegation, and autonomy."

The overriding interest of bureaucratic personnel in the countryside, as that of most people, is to perform well enough that they will be transferred back to the metropolis as soon as possible. They tend to practice upward orientation; they care mainly to please their superiors. And rightfully so, they are rarely rewarded for being responsive to local conditions or contributing toward the development of local institutional capacity. This is antagonistic to the requirements of participation, which mandates a focus toward the poor rather than promotion.

Change, especially structural change, involving the redistribution of power is inherently antagonistic to the need for continuity. An organization's need for self-perpetuation necessarily requires the continued existence of the larger system of which it is a part, which it serves, and from which it benefits. Consequently, even minor change is a sensitive issue in discussion, and often a revolutionary one in advocacy. But it is quite simple, convenient, and popular to place all fault with existing structures—with much "wringing of the hands"—which, in turn, blames the intransigence of the people, who, in turn, blame the government, and so on. These patterns of reciprocated blame wreck the kind of coordination necessary to achieve development objectives.

Again, structural change alone will accomplish little. It is not enough to provide participation in the system, even if this can be made less formal and more substantial; the aim is to create a more just society. Participation is necessary but not sufficient for this to happen. What is needed is self-government, a decentralized order through which the people involved are empowered. The "chicken and egg" paradox is that, although existing structures are a substantial impediment to participatory processes, valid, applicable restructuring can occur only through some degree of authentic participation. Therefore, unless policy making and the social process are themselves participatory, it is unlikely that the result will be a democratic pattern of communication.

Participation and Vested Interests

There is no magic formula for injecting participation into projects, it must come from within. Furthermore, barriers to participation are most certainly not limited to government-populace or powerful-powerless relationships. There is little substantive interaction among various governmental and private units and that which does occur is often continuous infighting over budgets, prestige and power. Therefore, sectarianism or/and propaganda interests of specific government departments often enmesh and destroy projects. Heim, Rabibhadana, and Pinthong (1983:20) explain:

> The budget is divided centrally, various departments vying for larger amounts of the limited fund by presenting and showing off their plans and schemes . . . such departmental jealousy and competition, cooperation and team work among officials of various departments at the local level are very weak or almost non-existent.

Nor do problems stop at the gates of the rural community. The same charges are applicable to the local context. Communities are seldom unified groups of people. To be avoided is "the romantic image of a community as one big happy family. . . . Each of the sub-communities or factions has its own self-interest to protect . . . an endeavor which may or may not serve the needs of the community at large" (Kennedy, 1984:85).

We see that elitist attitudes are not limited to exogenous leaders, and neither are elitist aspirations. Khan (1976:70) relates, in regard to the Comillia project, "wolves quickly volunteered to herd the sheep," and Nanavatty (1988:97) writes, as a result of democratic decentralization within development programs, "the dominant caste and class got a free hand to usurp the resources of development in its own interests." In other words, the local elites often hijack the struggles of the poor in order to meet their individual needs. More powerful community members take advantage of any available opportunity for influence, thus corrupting the purpose of the participatory approach and destroying the spirit of cooperative effort. In particular reference to the Indian context, Narula and Pearce (1986:43) write that within communities "partisan relationships, caste memberships, resentments . . . and the traditional power structure can preclude the cooperation necessary for popular participation." Furthermore, even though village *Panchayats* were established through egalitarian ideals and "are elected by the community . . . decisions are often governed by vested interests . . . panchayats no longer remain a democratic forum for village participation" (131).

Self-depreciation

Finally, from international to local contexts, the long-term existence of hierarchical structures have often conditioned rural people to see "themselves as 'consumers' rather than 'participants' in development" (Narula & Pearce, 1986: 21), and as a consequence, people often have lost the power to make decisions affecting their communities and expect solutions to come from above.

> Self-depreciation is another characteristic of the oppressed. . . . So often do they hear they are good for nothing, know nothing and are incapable of learning anything—that they are sick, lazy, and unproductive—that in the end they become convinced of their own unfitness. Because people are not stupid about how others regard them, the communication that operates according to these principles puts people's backs up. It may be much more effective at creating resentment than change. (Freire, 1983: 49)

Narula and Pearce (1986:149) define this as *learned dependency*. In Indian democratic socialism, there are "two mutually exclusive forms of action: providing for the masses' material welfare and eliciting active participation." The paradox is that often the development agents, intending to foster increased social welfare, participation, and self-reliance, and seeing themselves as the participation "experts," interject themselves into the local context and simply transfer dependency from local elites to government elites. "The pattern is such that the actions taken by various agents to change it themselves become the forces that perpetuate it" (183).

Development, participation, and such become, from the perspective of the poor, notions that are conceived, initiated, and controlled by the government. Why shouldn't it be the government's responsibility to carry them out?

Culture and Language (Once Again)

The nexus of intercultural communication is that any two individuals or groups can communicate effectively in so far as they share past experience and worldviews, but they differ culturally to the extent they do not share these same phenomena. As cultural variance increases, so does the difficulty of communication.

Earlier we conceived culture as the manifestations of a person's attempt to relate meaningfully to his or her environment. An excellent conceptual, though very poorly labeled, delineation of the differences in their orientation between agrarian and bureaucratic cultures is discussed by Howard (1986:241), who divides worldviews into *primitive* and *civilized*.

The primitive world view is essentially a personal view of the universe in which humans are seen as united with nature. ... [It] reflects the close social relationships that members of small-scale societies maintain with each other and the close relationship with nature that their technology and adaptive strategies entail. The civilized world view . . . reflects the impersonal nature of social relationships in large-scale societies . . . and a technology that allows people to become distant from nature. ... [It] stresses our separation from nature and our role of conqueror of nature. (Howard, 1986:241)

An association can also be drawn between these worldviews and Hall's (1976) *high-context* and *low-context* cultures. Operating from their worldview and a low-context culture, officials ("developers") analyze a situation as a discrete entity, existing "out there," something to be overcome with technology, "know-how," or sheer numbers. "He [or She] perceives and evaluates the promises and performances of development from his [or her] concrete, here and now, location in the factual order" (Ramashray & Srivastava, 1986:77). Khan (1976: 69-74) paints a picture of those with such an orientation:

Their proposals were precise; more assistants, more demonstration plots, more teaching of improved methods, more supplies. . . . The system seized them like a boa constrictor. They rushed from one time-consuming meeting to another, and, in between, read heaps of files and received numberless visitors and telephone calls. Always busy counting the trees, they never saw the woods.

The richness, complexity, and diversity of local life and self-help action often blend into highly aggregated statistics or are reduced to the abstractions of theoretical models, and once removed from consciousness, cease to exist in practical reality.

On the other hand, if the rural farmer, the developee, subscribing primarily to the another worldview and living in a high-context culture, sees the same situation as a problem at all, he or she may approach it as something to be tolerated or addressed in consideration of the total physical and social environment. He or she sees the situation in its social context. He or she is "guided more by intuitive understanding than by organized and systemized knowledge" (Ariyaratne, 1986: 32). It is important to recognize that this social intelligence of the farmer is often a more necessary possession than the abstract intelligence of the "expert." For example, the expert sees the social orientation—the time spent on the maintenance of relations with other community members—as laziness, as whiling away the hours in gibberish. The expert does not often realize that in the community, the production system is communal, that in many rural, agrarian contexts "sitting" is not a "waste of time" nor is it a manifestation of laziness. Sitting is having time together, time to cultivate social relations. Quite possibly ensuring good social relations is as important as producing food. In other words, different people see the same phenomena and, based on different cultural perspectives, indeed different realities, they arrive at different conclusions.

Cross-cultural Communication

To reiterate, we see that culture is a function of collective worldview, perception, logic, and language rather than geographical location or nationality. Therefore, there is an inverse relationship between cultural differences and communication ease. Whereas communication between national development institutions and rural populations is often assumed to be intracultural in nature, this is not often the case. Culture, when not understood, or seen as antagonistic as in the modernization paradigm, constitutes a substantial barrier both inter- and intra-nationally in development communications and participatory endeavors.

Halloran (1981:42) illustrates this variance in relating that scholars from different cultures "had difficulty in finding a level for mutual understanding, not only because their national languages differed, but because they classified reality in different ways." The cross-cultural communication effort par-excellence is the technical expert in the rural village; the man [or woman] whose thinking and acting are shaped in the concepts of the written language, trying to communicate with the people whose minds and behavior are molded by an oral tradition—or vice versa.

These incongruencies have profound implications for both communication and participation between exogenous development personnel and rural populations, as well as instances in which models, methods, and strategies formulated in the West are applied, largely intact, in other cultures.

> The exchange between government officials and their constituencies is conducted in a bureaucratic sub-language which has one meaning to the official and an entirely different meaning to the average citizen. . . . In this situation, communication has not "broken down"; it has never even begun. (Kennedy, 1984:87)

SYNTHESIS

1. The relative autonomy of a cultural analysis is recognized. Two basic types of cultural critique have been distinguished. The first is of a philosophical nature, posing as an epistemological critique of analytical reason, of the Enlightenment faith in pure reason, and the social progress that rationality is supposed to engender. This type of critique attempts to demystify power and ideology. The second approach uses more empirical and therefore more conventional social science techniques to analyze social institutions, cultural forms, and the modes of discourse in social life.

2. A research design is advocated that starts from a more dialectic and multicentered perception of power factors in the context of communication for social change. Such a framework also takes counter-power or empowerment from a bottom-up or grass-roots perspective into account. In general, three general problem areas can be discerned: (a) the mutual dependency between the macrolevel of the society or a given structure, and the microlevel of the social actions involved; (b) the position and the autonomy of organized subjects; and (c) the relationship of domination, dependency, and subordination versus liberation, selective participation, and emancipation of power and interest contra positions.

3. Such a research design builds on participatory approaches that call for upward, transactive, open, and radical forms of planning that encompass both grass-roots collective actions (i.e., planning in the small) and large-scale processes (i.e., planning in the large). This kind of planning and research is centrally conceived with human growth and learning processes through mobilization. The basic aim is to involve the people under study cooperatively in the planning and research process, with the planner or researcher as a facilitator and participant.

4. A number of obstacles have been identified that condition and sometimes even obstruct the successful implementation of a participatory approach: agencies, governments and bureaucracies, hierarchies and vested interests, self-depreciation, language, and cross-cultural communication.

Part III
. . . To Praxis

8

A Village in the Jungle: Culture and Communication in Thailand

There appears to be an almost insulting contradiction between the image of the delicate Land of Smiles, of exquisite manners and "unique hospitality", and the world of live pussy shows. Yet, to see these images as contradictory is perhaps to misunderstand Thailand. Patpong kitsch and Thai traditions coexist—they are images from different worlds, forms manipulated according to opportunity. The same girl who dances to rock 'n' roll on a bar top, wearing nothing but cowboy boots, seemingly a vision of corrupted innocence, will donate part of her earnings to a Buddhist monk the next morning, to earn religious merit. The essence of her culture, her moral universe outside the bar, is symbolized not by the cowboy boots, but by the amulets she wears around her neck, with images of Thai kings, of revered monks, or of the Lord Buddha. The apparent ease with which Thai appear able to adopt different forms, to swim in and out of seemingly contradictory worlds, is not proof of a lack of cultural identity, nor is the kitsch of Patpong proof of Thai corruption—on the contrary, it reflects the corrupted taste of Westerners, for whom it is specifically designed. Under the evanescent surface, Thais remain in control of themselves.
—Ian Buruma (1989: 30)

Though Thailand has never been "colonized" by a foreign power, external influences have always played a significant role.

Whereas historically the Chinese and Indian cultures heavily affected the local society, since the beginning of the so-called Ratanakosin period in 1782, Western values have been introduced. Especially during the reigns of King Chulalongkorn or Rama V (1868-1910), King Vajiravudh or Rama VI (1910-1925), and the regime of Colonel Pibul (1938-1945), the Thai were strongly "advised," not to say "forced," to assimilate through "fashion," language, and etiquette the forms and symbols of a so-called Western civilization: "Material progress, technical advancement and a high standard of living characteristic of the West make the Thai think that Western culture must be better than ours, and that it is our duty to follow suit and adopt it as ours." This statement was made by Kurkrit Pramoj, who as a former Prime Minister, president of the Social Action Party, actor in the film "The Ugly American" (with Marlon Brando), newspaper columnist, author of several historic novels, and expert in the traditional *Khon* pantomime art, can be considered one of the outstanding representatives of modern Thai culture. He continues by saying that "it must be admitted that Thai culture is in a state of utter confusion, and probably it has reached the highest degree of confusion ever known in our history" (Pramoj, quoted in Van Beek, 1983:93-94).

The Thai audiovisual market is no exception. Foreign movies (mainly American "action," and Hong Kong "Kung Fu" films) account for about 85% of films shown and distributed. In a special issue of the *Far Eastern Economic Review* about the Asian film industry, it was noted that most of the Thai films were "either comedies or soap operas; only very few would satisfy those with a sophisticated cinematic taste" (Bangsapan, 1984:63). In their turn, Thai movie and television producers tend to "blame" the audience for being *Nam nao* (polluted water). In other words, they claim to give the public what it wants.

As explained previously, each culture has to be analyzed on the basis of its own "logical" structure. Each culture operates out of its own logic. In each culture one must therefore focus on the so-called *archetypes* rather than on the formal and often officially propagated manifestations of a culture. Along with anthropological research methods, the study of cultural expressions such as art, folktales, film, video or literature (see, e.g., Anderson, 1985; Boonyaketmala, 1982, 1985; Diskul, 1986, Harrison, 1994; Rutnin, 1988; Seesawat, 1987; Servaes & Malikhao, 1989) can be of use in answering the questions that arise from this approach: How do the Thai construe and interpret their own "Weltanschauung"? How do they explain their world in terms of (wo)mankind, (wo)man to (wo)man relationships, and (wo)man to nature and (wo)man to supernatural relationships? And what are the formats, contents, and institutions in which such a worldview and value system are symbolically represented?

As the needs and values that various communities develop in divergent situations and environments are not the same, various cultures also manifest varying "identities." Far from being only a top-down phenomenon, foreign mass media and cultural influences interact with local networks in what can be termed a *coerseductive* (for coercion/seduction) way. Far from being passive recipients, audiences are actively involved in the construction of meaning around the media messages they consume. Consequently, such messages may have different effects and meanings in different cultural settings.

Expanding mainly on the cultural, anthropological, and sociological interpretations of Saneh Chamarik (1993), William Klausner (1983, 1997), Niels Mulder (1985, 1990), Seri Phongphit (1989), and Anuman Rajadhon (1968, 1987), I offer an analysis of the interdependency between Thai culture and its communicative expressions with the aid of two complementary, mutually interpretive, and influential dimensions from the traditional, rural, and animistic culture, which still fundamentally conditions modern-day Thailand. One dimension is of a spiritual-moral nature, the other of a sociological nature.

Thai Feudalism: The "Sakdina" System

Historically the Thai societal structure is rooted in the so-called Sakdina system. (Sak means status or power and na means land or ricefield. Sakdina could therefore be translated as "land status" or "status shown by land".) The major difference between the Sakdina system and the European feudal system is its dependence on the king and the changeability of status. Status was not possible unless one had royal blood. The king or *Chao Paendin* (the lord of the land) was perceived as infallible, semi-divine, and all-powerful. He was the only land owner. He distributed the right to use land according to the Sakdina status, which depended in turn on an individual's relationship by blood or by service to the king. The closeness of that relationship had to be ranked with great precision because the Sakdina status determined an individual's rights, wealth, political power, and responsibilities to the state as well as his or her relationship to the rest of society. According to Somsamai Srisootarapan (pseudonym for Jit Pumisak, a famous artist and critical scholar who was killed by the police in 1966), there are four major characteristics of the Sakdina system: (a) The king was the owner of all land, with absolute power over land and people; (b) The people did not have the right to own land. They had to rent the land and pay with produce at high rates; (c) There was an exploitive relationship between landlord and serf; and (d) The king's officials were given land, horses, buffaloes, and men so they could exploit common men for personal and royal benefits (Srisootarapan, 1976).

The introduction of capitalist modes of production has not fundamentally altered this Sakdina system (Keyes, 1989). The Sakdina system modernized materially without changing its psychological dependence on the old traditions of power. Therefore, Wedel and Wedel (1987:23) argue

> the monetization of the economy eventually forced the old system of land control to become one of private ownership. Land changed from the means of subsistence to just another commodity that could be sold. This change and the failure of the Thai peasant to understand it, at least initially, worked to concentrate land in hands of many fewer people. This created problems of land ownership that persist today.

The monetization of the economy also increased the power of at least a portion of the noble class who could siphon off profits from their political control over the capitalist class and were clever enough to convert their ancestral control of land in the king's name to actual ownership. Up to this day, the Crown property alone still represents the fourth largest corporation in Thailand and is comprised of 44 companies. The natural alliance of the Chinese capitalists and old aristocratic families began to be expressed in convenient marriages that joined economic and political power (Charoensin-o-larn, 1988). Therefore, "the transition from a feudalistic to a capitalistic society leaned on rather than destroyed the conservative force . . . (and) the formation of a public consciousness through State or military-owned mass media has also brought another form of feudalistic thought" (Lertvicha, 1987: 59). Television series and films that portray or promote the Sakdina values, like *Look Tas* (Slaves' sons) or *Poo Chana Sib Tid* (The king who conquered the world), have been very popular.

According to the Film Censorship Bill

> films whose character is against or may be against people's peace of mind and morality are prohibited. Even the production, projection and screening of films for advertising purposes, which are likely to bring about such an effect, are also prohibited. Films or advertisements produced in the country, if having such a character or likely to effect such a result, cannot be exported from the Kingdom. (Padmadim, 1984: 50)

Issues related to the national ideology, which centers around the nation, the religion and the monarchy, are very sensitive, and scrupulously screened. Therefore, the Censor Bill is so strict that producers dare not create new plots or fresh material, and "radio and TV are consistently employed to transmit nationalism, patriotism, the importance of the monarchial constitution and anti-communist propaganda" (Bunbangkorn, 1983:198). *The Bangkok Post* lamented in an editorial on October 29, 1990: "The cinema censorship regulations are so silly as to be ridiculous." This makes the filmmakers shy away from controversial issues and produce "safe" films, which in turn, makes the movie-going public bored with Thai movies. However, as a first step toward a new government media policy, the National Film Federation (NFF)—founded in mid-January 1989 and representing actors, dubbers, producers, directors, cinema owners, distributors, video business representatives, lawyers, entertainment news reporters, as well as mass communication scholars—proposed a new Board that would also include communication scholars, consumer specialists, and representatives of the NFF and the National Cultural Council.

A Rural Village Culture

In the Thai rural village culture, the family is the center of the local community. The family (or inner group) guarantees security and stability. All members of this inner group know their place and role and act accordingly. Social cohesion and group identification, as well as social control, are very great. Life is hierarchically orientated on the basis of mutual trust and moral kindness. In Thai this is termed *obe-oam-a-ree* or *pra-khun*. Outside of this protective and "safe" world of the family and the village the individual enters into a threatening and chaotic "outside" world. The principles of moral kindness, which are highly regarded in the inner group, are of far lesser importance in the world of the outer group. There, the so-called "law of the jungle" rules, the amoral and sometimes also the immoral worldly and supernatural power (*am-naj/pra-dej*). To be able to survive personally and socially, the individual has to beg for the protection and the favors of these powers and not upset them in any way.

Power is the most central element in the Thai worldview. The way in which Thai deal with power and submit themselves to it is essentially animistic. Animism does not attempt to explain the complexity of everyday reality on the basis of "rational" and universal principles, but reduces the world into simplistic categories like us and them, insiders and outsiders. The insiders and their ancestors form the natural center of the universe. The inner group offers continuity, stability, and protection; outside of that there is chaos and danger and the Thai feels threatened by all sorts of supernatural powers. In this realm of "phi" (spirits), there are many amoral, and immoral spirits who each are supposed to be favored with a certain function or quality. Some are more active than others, but no definite hierarchy can be perceived. So what matters most for the Thai is to try to stay on friendly terms with as many as possible, or to protect against them. The very first word almost every Thai child learns is "phi" and to this word is generally appended the adjective "laug" (deceiving). They are warned that if they do not behave in a pleasing and appropriate way, they will have to give account to the "phi laug" (deceiving spirit), who will mete out the severest punishment. In almost every house one will find a *praphoom* or temple for the house spirit. The house spirit is believed to protect the house and its inhabitants for as long as they honor him in a suitable manner (e.g., by paying homage to him and/or bringing him some food). Some spirits are believed to protect certain places such as woods, ricefields, factories, cars, and so forth; others cure illnesses, assist in finding a job, or "reveal" the winning lottery numbers. At the same time, the Thai can, with the aid of objects, actions, or persons of influence, protect themselves to the possible danger of deceiving spirits. Holy objects (sing saksit) such as Buddha images or amulets, tattoos, Buddhist sayings, astrologers, monks, or the King (or his portrait) are believed to offer protection. In this way the Thai surround themselves with a sort of protective aura.

Everyone, that is, people with both good or bad intentions, can invoke protection or favors of a higher power, or can try to neutralize a potential negative influence in the outer world. To do so they have to follow a clearly laid out ceremony or ritual that can be different from spirit to spirit. For instance, some spirits are believed to like flowers, others prefer images or replicas of elephants or phallic symbols. As the artifacts of the society change, the "taste" of the spirits also changes. Therefore, today most of them are also said to appreciate money. If a wish is not granted, the Thai dare not question the expertise or power of the spirit, rather they look for a cause or explanation in their own behavior. Perhaps the individual did not honor the spirit in the correct way, or perhaps the spirit's pride was, for unknown reasons, injured. Another often quoted explanation is that another power stood in the way of the fulfillment of the wish. As it is characteristic of these spirits that their power does not come from elsewhere, no higher legitimation exists. Therefore, different powers can exercise opposing influences and thwart the fulfillment of a wish. In other words, to survive in this threatening and chaotic world, the Thai has to make a sort of allegiance with these powers. This allegiance is of a business-like, nonemotional, and limited sort. Moral judgments form no part of the contract.

Complementary to this amoral power is the dimension of moral kindness and mutual trust in the inner group. Everyone is daily confronted with both. Whereas *pra-dej* represents the amoral order and immoral chaos, *pra-khun* represents moral backbone and stability. Whereas power is mainly symbolized by supernatural projections, one finds *pra-khun* mainly in worldly manifestations. Power is strong, kindness is weak. Power is masculine, kindness is feminine. The main symbol of moral kindness is the mother. The love she has for her children is pure, disinterested, and unconditional. Also, elderly people and "educators" because of their unconditional efforts, their knowledge and morals, are regarded as *khun* (morally good). Because relations based on kindness are not business-like but moral, they have to be valued in an appropriate way. For example, a lack of respect or gratitude (a-*ka-tan-yu*) is regarded as disgraceful and punished on the basis of moral justice principles. Psychologically, this is a source of many guilt feelings.

The Power of Beliefs

Instructions on the way in which to observe kindness and morality are embodied in Buddhism. The *Dhamma,* the Buddhist dogma, provides the moral instructions by which each individual can surpass the worldly order of passion and preconceptions (*kilesa*), rebirth (*sangsara*), and fate (*karma*). If one follows the instructions of the Dhamma and lives according to the eight noble principles, one can reach the highest worth, the *nirvana*, the goodness of pure worth, pure humanity and pure wisdom. In *Hinayama* or *Theravada* Buddhism this path has to be walked individually; salvation is not a gift from heaven but a permanent, lifelong mission. Sulaksa Sivaraksa (1981:72) summarizes it as follows:

> Buddhism emphasizes the middle way between extremes, a moderation which strikes a balance appropriate to the balance of nature itself. Knowledge must be complete knowledge of nature, in order to be wisdom; otherwise, knowledge is ignorance. Partial knowledge leads to delusion, and encourages the growth of greed and hate. These are the roots of evil that lead to ruin. The remedy is the threefold way of self-knowledge, leading to right speech and action and relations to other people and things (morality), consideration of the inner truth of one's own spirit and of nature (meditation), leading finally to enlightenment or complete knowledge (wisdom). It is an awakening, and a complete awareness of the world.

For more details about Thai Buddhism, I recommend reading Buddhadasa (1986), Punyanubhab (1981), Rajavaramuni (1983), or Sivaraksa (1988).

But as, in my opinion, the Thai's common beliefs are more of an animistic than a Bhuddist nature, the Thai is more oriented toward the exterior, institutionalized norms of Buddhism (the temple, Buddha images, monks, ceremonies) than the moral principles of Buddhism. Supernatural elements like spirits and ghosts form a substantial part of many videos that are shown on television, like *Mitimued* (Dark Dimension) or *Peesad Saen Kon* (A tricky ghost). An example of a communication campaign in which "animistic" symbols have been successfully used is the *Magic Eyes* or *Keep Thailand Clean* campaign, which was launched in 1984 and organized by the Thai Creative Society. Magic Eyes conforms to the belief that when Thais do something wrong a spirit will watch them. This campaign, which ran on all four television channels and made use of cartoon films, strove to introduce the belief that somebody will watch you whenever you are careless about the environment.

That does not mean that the Thai's animism does not correspond with Buddhism. Rather it is the other way around. Certain basic principles of Buddhism such as *Anijjang* (everything is perpetually changing; hence, continuity=change, change=continuity), *Dukhkang* (life is full of suffering), and *Anatta* (everything is relative, certainty does not exist) fit in completely with the Thai common belief. Therefore, Niels Mulder (1985:44) concludes that

> the Thai Weltanschauwung combines the sophisticated elegance of a universal principle with the primordial directness of animistic thinking; somehow Therevada Buddhism and the Buddhist animistic heritage have corroborated and concluded a perfect marriage. The Buddhist message does not endow this universe with a center to cling to; but characterizes this-worldly and this-cosmic existence as impermanence, suffering, and nonself, guided by the impersonal this-cosmic principle of karma.

In other words, the Thai Buddhist perceives his or her worldview as essentially "supernaturalistic." He or she "sees" all phenomena as an integrated whole, in a "sacred" rather than a "secular" world, a cosmos that is to a large extent governed and controlled, not by just the human powers-that-be, but by the supernatural powers. Additionally, John Davis (1993:35) argues that the Thai religion has three components or subsystems, comprising Therevada Buddhism, Brahmanism, and animism, which mutually support each other without conflict. For a summary, based on Davis, see Table 8.1.

The Amoral Power . . . and Moral Kindness

The institutionalized way of living of the Thai is set in this continuum with, on the one hand, the moral order and, on the other hand, the

Table 8.1. Summary of the Three Religious Subsystems of Thai Religion.

	Buddhism	Brahmanism	Animism
1- Goal orientation	Other worldly	This worldly	This worldly
Worldview	Rational/ Certain	Rational/ Certain	Capricious/ Uncertain
Ritual	Standard/ Routine	Standard/ Routine	Tailored to individual
2- Specialists Recruitment	mainly male Universalistic achievement	mainly male Universalistic achievement	mainly female Particular ascription
3- Participants Involvement	laity constant	client intermittent	client intermittent
4- Attitude toward	highly favorable	favorable	ambivalent
Social focus	whole society	bridging local and society	highly local

amoral power. Relations in the *khuna* dimension, inside the hierarchy of the inner group, are based mainly on mutual trust and informal dependency. Relations in the *pra-dej* dimension, inside the hierarchy of the power-based outside world, are characterized by mutual distrust and formality. Because the Thai view of the world lacks a center in which the opposites between power and morality can be overcome, they have to take notice of both in everyday life and act according to the situation in which they find themselves.

This does not mean to say that relations of which both dimensions are part do not exist. In the mass media, the symbol of the "good and rightful" leader, father, village elder, manager, minister, or general, who manages to combine kindness and power inside one person, often appears. However, the outcome of this kind of story is very often rather negative. An explanation for these failures is given neither in the media products nor in reality. In view of the fact that the Thai worldview is mainly controlled by supernatural powers, the Thai do not have a need to look for "rational" explanations. They accept the world as it is and adopt a rather fatalistic attitude toward social change. In the given circumstances they try to make the best of it for themselves and their immediate relatives and friends. For instance, in the novel "The Judgment" by Chart Kobjitti, which has also been turned into a hugely popular film, the moral advice underlying the story can be summarized as follows:

> This is your karma. This is what I spoke with you about. The world outside is in a state of turmoil. At that time you weren't prepared to believe me. . . . Who do you want me to tell? If what you've told me is not true, then—I don't want to get a reputation as a monk who lies. But if it is true, how will I force them to believe me when they've already decided that they don't want to believe you? Just try to do good every time you're in their presence. You'll feel better. (Kobjitti, 1982: 38-39)

Interpersonal Communication: Mai Pen Rai

Some people explain the friendly, superficial, and conflict avoiding way in which the Thai behave in public life as being in accordance with the Buddhist principle of the middle way. To me, however, it seems as if an explanation based on Thai animism is more appropriate. Contacts with people in the power circles are business-like, formal, and instrumental. To engage oneself for long periods or to show any feeling is, therefore, not necessary. But on the other hand, one has to be careful not to upset the power's feelings and to honor it in the proper way. For that reason children are taught at a very early stage in life to suppress their emotions and to avoid open conflicts. This behavior, known as jai yen (literally: cool heart), is a fundamental contrast to the Western more assertive way of communicating. Besides avoiding conflicts (kreng-jai), social interactions are characterized by formality, superficiality, and an easy-going atmosphere. This attitude can be best typified by the common saying, mai pen rai (never mind, take it easy). Two of the concepts that appear in virtually every conversation, and are a gauge of the way in which the Thai dream about life, are sanuk (fun, amusement) and sabai (pleasure, comfort). Therefore, the ingredients that form a substantial part of almost all popular Thai film plots, and which are considered sanuk by Thai standards, are violence, romance, superstitious events, and talok bababobo (that is, a kind of humor that could be defined as silly or slapstick by Western tastes). Also Western (especially American) film and TV formats are copied and adapted to Thai tastes. The popular Thee Nee Krung Thep (This is Bangkok) or Si Toom Square (The 10.00 PM square) talk shows, for instance, imitate the American "Entertainment Tonight" and "Tonight" with Johnny Carson shows. All it adds to the American format is more gossip and silly games. For those interested in a combination of silly games and stars there are *Mar Tarm Nad* (Rendez vous), the *Wig 07 Show*, or *Ching Roi Ching Larn* (Compete for 100 million). Also "weird" performances like *Tarm Pai Doo* (Follow to take a look), *Thar Phisoot* (Challenge to proof), or *Khun Ko Maa* (You ask for it) are very popular. Seksan Prasertkul (1989:64), one of the student leaders in the 1970s, observes:

> whenever Thais meet, they try to make others laugh even though the subjects they are talking about may not be relevant for jokes. Life talk shows are very popular, especially during election campaigns. . . (also) Thai newspapers have a special expertise in transforming news into entertainment.

Additionally, in interpersonal communication the end product, the content, often tends to be overlooked. However, in Thai society, the social achievement, the form, the show element are that much more important. Therefore, false modesty has no place in Thailand. Outward characteristics of status and power are fully and emphatically shown. Despite the superficiality and "showing-off" the power expects to be recognized and respected in a suitable fashion. Moreover, power is amoral; value-verdicts have no part in the power game.

It is often difficult for an outsider to distinguish among the different, moral, or amoral relation patterns. The outward signs are often the same. But for the Thai the subtleties and nuances are immediately clear. The differences also appear in the use of language, not only in the manner of address, but in the description of the different behavior patterns. To show respect for elders or teachers is described as *krengjai* (to respect somebody with the heart), to render honor to a representative of power, on the other hand, is called *krengklua* (to respect out of fear). The meaning behind certain actions can differ completely as well. Showing gratitude (*boen-khun*) in an inner group relation is based on the principles of morality and commitment. In an outer group relation this is, however, of a formal and business-like character. The Thai do not approach prostitution, for example, from a moral criterion, but on the basis of relations within the power sphere (Meyer, 1988). More of these everyday situations, which are often said to be "incomprehensible" to the Western world, are described in Cooper and Cooper (1982), Holmes and Tangtongtary (1995), Klausner (1980), and Segaller (1981, 1982).

In Figure 8.1 I sum up the most important characteristics of the Thai culture.

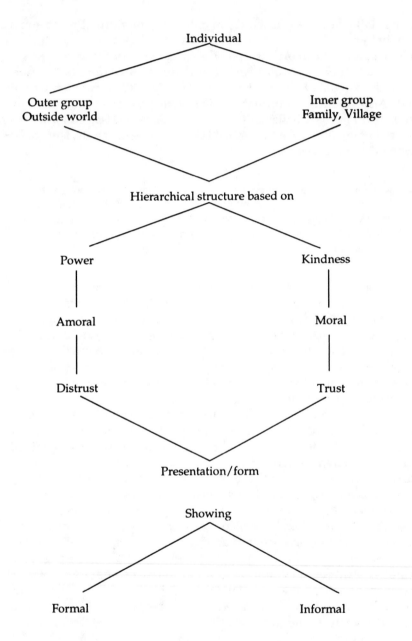

Figure 8.1. Main characteristics of Thai culture

Likay Drama

Buddhists and animists stress the progression and the temporality of life. Having fun cannot last long enough. Therefore, most Thai movies easily last for two to three hours. They have adopted the format of the *likay* drama play, which is still very popular in rural areas. Likay is a traditional theater form or folk opera of Malay or Indian origin, thought to have been introduced to Thailand toward the end of the 19th century. It combines music, singing, drama, and narration, with the performers dressed in traditional Thai costume. Its plots are based folk legends. Often the story will be serious, with the costumes identifying the villain, the victim, and the hero. Spectators get so caught up in the dramatic presentation that they often weep and may even threaten the villain from the audience. Levity is also included, usually through one or two simple-minded characters. (For more information, see Virulrak, 1975). In likay the message and the medium are closely tied. Therefore, John Davis (1993: 114) argues

> to effectively communicate the message it needs to be packaged in a medium that will be culturally acceptable. For Thai this medium is drama. There seems to be no other means of communication which makes such a powerful impact on Thai audiences as the dramatic arts.

Growing Pains: Modernization and Tradition

Modernization and Westernization have strengthened the animistic concept of power rather than weakened it. Unemployment and economic and political crises have made life for the majority of the population even less attractive, so the need for worldly and spiritual "protection saints" has increased proportionally, just as the struggle for status and prestige under the growing Westernized middle classes has increased. Whereas before one fought with traditional "power-means," the power of money is undermining many traditional relationship patterns. Impersonal and uncontrollable money is ever present and even throws a shadow on certain khun relationship patterns. Thus it is not surprising that corruption and the misuse of power are on the rise:

> The prevalence of bureaucratic corruption stems from the systems of self-remuneration in the traditional bureaucracy. Officials were expected to remunerate themselves by taking a cut from revenues they collected, and extracting fees for services performed. In the tran-

> modern form of bureaucracy, these practices were never erased.
> Meanwhile the systems for imposing moral and conventional limits on
> the extent of such self-remuneration have tended to decay. . . . The rise
> of corruption as an issue was more a function of increasing competi-
> tion for political power and corruption revenues between the old
> power-holders in the military and civilian bureaucracy, and the new
> challengers in civilian politics, particularly those with a business back-
> ground. (Phongpaichit & Priryarangsan, 1994: 173)

In the hierarchically structured Thai society, in which form and performance play a major role, the individual is regularly confronted with situations that cause heavy psychosocial stress. Because Thai rationalize
these psychosocial problems in an animistic and fatalistic way, as the
work of a bad spirit and so on, they do not seem to be able to address
these tensions. The only way to solve such a problem is, in their opinion,
to get rid of the bad spirit by eliminating it (or its personification) combined with the propensity to suppress anger, frustrations, and so on,
until they literally burst. Whenever this happens the outcome is usually
very extreme and this, for instance, is one of the explanations for the fact
that Thailand has one of the highest crime rates in the world.

As more people fall by the wayside in this power struggle, the
longing for a "safe" life in the inner group increases. On the political front,
this tendency has given rise to the revival of conservative and nationalistic
ideas. On the personal level, it leads to the strengthening of Brahminical
and spiritual practices. The result of a survey on values among urban and
rural Thai indicated that certain superstitious behaviors like fortune-telling
and lucky numbers are practiced more among Bangkokians than among
farmers. No difference was observed in terms of educational level.

> This casts some doubt on the theory that postulates a negative corre-
> lation between education and supernatural belief and behavior.
> However, it is a dominant value behavior characteristic of the Thai.
> In addition, it is a known fact that a number of highly powerful peo-
> ple in Thailand have their personal well known fortune-teller.
> (Komin, 1988:171)

According to the daily *The Nation* (1989:15), there even is a strong element of superstition in the stock market. For example, securities with the
word *Siam* attached to their names, such as Siam Foods and Dhana Siam
Finance, are branded as *Sayoeng*, meaning horror, when their share
prices tumble.

Public life, or so-called *patronage system* (Chaloemtiarana, 1983), is
organized on the basis of friendship circles with an influential leader on

the top. The Thai do not follow political programs or abstract ideas but leaders and charismatic figures on the basis of the "right or wrong, my group" principle. For example, Minister Chalerm Yoobumrung, who was in charge of the Mass Communication Authority of Thailand which controls TV channels 3 and 9, used these stations to fight against newspapers that dared to criticize his policies and to promote his political party. The majority of the military coups and political fractions are explicable through this perspective as well. John Girling (1981, 1984), who applied the Gramscian hegemony principle to the Thai society, came to the conclusion that the production basis is integrated in and determined by the cultural-ideological superstructure of the civil society: "The result, in Thai terms, is the 'bureaucratic policy', or what Gramsci calls 'transformism': a ruling class that grows ever more extensive by absorbing elements from other social groups who then operate within the established framework" (1984:445). He decides that in these circumstances there is little chance for social change. From a cultural perspective this view is confirmed by Amunam Rajadhon (1968:29): "The social system, habits and customs as seen in modern times are superficial modifications of the fundamentals and in a comparative degree only."

The Thai Value System

Generally speaking, the Thai social system is essentially a society in which "self-centeredness" and interpersonal relationships are of utmost importance. Even though the Thai self-image is often described as individualistic, we prefer to term it a weak rather than a strong personality. This is also the opinion of Hans ten Brummelhuis:

> The individual's preoccupation is not so much with self-realization and autonomy as with the adaptation to the social or cosmological environment. If a notion of Thai individualism is to have any specific meaning it is in designating that particular mode of retreat, avoidance and distrust, which colors so many forms of behavior and social relationships. (1984:44-45)

Seksan Prasertkul (1989: 64) is more critical:

> Our national traits, which I think are very strong, are: firstly, Thais do not like serious matters; they like to crack jokes and talk about sensational matters, especially dirty 'under the belt'-matters. Secondly, they are egotists. They use group benefits to be their norms. If matters are not relevant to their own lives, they will not take them into account.

Referring to the earlier Thai Value Study, Komin (1988, 1991) identified nine value clusters according to their significant positions in the Thai value system: (a) ego-orientation (which is the root value underlying various other key values such as "face-saving," *kreng-jai*, etc.); (b) grateful relationship orientation (*bun-khun*, reciprocity of kindness, *a-ka-tan-yu*); (c) social smoothing relationship orientation (caring, pleasant, polite); (d) flexibility and adjustment orientation (situation-orientedness); (e) religio-psychical orientation *(karma*, superstition); (f) education and competence orientation (form is more important than substance); (g) interdependence orientation (peaceful coexistence of ethnic, religious, etc. groups); (h) achievement-task orientation (achievement is the least important value among Thai, it connotes social rather than task achievement); and (i) fun-pleasure orientation (fun loving is both a means and an end in itself). "These are the major value orientations registered in the cognitive world of the Thai, and serve as criteria for guiding behavior, or as the blueprint that helps to make decisions at the behavioral levels" (Komin, 1988:172). She argues that these value orientations have to be taken into consideration in any development program as they often prove to be stumbling blocks to social change.

SYNTHESIS

1. An analysis of the interdependency between Thai culture and its communicative expressions is offered with the aid of two complementary, mutually interpretive, and influential dimensions from the traditional, rural, and animistic culture, which still fundamentally conditions modern day Thailand. One dimension is of a spiritual-moral nature, the other of a sociological nature.

2. Power is the most central element in the Thai worldview. The way in which Thai deal with power and submit themselves to it is essentially animistic. Animism does not attempt to explain the complexity of everyday reality on the basis of "rational" and universal principles, but reduces the world into simplistic categories like "us" and "them," insiders and outsiders.

3. The institutionalized way of living of the Thai is set in a continuum with, on the one hand, the moral order and, on the other hand, the amoral power. Relations in the khuna dimension, inside the hierarchy of the inner group, are based mainly on mutual trust and informal dependency. Relations in the pra-dej dimension, inside the hierarchy of the power-based outside world, are characterized by mutual distrust and

formality. Because the Thai view of the world lacks a center in which the opposites between power and morality can be overcome, they have to take notice of both in everyday life and act according to the situation in which they find themselves.

4. Modernization and Westernization have strengthened the animistic concept of power rather than weakened it. Unemployment and economic and political crises have made life for the majority of the population even less attractive, so the need for worldly and spiritual "protection saints" has increased proportionally, just as the struggle for status and prestige under the growing Westernized middle classes has increased. Whereas before one fought with traditional "power-means," the power of money is undermining many traditional relationship patterns.

5. In Thailand, as documented in other parts of the world as well, one observes at least two interrelated developments with regard to the production and consumption of media software and hardware. On the one hand, there is a tendency to import cultural content and technology and develop local imitations, that is, an attempt to forge a more autonomous culture, independent of but at the same time borrowing from foreign (mainly Western) cultures. On the other hand, as is the case in the West, one observes that in spite of the better production quality the majority of local audiences prefer programs produced in their own culture. Furthermore, as William Klausner (1983: 289) contends: "Films are not only a reflection of economic, social and cultural realities but also an outlet for repressed feelings and desires. Thai films are not exceptions."

9

Broadcasting in Bhutan: Between Tradition and Modernization

The methods of planning, analysis, and management introduced during the 1960s and 1970s—and which still dominate the procedures of most international organizations and governments in developing countries—were not primarily concerned with flexibility, responsiveness, and learning. They were more concerned with efficiency and control. Rationalistic approaches were introduced not only because they were compatible with economic growth strategies that were prevalent during the 1950s and 1960s, but also because they were perceived to be effective methods of reducing uncertainty and increasing efficiency. Administrators embraced control-oriented planning and management techniques that were either ineffective or inherently incapable of reducing uncertainty at the same time that development policies were becoming more complex.
—Dennis Rondinelli (1993: 7)

Radio broadcasting began in Bhutan on November 11, 1973 when a group of young people from the National Youth Association of Bhutan started with a weekly one-hour transmission of entertainment programs in English. They operated in a makeshift studio and used a 400-Watt Short Wave transmitter. The staff at that time was untrained and no pro-

227

fessional equipment was available. Subsequently, programs in *Dzongkha* were introduced. In the following years, the language of the southern region, Nepalese or *Lhotsham*, was added, and in 1979, the eastern language, *Sharshop*. In the same year the radio station came under the auspices of the Ministry of Communication and Tourism of Bhutan. Broadcast hours were expanded to nine hours weekly, with three hours of programming on Sundays, Wednesdays, and Fridays.

Since 1983, the staff members of the radio station and Kuensel, the national newspaper, have been benefiting from a United Nations Development Program (UNDP) training project that develops professional manpower in the country. Gradually the amateur station became more professional.

On June 2, 1986, the station was renamed the *Bhutan Broadcasting Service* (BBS). That same year the government of the Kingdom of Bhutan submitted a request to UNESCO for assistance to the national radio. Although the request was only a modest one for equipment, the background document submitted by BBS provided further information on the need for developing the entire radio service as a whole, particularly in the context of bilateral Indian assistance to provide a new studio building and a 50-kW Short Wave transmitter. Transmission hours for the BBS were increased to four hours during weekdays and six hours during Sundays in 1987. The clarity of reception improved when BBS changed its frequency to 60 meter band or 5025 KHz in 1989 and FM transmission was introduced in the capital of Thimpu. The main development during the Sixth Five-Year Plan (1987-1992) was the inauguration of the new 50-kW broadcasting station on March 15, 1991.

To ensure continuous input and a coherent program of training and standardized broadcasting principles, BBS had the foresight to affiliate with a suitable broadcasting organization, already experienced in projects of this type. The Danish Consultancy Agency, DaniCom, which had previously been associated with UNESCO in the Sri Lankan project, *Mahaweli Community Radio*, was selected for this task. DaniCom provides assistance and services in specific areas identified by the BBS. UNESCO has overall responsibility for the project.

On October 1, 1992, however, BBS, together with the national newspaper *Kuensel*, was detached from the Communication Ministry, and both were to be governed by an independent Editorial Board. In accordance with the objectives of the Seventh Five-Year Plan (1992-1997), the decision to grant autonomy to BBS apparently meant that BBS would eventually have to seek its own funds for operations.

This chapter presents the history of the BBS, the objectives of the radio station and a review of the present situation. However, a basic understanding of the societal and communication context is needed to get a clear and realistic perspective of the problems BBS is facing. Therefore, by way of introduction, some basic information on Bhutan in general, as well as its communication sector, is first provided.

Bhutan, a Himalayan Kingdom

Bhutan is a rather unknown and inaccessible Buddhist kingdom in the eastern part of the Himalayas with approximately 1.5 million inhabitants (*New Encyclopedia Britannica*, 1992). The majority of the population, the *Bhutias*, derive from Tibet but have always lived in Bhutan. The most important minority, the Nepalese, live in the south. Several Tibetan dialects are spoken, of which Dzongkha is considered the official national language. Dzongkha, which was formerly only an oral language, has become a written language in the last 30 years or so, and the government has made great efforts since the 1960s to standardize it and encourage its use. However, no contemporary literature in Dzongkha is yet available. Dzongkha has replaced more and more the immigrants' own languages (especially Nepalese) at the schools in the south. One of the big problems in learning Dzongkha arises from the complexity of its orthography, which requires a great deal of memorization. Consequently, many educated people, especially those with foreign degrees, feel reluctant to speak Dzongkha in public.

The Nepalese speak their language, Nepalese or Lhotsham. Because there is a shortage of Bhutanese, many (Nepalese) immigrants work at the construction and maintenance of bridges and roads (Shaw, 1992). Differences in religion, language, and ethnic origin have an obvious effect on the Bhutanese culture.

Up until now, the state religion in Bhutan, a Tantric version of Mahayana-Buddhism, has had a major influence on the Bhutanese culture. The highest religious authority or leader is the Je Khempo. The king will not make an important decision without respecting the advice of the *Je Khempo*. The other important religion is Hinduism. It has followers among the immigrants from India and Nepal. The authorities try to integrate them into society. An example of this is the obligation for ethnic minorities to wear the national dress at public holidays and official functions.

Large parts of the country are inhospitable. The majority of the Bhutanese live in about 4,000 small isolated villages or in four "boom-towns" of more than 10,000 people. As a consequence, Buddhist monasteries occupy a central place in the social, cultural, and religious life of the people. They are often the only place where young people can be educated (especially in the eastern region). In the larger places more and more "normal" schools have arisen. In 1989 Bhutan had approximately 1,500 primary schools, about 30 secondary schools, one college of technology, and one teacher training college. No university degrees at master's level are offered within the country.

Bhutan has for centuries been closed to foreign countries. Like Nepal, it managed to maintain its independence from British India. Although under the terms of a treaty concluded in 1910, Bhutan agreed to be guided by Britain in external affairs. In 1949 a treaty between India and Bhutan repeated this willingness to accept guidance, while guaranteeing New Delhi's noninterference in Bhutan's internal affairs. Since the Chinese-Indian war in 1963, India tries to obtain a favorable military position in Bhutan. Further motives are grounded on economic interests. The biggest part of Bhutan's exports goes to India, whereas most import comes from India. India also provides the most development aid for Bhutan. Almost half of the annual budget consists of Indian development aid. Many Indian civilians are also acting in various advisory capacities.

However, the government of Bhutan is still very reserved toward foreign influences and does its utmost to protect the Buddhist religion and culture. Although foreign investments are not allowed, there is a big need for foreign know-how. Bhutan lacks human resources at all levels. Training in Bhutan is being emphasized as part of the Royal Government's human resource policies because of its concern about its domestic situation. The input of foreign development organizations is strictly tested on this criterion. Next to Non-Governmental Organizations from India, Switzerland, Japan, and other countries, several United Nations organizations (FAO, UNDP, UNESCO, UNICEF, UNFPA) are active in the country.

Development Planning

Bhutan has been a hereditary monarchy since 1907. In 1969 the king, Jigme Dorji Wangchuck, gave up part of his absolute power by establishing a council of ministers. The king is head of state and head of the government. The *Tshogdu*, or National Assembly of 155 members, is chosen indirectly (through the local chiefs) by the people. Through the year the king and his government are advised and controlled by the Royal Advisory Body, of which the members are partly chosen. The government administers the country from Thimpu, the capital of Bhutan. There are no political parties.

Since 1961, the Bhutanese Government has drawn up and worked toward goals set by its Five-Year Plans. The Fifth Five-Year Plan, covering the years 1982-1986, was a turning point for the country.

The Government was not only concerned about implementing projects and achieving economic growth for greater economic self-reliance, it was also intent on distributing to the population its fair share of the progress. Hence, it recognized the necessity to involve the people in the implementation of its plans. The Sixth Five-Year Plan (1987-1992) flows from the objectives of the Fifth, placing an even greater importance on the promotion of national values. Concerned by the growing spread of foreign influences on local lifestyles, the Government stressed the need to protect the Buddhist religion and culture through the Bhutanization of the school curriculum and the promotion of Dzongkha as the national language.

The Communication Infrastructure

Although there are many laudable and wide-ranging goals set by the Government, there are also many constraints besetting the country's communication sector, including BBS. However, the remote and scattered population, combined with the transport constraints imposed by a mountainous terrain, makes the development of all forms of communication a most vital aspect of development.

As of December 1990, the number of institutions in the communication sector were as follows: 86 post offices and 25 branch (part-time) post offices; 44 civil wireless stations; eight telegraph offices; one weekly newspaper (*Kuensel*); many institutional bulletins, newsletters and journals; four printing presses; one broadcasting station (BBS); and 2,461 working telephone connections served by 13 telephone exchanges. In addition to printing presses, wooden block prints are also used extensively, especially in monastic institutions and villages.

Neither radio nor written press has a big range of distribution. The country has no television (although some rich families have bought satellite dishes to watch international television channels), but videotapes with Western and Indian movies are available through a booming network of video rental shops.

Communication Policymaking and Planning

Faced with the tasks of achieving greater economic growth and the preservation of local values and national identity, the Government confirmed that the media would play an essential role in development. It was proposed in the Sixth Five-Year Plan (1987-1992) that video and cinema be used to promote the country's rich culture and traditions, to counter the popularity of foreign films. It was pointed out that although maintaining and promoting cultural values was of the utmost importance, the increasing popularity of foreign cinema and video programs was posing a serious threat to the erosion of these values. It was argued that promoting indigenous audio-visual programs would not only counter the negative influences of foreign audiovisual programs, but the revenue generated from indigenous programs would also remain inside the country. As the audiovisual media have become the most important and effective means of disseminating information, it is the policy of the government to strengthen and develop the media in Bhutan. More importantly, the objectives of the Government highlighted the bigger tasks that lie ahead for the press, both print and broadcast, to foster better communication between government and people. It has to disseminate information about government policies and programs, provide a public forum for discussions on issues of interest, and enable greater understanding of the cultural, social, and economic issues affecting the country. In all its functions, the media have to be at the service of *Tsa Wa Sum*—the country, the King and the people. The services of both the national newspaper, Kuensel, and the radio station Bhutan Broadcasting Service (BBS) are vital.

Autonomy for National Media

On August 1, 1992, the Development Support Communication Division (DSCD), which was the audiovisual wing of the Information Department, was delinked from the Communication Ministry. At the same time the Ministry of Communication expressed its interest in encouraging and extending all possible assistance to private companies making audiovisual programs that would strengthen and promote the country's rich cultural heritage.

Two months later, on October 1, 1992, Kuensel and BBS, were also delinked from the Ministry of Communication and established as autonomous corporations. *Kuensel* and BBS are governed by an independent seven-member Editorial Board comprising scholars, eminent citizens, media professionals, and two representatives of the civil service.

The Communication Minister, Lyonpo T. Tobgyel, explained that this move had been initiated by the King to strengthen the Bhutanese media and ensure that both the national newspaper and broadcasting service would play a more responsible and important role in the socioeconomic and political development of the kingdom. It was assumed that the decision would also contribute to more professionalization of the media. The Minister added that the establishment of an independent and effective media would also be a significant achievement of the king's policy of decentralization, which aimed at involving the people in the national planning process.

The Seventh Five-Year Plan (1992-1997)

The earlier decision appears to be in line with the new Seventh Five-Year Plan (1992-1997), presented during the 71st Session of the National Assembly of Bhutan from October 16 to November 6, 1992. Stating that some of the objectives of the Sixth Plan overlapped into the Seventh Plan, the Planning minister summarized the important objectives of the Seventh Plan as follows:

1. Self-reliance with emphasis on internal resource mobilization;
2. Sustainable development with emphasis on environmental protection;
3. Private sector development;
4. Decentralization and people's participation;
5. Human resource development;
6. Promoting balanced development in all the dzongkhags; and
7. Ensuring the security of the nation.

In addition, the objectives of the Information Services of the Government are:

1. To disseminate policies, strategies, and programs of the government and bring about better communication between the government and the people.
2. To provide a public forum for discussion on issues of interest.
3. To enable greater understanding of cultural, social, and economic issues throughout the country.

Radio Program Policies

In order to accomplish these objectives in the context of the development approach adopted by the Seventh Five-Year Plan and also in accordance with the overall objectives set for the communication sector, the radio programs broadcast are supposed to conform to the following policies and guidelines:

1. BBS will produce and broadcast programs and organize related listener activities to help foster individual and community endeavors geared toward the pursuit of goals of the Seventh Five-Year Plan in particular, and *national development* in general. Accordingly, BBS will help disseminate information and provide a channel for the exchange of experiences necessary to enhance living standards of the people in relation to their

habitat, health, sanitation, and to upgrade their operational skills. Similarly, BBS will allow access to all relevant and responsible points of view on development issues and act as a forum to improve two-way-communication between the government and the people. In making relevant programs, BBS will take all possible steps within its resources to ensure the participation of people from all regions of the country.

2. In its programs BBS will preserve and promote *Bhutanese identity* in culture and help foster the development of the *national language* and the spiritual needs of the Bhutanese people. The radio programs will facilitate the preservation and promotion of Bhutan's cultural heritage and age-old values.

3. Similarly, BBS will disseminate information necessary to enhance the universal perception of its listeners in order to promote *intercultural understanding and tolerance.*

4. Through its broadcasts BBS will ensure the advancement of the aesthetic needs and the creativity of its listeners. Accordingly, BBS will facilitate and develop *local talents* with regard to music, songs, creative literature, and other aesthetic and recreational activities.

5. BBS will make provisions in its broadcasts to cater to *children's needs* and foster their constructive perception to help them develop into responsible citizens of Bhutan. Accordingly, BBS will provide supplementary programs, both in the fields of nonformal and formal education, in accordance with the National Education Policy.

6. In all its functions BBS will always be at the service of the *Tsa Wa Sum* (country, king, and people).

For the program and news staff, more detailed guidelines were approved in May 1992. These ensure that no program broadcast by the BBS shall: (a) Denigrate religious faith or beliefs or make an attack on religious sects; (b) disrespect the feelings of listeners; (c) include anything amounting to contempt of court; (d) include criticism of friendly countries; (e) include anything obscene or defamatory; (f) incite any person to violence; (g) simulate news and events in such a way as to mislead or alarm listeners; (h) present as desirable the use of intoxicating liquor, smoking, or narcotics, except under medical direction; (i) include the use of horror for its own sake; and (j) include anything amounting to denigration of Tsa Wa Sum. Furthermore, when interviewing individuals for the purpose of simultaneous or subsequent broadcast the interviewer should inform them of the purpose of the interview and obtain the consent of the interviewee. Similarly, every effort should be made to inform the interviewee/participant of the date and time of the broadcast in which the interview/insert would possibly be included. Finally, in dealing with controversial issues the program producer should take all possible actions to provide opportunities for adequate and fair representation of all significant and responsible points of view by the persons or organizations affected.

Broadcasting in a Time of Change

In addition to the already identified contextual factors, the following interrelated constraints condition the present activities of BBS: the Bhutanese culture, the poor educational context, the Civil Service System, the lack of experience in media/radio communications, and language problems.

Institutional Culture and Organizational Structure

The Director of Information and Broadcasting under the Ministry of Information is the national coordinator of the BBS project and responsible for all policy decisions concerning its operation, including final approval of all consultants and equipment to be purchased. The Deputy Director of Broadcasting and Manager of BBS has been nominated the Project Manager and is responsible for all operations of the project. The Project Manager is assisted by the Technical Director, Program Director, and the Director of News, Research and Public Relations, for specific activities concerning these departments. Given the hierarchical structure of the Bhutanese society, the "personality" and "leadership qualities" of the Directors have been very important for BBS operations.

Under the guidance of DaniCom, BBS underwent a basic restructuring of its management. A new organizational chart was drawn that focused on shared management among the key work areas: news, program, technical. Each would have a new head who would work under a new Joint Director of Broadcasting. After a three-week management workshop organized at DaniCom and Radio Denmark in January 1991, the formal appointment of the new officers according to the new management structure was announced. The workshop covered basic concepts of management, supervisory methods, and working partnerships and relations (Hamarsaa & Ebbesen, 1992).

This overall institutional organigram needed reconsideration: a more established audience research section and, in view of the autonomy, a commercial and PR section. Also the engineering section needed another organization of different tasks and responsibilities according to the more popular division in maintenance, operations, and production sectors. Therefore, a *new organigram* was agreed on (Servaes, 1993).

However, it remains to be seen whether this new organigram can be implemented smoothly. For instance, it would be ideal if the section heads could be released from their daily production assignments. They could delegate responsibility for the daily production to senior producers and instead concentrate on supervision and planning. The existing lack of manpower (cf. infra), however, may prevent the speedy implementation of this plan.

Human Resources

It is safe to say that the educational level in Bhutan is low. Some of the necessary (professional and technical) qualifications/skills for radio making are not available. Therefore, one of BBS' major problems is getting qualified staff. Consequently, DaniCom/UNESCO has provided programming, technical, and management training. Training (in-house and abroad—almost all staff has been on training tours abroad) could partly solve this problem. However, a related problem seems to be that some of the people who receive training afterward resign. This high turnover of staff poses the problem of cost effectiveness.

However, although according to the target set by the Sixth Five-Year Plan 82 people would be needed, in early 1993 BBS employed 52 people. Five people who joined BBS before 1986 are still working at BBS; the majority of the staff was newly employed in 1989. One of the most pressing problems remains the continuing low morale of the majority of the staff. Fortunately, this is slightly balanced by the hard work and commitment of a relatively young team of about 10 people. All staff members of BBS are civil servants. In the Bhutanese Civil Service system seniority and hierarchy are preferred. Therefore, qualified and committed people are sometimes bypassed by senior colleagues. At the same time, passivity and submission is preferred. This not only creates tensions within the existing organizational structure, but also affects programming and production.

The transfer from one job to another is easily granted by the civil authorities. This happens more often than regularly within BBS because the station is regarded by many civil servants as too demanding (long and irregular working hours for a basic salary). On top of this is the fact that BBS is not regarded as a status position within the governmental system. For all these reasons, it is hard to find new and qualified staff.

Only 6 of the 14 producers understand English, and 8 can write in acceptable Dzongkha. For most of the Bhutanese population, Dzongkha is still considered an elite language. One of BBS's objectives—to create through the promotion of Dzongkha unity in the country—may therefore be difficult to achieve. Another aspect of this problem is that many people (especially civil servants who are educated abroad) are reluctant to be interviewed in Dzongkha on the radio. As a result, many producers have a hard time finding the "right" people for their programs.

Moreover, staff salaries and other forms of financial benefits are not very high (certainly not competitive to salaries offered in the private sector). For instance, the daily allowances for field trips do not cover the most basic expenses. As a result, most producers are not eager to schedule field trips for programming purposes. Consequently, most programs are produced in-house.

The Management Team is aware of all these constraints. It hopes that the new corporation structure may solve some of them (e.g., the hiring and firing of people could be organized in less bureaucratic ways). Furthermore, the Management Team has taken a number of steps to increase the level of professionalization, especially in the news section (cf. infra).

Increase and Change in Transmission Time

Transmission hours for the BBS were increased to four hours on weekdays and six hours on Sundays in 1987. According to the Sixth Five-Year Plan, BBS would be on the air six hours daily by mid-1992 (Jayaweera, 1992b). However, by November 1992, this still was not the case. Therefore, in its meeting of December 3, 1992, the staff agreed to an increase and change of hours from January 1, 1993 onward (see Table 9.1, Servaes, 1993: 7).

An increase of up to 9 1/2 hours a week (or 39.5 hours a month) meant increasing to a level beyond the target of the Sixth Plan. The goal of the Seventh Five-Year Plan is to extend the transmission time by an hour every year during the first period, with a final increase of two hours in the last 12-month period (from mid-1996 to mid-1997). This will bring the total number of transmission hours by the end of the Seventh Plan to 12 hours daily.

In general, the expansion of transmission time should be considered a right and positive move. However, in the short term it may create manpower and programming problems.

Programming

The objectives and program policies of the BBS have been described earlier. Though one cannot deny the progress made during the past few years, many of the program objectives of the project, or those of the Sixth Five-Year Plan, will probably not be met.

Table 9.1. New Transmission Time Schedule (as of January 1, 1993).

	Summer	Winter	Sunday
Dzongkha	4.30 - 7.30 p.m.	4.00 - 7 p.m.	10 - 2 p.m.
Sharshop	7.30 - 8.15	7.00 - 7.45	2.00 - 2.45
Lhostham	8.15 - 9.00	7.45 - 8.30	2.45 - 3.30
English	9.00 - 10	8.30 - 9.30	3.30 - 4.30

Despite initial planning and regular training, there is still no clear direction or format in many of the programs. There is not enough planning and research, and some producers find it difficult to select topics for their programs. Furthermore, there is very little monitoring of individual programs. Due to lack of individual supervision, there is no uniformity in the quality of programs.

The news and current affairs section seems to have the best organized, qualified, and committed group of people. However, the news section may face major editorial "challenges" once autonomy is fully implemented. The division has accepted a set of guidelines/policies for the production of its current affairs and daily news programs:

1. As the radio is one of the fastest means of communication, BBS news will provide the latest and most up-to-date information.

2. BBS News will maintain a balanced, accurate, and objective coverage of events and will strive for credibility.

3. BBS News supports the goals and objectives of the Royal Government and will serve as a link between the government and the people.

4. Even though many stories and programs will be related to government activities, the section will pay attention to getting the views of the people on current issues.

5. The news programs will reflect the cultural, social, and economic developments in Bhutan. Emphasis will be given to all the major issues in Bhutan's development such as women and children, health, agriculture, and the environment.

6. Keeping in mind the difficulties in communication, BBS news programs will seek through increased national news coverage to keep the kingdom better informed of happenings within the country. National coverage will make up the major portion of the news bulletins and programs.

7. Development news will remain the focus of the division with programs on development plans and activities. The programs

will provide a forum for discussion and feedback on developments throughout the kingdom.

8. The news section will also provide in-depth and analytical programs as well as investigative reporting.

9. To promote a better understanding of world affairs, BBS news will also cover major international events so that Bhutanese are kept informed of international developments. This will, at the same time, help foster an awareness of Bhutan's international relations and promote an understanding of other people, their lives, and culture. Whenever possible, BBS news will also attempt to show the implications of international and regional events to Bhutan.

10. The section will serve the interests of the public by relaying and providing public service announcements and messages in keeping with guidelines laid down by the station.

Additionally, the news section agreed to the following goals for the coming years: to keep up a core of corespondents from around the country; to keep listeners abreast of the latest developments both within and outside the kingdom; to support the government's development plans and policies with in-depth, analytical programs; to complement development activities with educational/informative programs; and to provide a forum for discussion and feedback on developments in the kingdom (for more details, see Pek, 1991).

BBS news is broadcast daily in English (15 minutes), Dzongkha (15 minutes), Sharshop and Lhotsham (10 minutes each). News is edited in English and translated and reedited into the three other languages by producers from the program section. Although the aim is that on average 70% of the material is local news and 30% is international, it was argued that a more realistic estimate for the English news broadcast is 50-50. International news is mainly monitored from BBC World Service, All India Radio, and Radio Nepal. More diversity in BBS' international news sources may be necessary. The sources of local news are government offices and other official institutions. Local gatherings, new projects, and sports are recurrent topics. In principle, producers take full operational responsibility for their programs: recording, editing, and continuity. As for the program section, specialization will be needed in the future.

The program section seems to be facing the most problems. There is, for instance, an imbalance in workload among the different producers. Some producers are responsible for the production of two to three programs a week, whereas others have a whole week to produce only one program. Furthermore, every producer is responsible for the overall production (including recording, editing, translation, presentation, etc.) of his or her program.

Some producers repeat the same programs that have been broadcast with an interval of a few weeks. The previously mentioned "shyness" among many educated people to speak Dzongkha in public and, therefore, their reluctance to be interviewed creates programming problems for BBS (for more details, see Jayaweera, 1991a, 1991b, 1992a).

Music programming and programming on nonformal education need special attention: since 1973 BBS has recorded and filed approximately 1,000 pieces of local music. The daily BBS broadcast includes quite a lot of music (according to some informants, more than 60% of the total broadcast time; Reitov, 1990). The English section mainly presents western music, whereas local music is used almost exclusively in the other sections. It is almost impossible to buy cassettes or records with Bhutanese music in Bhutan or elsewhere.

There is a great demand for distance language education in Dzongkha and English, and it is expected that radio can play a key role. However, a popular Dzongkha program, produced in close cooperation with the Commission for the Development of the National Language, was cancelled.

Training and Technical Assistance

From the start of the UNESCO/DaniCom project it was decided not to have a resident expert as project coordinator but instead have these functions under the charge of the Director of Information and Broadcasting. At the same time it was also planned that, as much as possible, there would be a regular flow of consultants in the areas of expertise required and that this continuity of consultants would compensate for the absence of a full-time expert.

Radio production training was identified as one of the key components of the project. Therefore, it was planned to have regular training in this field every year, starting with the basics of production and moving to advanced techniques and innovative program formats. Training covered basic program formats, basic journalism and radio news, music production and use of spots, interviewing techniques, and field recording.

Technical training was similarly identified as a key need. Consequently, courses on basic electronics, the use of measuring instruments, and transmitter maintenance were organized.

On several occasions it was observed that the work procedures and the training levels of the staff at BBS were different from other stations. Therefore, it was argued that the training provided did not sufficiently link to the knowledge and cultural background of the BBS staff.

However, in general, the work done and assistance/training provided by the DaniCom and UNESCO consultants has been evaluated positively.

Technology Development and the Provision of Equipment

Given the isolation of the country and the need to ensure not only operation and maintenance of equipment but creative design and application of electronics, a system for electronic mail, coupled with a laptop computer was installed. The same system can also be used within the country for sending news dispatches, program scripts or simple communication, or for communication between BBS and Kuensel.

In 1987, BBS was provided with a 10-watt FM transmitter to ensure permanent service, at least in the capital Thimpu. Initial problems with the vertically polarized antenna were solved after it was replaced by a horizontally polarized antenna that made a significant improvement in reception quality.

Additionally, an operational network of Macintosh computers and laptops and a few IBM PCs has been delivered and installed. The Macintosh computers are mainly used in the newsroom. A special workshop on archiving and documenting BBS news and programs was organized in 1992 (see Hartwell, Arnoldo, & Boston, 1992).

Compared to many other radio stations, BBS is "over-equipped" with new technology (especially computers, which are mainly used for word processing). One reason for this technology "richness" seems to be the lack of coordination between the different funding agencies (some equipment is provided by the Indian government, some is part of the UNESCO/Danida project). Equipment to supplement that supplied by the Indian Government in the new building has been delivered. This includes field radio production equipment, field recording consoles and taperecorders, spares for transmitters, computers, electronic mailboxes, laboratory measuring instruments and equipment, FM transmitters, and amplifiers.

It should be noted that the new studios were built to specifications indicated by All India Radio. This means that even studios used for editing were built for a two-man operation, a technician and an announcer, whereas BBS procedures require only a single producer who can handle the technical equipment. Moreover, the current room used for editing is not actually an editing suite but a dubbing room, with a patch junction, not a console. This is why the engineering consultant had to improvise by installing a console and temporarily patching taperecorders and microphones. Because the matching impedances were not the same for all equipment, a number of taperecorders (Indian made Studers) became useless.

Furthermore, some of the equipment is underused (consoles, synthesizer, cars) for a number of reasons (technology illiteracy, heavy maintenance cost, lack of training, etc.). For instance, UNESCO ordered vehicles for field work, but there were problems with the specifications. The ones delivered were unsuitable for duties outside of Thimpu and nearby towns. Therefore, additional vehicles were ordered.

There is a certain interest at the BBS to introduce stereo production in view of the planned cassette music production for nonbroadcast distribution that would compete with imported stereo-recorded music. However, going stereo would mandate certain modifications of the studios in the new radio station (e.g., adding speakers in control rooms and studios, adding stereo signal control meters to the consoles, rewiring, etc.).

Research

BBS expressed the need for a better understanding of their listening audience. Two limited audience surveys (one in 1987, another in early 1992) have been executed. They had a number of serious limitations, partly due to the low educational level and the lack of a research tradition in the country.

Furthermore, in view of the "autonomy"-decision and the extension of the transmission time (and the switch between summer and winter time schedules), audience research was put on the agenda as a priority issue. The staff also felt that more and better self-evaluations of individual and group performances and evaluations of programs should be organized on a regular basis.

Therefore, a plan for internal and external evaluations has been worked out. Internally, two types of evaluations will be organized on a regular basis: in-depth evaluations of individual and group/section performances, and qualitative product (content/form) analyses of individual programs and program types.

As little information is available about the listening audience, a more in-depth and qualitative audience survey is also needed. The central questions for this research might be: What is the need of the public regarding radio? Are the radio programs attuned to those needs?

A critical assessment of the Bhutanese mass media situation and its communication policies has to pay attention to the following points: (a) the sociocultural context of a developing country, with a real lack of trained and educated persons to recruit; (b) the frequent call on the few talented persons in higher management positions, making them less available for daily management duties; (c) the difficulty of imposing managerial authority by new recruits and younger graduates on older though less experienced broadcasters; (d) the lack of financial and career incentives in a civil service atmosphere; (e) the consequent inability to recruit outside talent; (f) the lack of experience in radio/media communication; and (g) the possibility that the inability to define and implement explicit program policies may be due to real cultural constraints and not merely omission.

Given the targets of the government, the responsibilities of BBS are now greater. In addition to the tasks mentioned in the Seventh Five-Year Plan, BBS has to produce and broadcast programs and organize related activities to foster individual and community endeavors toward fulfilling national development goals. Some of the major objectives of Bhutanese communication policies are to ensure the participation of people from all regions, to promote intercultural understanding and tolerance, and create a forum between the government and the people of Bhutan. BBS also has to disseminate information and provide a channel for an exchange of experiences necessary to enhance the living standards of people. Moreover, it has to be an instrument through which the government can learn what the people think. Not only should it attend to the needs of its adult audience, BBS has to be attentive to its young listeners, to help them develop into responsible citizens. Regular contacts could be established with local Ministerial Departments, NGOs, and UN and other international agencies, for instance, to organize and sponsor campaigns. Cooperation with other media groups will be necessary for BBS to successfully implement some of the objectives of the Seventh Five-Year Plan: to consolidate and widen the network of stringers, to negotiate international news subscriptions, to organize joint research, and to organize multimedia campaigns. At the international level, BBS could become a member of international organizations (e.g., ABU, AMARC, or AMIC). It is imperative that management attitudes change in accordance with the latest developments. Ultimately, how broadcasters adapt to the changes is what will determine the future of BBS.

SYNTHESIS

1. The case of Bhutan Radio BBS shows that the traditional theories on modernization and development need to be reconsidered. The classic modernization paradigm considered underdevelopment in terms of perceptible, quantitative differences between rich and poor countries. Development meant bridging the gaps by means of imitation processes between traditional and modern sectors, and between retarded and advanced or barbarian and civilized sectors and groups to the advantage of the latter. Here, the developing countries must gradually meet the

"qualities" of the industrialized countries. However, as discussed throughout this book, there are no countries that function completely autonomously and are completely self-sufficient, nor are there any nations whose development is exclusively determined by external factors. Every society is dependent in one way or another, both in form and in degree. Therefore, one has to accept that "internal" and "external" factors inhibiting development do not exist independently of each other.

2. This also implies a new understanding toward an integration of distinct means of communication: Modern mass media and alternate or parallel networks of traditional media or interpersonal communication channels are not mutually exclusive by definition. Contrary to the beliefs of diffusion theorists, they are more effective if appropriately used in an integrated fashion, according to the needs and constraints of the local context. The modern mass media, having often been mechanically transplanted from abroad into Third World societies, enjoy varying and limited rates of penetration. They are seldom truly integrated into institutional structures, as occurs in most Western societies. However, they can be effectively combined, provided a functional division of labor is established between them and provided the limits of the mass media are recognized. This recognition of dualistic or parallel communication structures also implies that governments or rulers are no longer able to operate effectively, to control, censor, or to play the role of gatekeeper with regard to all communications networks at all times in a given society.

10

Institutional Perspectives on Development Communication: The German Friedrich Ebert Stiftung

We have now reached an ironic situation in which the global significance of communication and information has been acknowledged, as well as their role within economic and social structures, but this significance is still not reflected operationally, in our educational, political or technical assistance structures. Communication has only recently been recognized even by the United Nations system as a programme classification sector in its own right, and it is still not treated as a critical vector of development by any United Nations or bilateral agency. There are still far too few educational programs in the field of communication for development (especially at an advanced level). Recognition of the field is normally expressed in restricted technical or technocratic terms, with communication perceived in the context of telecommunications or informatics, divorced from its social milieu, and looking, often uncritically, for the bonanzas of an ill-defined information society.
—Alan Hancock (1992: 217)

The theoretical changes in the perspective on development communication described earlier, have also reached the level of policymakers. As a result, different methodologies and terminologies have evolved, which often make it difficult for agencies and institutions in the field of development communication, even though they share a common commitment to the overall goals of communication for development, to identify common ground, arrive at a full understanding of each other's objectives, or to cooperate effectively in operational projects. Therefore, in 1989, UNESCO started a UNFPA-financed project on Integrated Approaches to Development Communication. Its objectives were to review the various approaches and methodologies, to identify their differences and common features, and to create a framework for integrated and cooperative action.

The project analyzed the following agencies and projects:

Seven United Nations agencies: the Food and Agriculture Organization of the United Nations (FAO), International Labour Organisation (ILO), United Nations Development Programme (UNDP), United Nations Educational, Scientific and Cultural Organization (UNESCO), United Nations Population Fund (UNFPA), United Nations Children Fund (UNICEF), World Health Organization (WHO)

Three Governmental agencies: Agence de Coopération Culturelle et Technique/Agency for Cultural and Technical Co-operation (ACCT), Canadian International Development Agency (CIDA), United States Agency for International Development (USAID)

Nine Nongovernmental organizations: African Council for Communication Education/Conseil Africain d'Enseignement de Communication (ACCE), Asian Mass Communication and Information Centre (AMIC), Association Mondiale des Radiodiffuseurs Communautaires /World Association of Community Radio Broadcasters (AMARC), Friedrich Ebert Stiftung (FES), Instituto para America Latina (IPAL), Radio Nederland Training Centre (RNTC), Women's Feature Service (WFS), World Association for Christian Communication (WACC), Worldview International Foundation (WIF)

Nine Case studies: Elaborated case studies of development communication in action, presenting a range of strategies in different world regions: Brazilian Telenovelas, Expanded Programme on Immunization (EPI) (BanglaDesh), Inter Press Service (IPS), Kheda Communications Project (India), Mahaweli Community Radio (Sri Lanka), Radio Enriquillo (Dominican Republic), Rural Communication System for Development in Mexico's Tropical Wetlands (PRODERITH), Social Marketing Campaigns, West and Central Africa News Agencies Development/Developpement des Agences de Presse en Afrique de l'Ouest et Centrale (WANAD)

Some of the communication for development approaches used by these agencies and communication media can be grouped together under the heading of the diffusion model, others under the participatory model. For more information on the distinct approaches and media used, one is advised to consult the orientation and resource kit edited by Mayo and Servaes (1994). In the following I present the communication and development strategies used by the German Friedrich Ebert Stiftung.

The Context of the Friedrich Ebert Stiftung

Although the bulk of the German development aid for communication development goes through official channels, some of the most innovative work is carried out by political foundations and church organizations, financed in part by the Government of Germany. There are five political foundations active in the development communication field: the Friedrich Ebert Stiftung (FES) based on the philosophy of social democracy, the Friedrich Naumann Stiftung (FNS) linked to the FDP, the Konrad Adenauer Stiftung (KAS) linked to the CDU, the Hanns-Seidel Stiftung (HSS) linked to the CSU, and the Stiftungsverband Regenbogen linked to the Green Party. The Friedrich Ebert Foundation is the largest of the five political foundations in Germany. It receives its funding from public (Ministry for Economic Cooperation, Länder) and private (industry, individuals) sponsors. In addition to international work carried out in 105 industrial and developing countries all over the world, the FES also supports political education and scientific efforts in Germany. Especially since the fall of the Berlin Wall in 1989, the FES is actively involved in socially integrating the two former states.

In 1990, 20 media and communication projects amounted to 13% (DM 11 million) of the Foundation's annual budget for cooperation with developing countries. Within its central aim to promote the basic values of social democracy and the labor movement, the Friedrich Ebert Foundation's media and communication department regards unhindered communication between people and states as a prerequisite for social justice and solidarity. Its activities include training, consultancy, scientific research, and international conferences with partners in the Third World. These FES activities are accompanied by specialized literature and learning manuals. They extend to Africa, Asia, the Pacific, Latin America, and the Caribbean.

Background

The FES was established in 1925 and named after the first German Reich president, Friedrich Ebert. As the oldest political foundation in Germany, the FES initially concentrated on sponsoring young working class students with scholarships. Its sociopolitical aims were not tolerated by the upcoming National Socialists. This resulted in the prohibition of the FES in 1933. After World War II the FES was reestablished and its education program rapidly expanded. During the 1950s the FES initiated a number of international activities. With the inception of an educational television project in Ghana in 1965 the FES began playing a role in developing media in the Third World.

During the following 25 years the media and communication department established a major position in the FES' international division and today it supports some 20 projects in Ecuador, the Caribbean, Algeria, Ghana, Zimbabwe, Mozambique, Kenya, Sri Lanka, Malaysia, Indonesia, China, the South Pacific, and Senegal. In these countries and regions the FES cooperates with local as well as regional and international institutions in education, research, and the development of television news exchange organizations. Additionally, provides consultancy projects, which are again based on bilateral contacts with an aid-seeking partner.

Partners

Its main partners on the international level are the EBU (European Broadcasting Union), INTELSAT (International Communications Satellite Organization), UNESCO (United Nations Educational Scientific and Cultural Organization), IIC (International Institute of Communications), and ITU (International Telecommunication Union). With partners from the different regions FES promotes regional television news exchange projects. Its partners in Asia are AMIC (the Asian Mass Communication Research Information Center), which FES has supported since 1972; ABU (Asia-pacific Broadcasting Union), and AIBD (Asia Pacific Institute for Broadcasting Development), with which FES has promoted Asiavision since 1984. In Africa FES cooperates with URTNA (Union of National Radio and Television Organizations of Africa) in the Afrovision project and with FANA (Federation of Arab News Agencies). Arabvision is developed in cooperation with ASBU (Arab States Broadcasting Union). Finally, Caribvision was established with the partnership of CBU (Caribbean Broadcasting Union). To facilitate access for Third World countries in the central European media landscape, FES is supporting the Inter Press Service (IPS).

In other less structured projects, FES collaborates with the regional COMNET centers and various locally based organizations in the training, planning, and implementation of media in rural areas.

Although its political convictions are never hidden, FES is a nongovernmental body, which implies the great advantage of flexibility.

Objectives

Committed to the sociopolitical values of the labor movement and social democracy, the international activities carried out by FES all serve its general philosophy that peace and international understanding, democracy, pluralism, social justice, and solidarity are prerequisites for independence and the equal economic and social development of countries and people all over the world.

Unhindered communication is seen as essential for the peaceful coexistence of people. In striving to end limitations and dependencies within countries as well as between nations, FES promotes the basic principles of the *new world information and communication order* concept. Its central aim—to promote mass media and information systems in the Third World—stems from these ideas and can be specified through five objectives: (a) supporting the countries' development, (b) narrowing the information gap, (c) building up transborder information systems, (d) developing production areas, and (e) initial and follow-up training of media workers. Within this framework, professionalizing and self-help are seen as important conditions for a country's independence.

Communication Strategies Employed

In promoting communication and information systems in development contexts, FES finds the adoption of a mix of methods and channels the best way of reaching its goals. In general, this implies that the Foundation tries to collaborate with partners on international, regional, and local levels, working with mainstream as well as grass-root media organizations. By creating two-way communication between the governed and the governing it tries to open the dialogue where social change is required.

Media based strategies.

At the regional level, already existing telecommunication systems can be modified, adapted, and expanded to serve the needs of local and national groups. By using the existing infrastructure, no new expensive technology is needed. Setting up regional television news exchange networks implies reaching a consensus between authorities and TV corporations to make use of already existing satellite services and ground stations wherever possible. If additional infrastructure is necessary, it is important to implement the economically, socially, and culturally most preferable hardware.

In developing its media strategies, FES places strong emphasis on participation by the target audience. Interpersonal and group communication is important in addition to educational and informational media programs. In addition to cooperation at the grass-root level, FES also supports the professionalism of opinion leaders. Special efforts are made to consult on regulations for media use.

Training.

In cooperation with local training and development centers, initial and follow-up training systems are developed, implemented, and evaluated. This concerns training for broadcasting personnel and agency technicians, as well as the training of journalists. Within the central objective of improving the quality of news output and bilateral news flow, exchange programs are set up. Communication manuals written by experts from First and Third World countries serve as guidelines for scriptwriters, journalists, and educational radio workers. These handbooks often are the result of workshops and conferences held between local experts from different regions.

Research.

In close cooperation with regional COMNET centers, such as the Singapore-based AMIC and the more practically oriented broadcasting unions, communication systems are developed. This decentralized approach is regarded as essential for the development of socioculturally autonomous and situation-specific methods and strategies. Apart from conveying modern methods of training in program production and engineering, efforts are made to design blueprints for media laws and regulations.

Conferences held between different experts aim at projecting and forecasting the consequences of local and international communication developments from an interdisciplinary point of view. The outcomes of these meetings serve as starting points for further research.

Projects and Activities

In general, the Friedrich Ebert Foundation supports three types of projects. First, it contributes to bilateral projects at a national level. In cooperation with one or more partners, FES plans and implements media activities. The special focus in these nonstructural relations is on rural radio projects.

Second, FES has close ties with regional COMNET centers and other regional research institutes. Together they attempt to develop research, documentation, education (training), and publications on theoretical, but especially also on practical fields of communication.

Finally, FES places special emphasis on the development of regional television news exchange activities. FES' financial support and expertise contributed to the establishment of Asiavision in 1984. These types of projects are seen as essential for the flow of information and understanding between North and South, as well as between countries in each region.

Bilateral projects at a national level

At the national level, FES participates in projects that mostly aim at educating people in rural areas. Often radio is used as the predominant medium; as radio is a relatively cheap medium, it does not require long and difficult training nor is it dependent on complex infrastructures. Additionally, efforts are made to organize discussion groups that make interpersonal reflection on the programs possible.

Some 15 years ago, FES supported the development of a trade union radio station in the Philippines (DYLA in Cebu City), which had gained an international reputation for its work in adult education and development broadcasting. FES activities included the organization of training courses for reporters and technicians, the provision of equipment, and the implementation and evaluation of the projects.

An example of this type of project is Radio 4 in Zimbabwe. Set up in 1983 as part of the Zimbabwe Broadcasting Corporation, Radio 4 is an educational radio channel, providing two-way communication between the governing and the governed that deals with various aspects of daily life. As a result of its cooperation with FES and BBC broadcasters, Radio 4 has developed into a high-standard station, filling the information gap in the countryside, and it has become a basis for frequent interaction between radiomakers and the audience in the area. There are 25 listener's clubs initiated by women in the rural districts that actively discuss the programs and even contribute to the broadcasts by means of their own recordings.

FES cooperates within the framework of a training project by providing fully equipped studios, two outside broadcast vans, accommodation and experts, and by paying the salaries of the local personnel.

Research projects.

In addition to scientific work carried out by specialists in Germany, FES also supports regional research centers in Third World countries. FES has strong ties with different COMNET centers, with which it develops training programs, research projects, and documentation.

A typical project of this kind is the Asian Mass Communication Centre (AMIC). The center was set up as an NGO in 1971 in Singapore, and FES has been supporting it with about half its annual budget ever since. Its work is mainly focused on documentation research, development, publications and discussion about communication models for national and regional needs in Asia. It is also advising partners (NGOs and governments) on the use of communication, training of medium-level and high-leadership personnel working in the communication sector, and research and promotion of the Asian flow of news. AMIC has become a major partner with bilateral and multilateral research projects in Asia, and a platform for Asian mass communication and media development.

Television news exchange projects.

A major part of the work done by the Friedrich Ebert Foundation is related to the promotion of regional news exchange schemes. Using Eurovision as its model, FES cooperates with different regional broadcasting units and training institutes to set up continent-wide television news exchange systems in the Third World.

In 1984, Asiavision was the first TV news exchange system set up in a Third World region. It stems from discussions in the 1970s in Asia about the one-sided flow of information and the lack of South-South dialogue. In collaboration with the Asia Pacific Broadcasting Union (ABU), FES developed a TV news exchange scheme along the lines of Eurovision and EBU. The basic elements of this model are:

- Each member is free in selecting its news items for transmission.
- The selection, distribution, exchange, and mode of presentation of the agency news is determined by the contributing broadcasters alone.

- Exchange between different regional systems takes place on the basis of equal rights and is not bound by quota.

Before the actual start in 1984, the project was pretested by means of a large-scale experiment. For a couple of weeks several broadcasting units exchanged their news footage. The training of the agency personnel, costs and tariffs of national PTTs, and infrastructural complications turned out to be the major problems on the way toward a balanced and well-functioning TV news exchange system.

The actual implementation of the project in 1984 was supported by broadcasting units from 12 Asiatic countries. Due to political and economic reasons Singapore, Thailand, and the Philippines do not participate in Asiavision.

To meet international standards and the needs of industrialized countries as well, emphasis is on the training of technical personnel and journalists from the Asian states. The Asia-Pacific Institute for Broadcasting Development (AIBD), supported by FES since its inception in 1977, provides these training courses. Over 800 participants have been trained so far by German and other West European experts in TV news production.

Despite the problems outlined earlier and several other technical constraints (time-span, geographical distances, quality of the software, different selection criteria between states), Asiavision succeeded in bridging the information gap between the Asian nations and provided an opening for them in the First World-dominated international flow of news.

Besides Asiavision, FES supports similar activities in Africa (Afrovision), Latin America (Latinvision), the Caribbean (Caribvision), and the Arab region (Arabvision). Through training, research, and the promotion of hardware and software, FES tries to promote professionalism and cooperation between the different broadcasting units.

Political and economic restrictions require long-term planning, insight into a country's culture, and creative cooperation.

Consultancy projects.

FES is in a position to provide consultancy services to NGOs and local partners with expertise drawn either from Germany or abroad. In principle, any organization can approach the FES headquarters in Bonn to apply for such services.

Publications.

Publications support all the activities in which FES participates. Apart from theoretical studies, published as a result of conferences and scientific seminars, there is a whole range of handbooks and instruction manuals providing guidelines for communication development. These manuals, written by experts and published in several languages, are addressed to workers and students in the field of mass communication in general, or to trainees in specific courses organized in collaboration with institutes in the Third World.

THE RE-UNIFICATION OF GERMANY

The democratization of the Eastern European states and the unification of Germany on October 3, 1990, involved a shift in focus for FES. In 1992, FES initiated a consultancy and training project based in Prague for radio and television in Poland, Czechoslovakia, and Hungary. Educational and research activities have been extended to Eastern Europe and FES now tries to integrate the former GDR's media policy into its own development communication perspectives. The former GDR's approach to development communication—limited to training institutions in Leipzig, Berlin, and Dresden, and technical assistance directed by the government—has been almost completely abandoned. Projects carried out in Algeria, Angola, Argentina, Brazil, Democratic Yemen, Ecuador, Ghana, India, the Laos People's Democratic Republic, Mexico, Mozambique, Nicaragua, the United Republic of Tanzania, Vietnam and Zambia are also being phased out, with only a few of them integrated into the existing activities of FES.

SYNTHESIS

1. The presentation of the communication and development strategies used by the German Friedrich Ebert Stiftung forms part of a more general assessment of communication for development approaches within international agencies, commissioned by UNFPA and UNESCO. Some of the communication for development approaches of these agencies and communication media used can be grouped together under the heading of the diffusion model, others under the participatory model.

2. The Friedrich Ebert Foundation is one of the largest agencies emphasizing communication strategies in Europe, or even in the world. Committed to the sociopolitical values of the labor movement and social democracy, the international activities carried out by FES all serve its general philosophy that peace and international understanding, democratic pluralism, social justice, and solidarity are prerequisites for independence and the equal economic and social development of countries and people all over the world.

3. Unhindered communication is seen as essential for the peaceful coexistence of people. In striving to end limitations and dependencies within countries as well as between nations, FES promotes the basic principles of the *new world information and communication order* concept. Its central aim—to promote mass media and information systems in the Third World—stems from these ideas and can be specified through five objectives: (a) supporting the country's development, (b) narrowing the information gap, (c) building up transborder information systems, (d) developing production areas, and (e) initial and follow-up training of media workers. Within this framework, professionalization and self-help are seen as important conditions for a country's independence.

4. FES supports three types of projects: First, it contributes to bilateral projects at a national level, Second, it has close ties with regional research institutes. Together they attempt to develop research, documentation, education (training), and publications on theoretical, but especially also on practical fields of communication. Finally, FES also places special emphasis on the development of regional television news exchange activities. These types of projects are seen as essential for the flow of information and understanding between North and South, as well as between countries in each region.

5. The democratization of the Eastern European states and the unification of Germany on October 3, 1990, involved a shift in focus for FES. Educational and research activities have been extended to Eastern Europe, and FES tries to integrate the former GDR's media policy into its own development communication perspectives. Many projects carried out in the South are being phased out.

11

From Radio Schools to Community Radio: Participatory Research at Radio Enriquillo

My basic idea is that participation is an essential human need, and therefore a human right. It is not merely a set of methodological procedures to achieve more efficiency and productivity. I believe that at the root of participation is (wo)man's eternal need for love and to be a whole person through love. Because of this need, participation and communication are at their best when they have a foundation of a solid humanistic philosophy linked to a transcendal view of man and universe.
—Juan Diaz Bordenave (1994: 47)

Radio Enriquillo in the Dominican Republic is considered a role model in the Latin American radio movement. Other participatory radio stations passed through phases similar to Radio Enriquillo, including Radio ERPE in Riobamba in Ecuador, "La voz de la Selva" in Iquitos in Peru, and Radio San Gabriel in La Paz in Bolivia. The emergent practice of genuine participatory peoples' radio in Latin America centrally involves issues of class, power, and cultural hegemony. The radios are an important part, but still only a part, of grass-roots struggles for fundamental social change in one's region and in one's country. The radios are used for direct political organization (to call a meeting, to organize a campaign), but using the radio also gives people self-confidence. Above all this involves the revaluation of their language and culture. This culture process may be a "long revolution"—the slow process of building a counter-hegemony to the dominant political culture. But it is also linked directly to political demands for fundamental social change. These demands of people in grass-roots organizations—which often find expression in local struggles for access to land and services, jobs and housing, clean water and schools—can be noticed throughout Latin America (for more information, see Beltran, 1993; Berque, Foy, & Girard, 1993; Cabezas et al., 1982; Ciespal, 1983; Fox, 1988; Girart, 1992).

After providing some general data on participatory communication projects in general, and the Latin American popular radio movement in particular, I elaborate on the way participatory research plays a role at Radio Enriquillo.

The Three Stages of the Latin American Popular Radio Movement

Like many other popular radio stations in Latin America, Radio Enriquillo has passed through the three phases typical of the Latin American radio movement. These phases are, in chronological order:

1. Radio schools (*escuelas radiofónicas*): Radio as a medium to support the education of the population. Specially formed listening groups received written material to support radio education. This material and the radio programs are designed to educate the poorer segments of the population.
2. Democratization movement (*radio popular*): In this period the radio was used as a propaganda medium against military dictatorships. Laborers (like the miners in Bolivia), farmers, and other opposition groups organized and used the radio to air their concerns and wishes.
3. Radio as a communication medium (*sistema de comunicacion*): Radio is part of the communication process as a whole: that is, radio is there for the people and made by the people. Although participation is one of the key concepts, it is recognized that radio is only one communication medium and that the population also has other means of sending and receiving information. What is most important in this phase is that people can be sender and receiver equally through one medium. Therefore, often this type of radio is also called a community radio system.

A Definition of Community Radio

At a more general level, the three phases the Latin-American popular radio movement went through are also discernable in other regions. Although there are notorious difficulties with the term community radio, it is used, for example, in the title of the World Association of Community Radio Broadcasters (AMARC). The movement of community radio encompasses a wide range of practices. In Latin America they are termed *popular radio, educational radio, miners' radio,* or *peasants' radio.* In Africa they refer to *local rural radio.* In Europe it is often called *associative radio, free radio, neighborhood radio,* or *community radio.* In Asia they speak of *radio for development* and *community radio;* in Oceania of *aboriginal radio, public radio,* and *community radio.* All these types of radio reflect a large diversity.

Furthermore, in Europe, for example, local or regional radio stations do not necessarily focus on social change. In England commercial broadcasters have appropriated the term *local radio.* One useful clarification, established in England during the days of the Greater London Council, is that "community" must be understood to mean community of interest rather than simply a geographically defined community. Even so, phrases such as "the gay community" or "the Black community" fail to clarify important issues of gender, social class, and other differences.

Therefore, the World Association of Community Radio Broadcasters (AMARC) characterizes community radio as:

- radio that responds to the needs of the community which it serves and contributes to its development in a progressive manner, favorizing social change
- radio that offers a service to the community it serves or to which it broadcasts, while promoting the expression and participation of the community through the radio

In other words, community radio is "a type of broadcasting that responds to community concerns because it belongs to and is part of the community." AMARC tries to facilitate access to and participation in their organization for all community radio broadcasters so that they can exchange information and experiences with each other. The whole movement must be reinforced, which means that it is an umbrella organization with members from all kinds of cultures. This can lead to cultural constraints as well.

AMARC's Declaration of Principles states, in part, that members of AMARC:

- believe in the need to establish a new world information order based on more just and equitable exchanges among peoples
- contribute to the expression of different social, political, and cultural movements, and to the promotion of all initiatives supporting peace, friendship among peoples, democracy, and development
- recognize the fundamental and specific role of women in establishing new communication practices
- express through their programming the sovereignty and independence of all peoples; solidarity and nonintervention in the internal affairs of other countries; cooperation based on the creation of permanent and widespread ties based on equality, reciprocity, and mutual respect; nondiscrimination on the basis of race, sex, sexual preference, or religion; and respect for the cultural identity of peoples.

AMARC uses a communication strategy that has participation as its main objective. This type of participatory communication is not limited to sending messages to the public; it is an agent for social change, cultural development, and democratization. This implies for every community radio broadcaster a democratic dimension; popular participation in the management of the station and in the production of its programs. Community radio is accessible; it is neither the expression of political power nor the expression of capital. It is the expression of the population. It is a third voice between state radio and private commercial radio. Community radio is an act of participation in communication. It is controlled democratically by the population it serves. It is based on a noncommercial relationship with its audiences. Its mission is essentially one of community and group development. It informs, motivates discussion, and entertains while broadcasting music and poetry that regenerate the collective soul.

Characteristics of Participatory Communication Projects

Community radios are only one of the media that can be grouped together under the heading of participatory communication projects. Alan O'Connor (1990) has produced a short list of characteristics of participatory communication projects. This does not mean that every participatory communication project contains elements of the below characteristics listed next. Rather it means that there is a diversity and variety of participatory communication projects and that each particular project can be evaluated along technical, cultural, linguistic, and social lines. These characteristics are:

1. *Small technologies:* This is mainly a technological focus. It points out that grass-roots movements for social change need to be aware of the possibilities opened by the availability of such technologies as low-power VHF FM radio, low-cost video equipment (camrecorders), and desk-top publishing using personal computers. The main point seems to be to counter a possible antitechnological bias within some social movements. These new low-cost technologies have to some extent changed the rules of the political game. But clearly conservative as well as radical social movements take advantage of the possibilities of video and desk-top publishing. However, having said this, one also needs to counter a possible antitechnological bias within some social movements.

2. *Local or community projects:* As explained earlier, this characteristic must be understood in terms of "identity" or "interest," rather than in dimensions of "space."

3. *Projects of the new social movements/media for empowerment:* This identification is sometimes used within feminist and ecological discussions. For instance, what changes have been made to radio as a cultural form in order to provide access not only to women broadcasters but to women's culture? These kinds of issues need a perspective that is anthropological rather than simply an evaluation of the organizational structure of each radio station. The phrase "media for empowerment" seeks to become part of a broad coalition for fundamental social change.

4. *Defense of language:* The preservation or rehabilitation of minority or aboriginal languages is often a key strategy for ethnic minorities and native peoples. Because radio especially involves crucial choices of which languages are to be used for broadcast programs, it has been a key issue in many parts of the world, including Canada, Latin America, and throughout Africa. Although this is a very important issue, the use of a minority or indigenous language itself is no guarantee of genuinely participatory communication. Many missionary radio stations, for instance, broadcast in native peoples' languages. In Latin America even some commercial radios broadcast in indigenous languages.

5. *Communication and dialogue:* These terms are from Latin American philosophies of communication. Antonio Pasquali (1980) made a distinction between information that is passed down in a hierarchical manner

and genuine communication, which implies a horizontal human dialogue. The earlier mentioned Freirean arguments for a dialogical
approach to social change are well known.

Although we have gained a great deal from the philosophies of
Pasquali and Freire, they have a tendency to emphasize group communication for its own sake, on the lines of Catholic Church-based communities in Latin America. However, any attempt to build a broad coalition
for social change must move beyond communication within homogeneous groups and work out the organizational structures that are necessary for broad multicultural movement.

6. *Access and participation:* Again, these are important keywords that can
mean many different things. In India, women's access to radio often
means simply that they will be permitted to listen to the radio set. The
important issue is not simply that people have access to the station with
their opinions or personal messages, nor that some local people participate on a paid or volunteer basis on radio programming. The crucial
issue is the institutional structure of the communication project. Who is
in control? Is it democratically managed? Is there a mechanism whereby
it is accountable to those it serves? (For more information on women's
projects, see, e.g., Gallagher & Quindoza-Santiago, 1994; Mata, 1995.)

7. *Defense of culture:* An argument is often made for the defense of a
national culture or an indigenous culture through the use of communication media such as radio. As we have argued earlier, the keyword
"culture" is one of the most difficult words to define in any language. It
can mean the arts or everyday life, artifacts or processes. Without entering into these debates again, we would suggest that culture must always
be considered relative to institutions of decision making.

Participatory Research at Radio Enriquillo

The island of Hispaniola in the Caribbean region is divided into a
Haitian and a Dominican part. From 1930 until 1952, R.L. Trujillo was
the president of the Dominican Republic. He led a terroristic and dictatorial regime. After 1952, his brother became the president, but the former dictator kept the power behind the scenes. In 1960 the Dominican
people stood up against the repression, and Trujillo was murdered in
1961.

Since 1966, the Dominican Republic has been a presidential
republic by constitution. Legislative power belongs to the Congress (an
institution similar to that in the United States). The political situation in
the Dominican Republic has been unstable for the last 30 years.

Cooperation between the 20 political parties seems impossible, but despite the problems, the politicians are still striving to attain a more orderly and democratic situation.

The Dominican Republic is economically dependent on the United States, with the export to that country accounting for 90% of total export. Agriculture is the most important sector of the economy, absorbing 70% of the working population. The main export product is sugar-cane. Other products are cacao, coffee, and tobacco. In the poor southwest region, where Radio Enriquillo is located, the farmers produce sugar-cane. There is much landlordism, so no matter how hard the farmers work, they remain poor.

Origins of Radio Enriquillo

Radio Enriquillo was founded in 1977 in the village of Tamayo, in the southwest region of the country. The *Surenos* (the inhabitants from the southern province) were until then "the forgotten people" because the area was quite isolated and underdeveloped. Radio Enriquillo (named after a 16th-century Indian rebel) was established by Humberto Vandenbulcke, a Belgian missionary who later also founded the Latin American Association of Radio Education (ALER), an Ecuador-based group that specialized in participatory research for community radio stations.

Radio Enriquillo consciously seeks to support grass-roots organizations in their social and economic demands. Observers agree that Radio Enriquillo was instrumental in the tremendous growth in the number of peasant associations and women's groups in the decade after its founding. In 1972 there were only a dozen associations of organized campesinos in the region. Ten years later there were some 110 associations. Its programming is produced in coordination with local organizations. This includes participation in planning the program by regional and local organizations, participation in production by the leaders and representatives of the various organizations, as well as the ordinary participation of the "voices" of many people in the region. It often broadcasts "live" and therefore completely unedited interviews. These interviews are about everyday things—the reality and the problems of the region. Mistakes, misunderstandings, everyday language, all go on air. Therefore, over the years, Radio Enriquillo has developed a highly participatory working style, involving youth, women, and peasant groups in the identification of themes and content of programs including news, debates, folk music, poetry, and drama.

For instance, after the military coup against the democratically elected Haitian President Jean-Bertrand Aristide in 1991, Radio

Enriquillo exploited a journalistic loophole in a ban by the Dominican Republic on newscasts in Creole, the patois spoken by most Haitians. Musical broadcasts were permitted, so Radio Enriquillo reporters began singing the news in Creole twice a day to the accompaniment of guitars, flutes, and drums. It aired musical propaganda in support of Aristide's reinstatement.

The expected spill-over of Radio Enriquillo is that local or national grass-root organizations recognize their collective problems. Through listening to and working with the radio, people can learn they are not the only ones to experience specific problems. When they get to know people who go through the same difficulties, they can organize and find solutions for their collective problems. This cooperation does not necessarily find its way through radio interaction, but it is possible that the radio establishes the first contact or recognition.

Appropriately, the station calls itself La *Amiga del Sur,* or Friend of the South. However, because of its clear identification with the poor, those in power have accused it of "agitating" and generating conflict.

Objectives of the Radio Enriquillo Project

Radio Enriquillo is an audience-centered, participatory project. Radio Enriquillo recognizes that *the public* or "audience" is, in fact, made up of tendencies, tastes, and class interests that are often antagonistic to each other. The audience is not one of individuals but of people who are already organized into associations that are both communicative networks and political entities. What is different about Radio Enriquillo is that it does not pretend to be neutral. It takes the side of the majority of the people. It respects and helps to strengthen the people's own political organizations, without making an explicit option for one ideological or political "party." The basic philosophical position of Radio Enriquillo is not a theory of "underdevelopment" or "dependency," but a diagnosis of the actual situation in the region. The diagnosis is that the dominant bloc is made up of an alliance of landlords, state functionaries, military men, and industrialists. The dominated bloc consists of small farmers, laborers, unemployed people who seek day labor, illegal Haitian immigrants, small traders, and employees. The most important political organization in the dominated bloc is the campesinos' associations. Radio Enriquillo allies itself with these associations in a process of social change.

Radio Enriquillo is dedicated to *horizontal communication* between the radio and its listeners. This means that the radio and its listeners are on the same level. There is no hierarchical structure with a teacher-student relation—anybody can learn from anybody. Everyone's voice is heard and everyone's ideas are seriously considered.

Participatory Communication Research Strategies Employed

Generally speaking, participation is the main concept of Radio Enriquillo. *Evaluation* is a very important concept for a radio of the people. To encourage participation, the audience should be known. It is also an obligation for the radio station to make itself known and to know how the programs rate with the audience in terms of its needs and aspirations.

At first these evaluations were initiated by the financiers of Radio Enriquillo, but later the radio wanted to evaluate its own work. For example, regular meetings are held to examine the station's relationships with local and regional citizen's organizations. In 1982, the station undertook an 18-month research project with the assistance of the Latin American Association of Radio Education (ALER). The evaluation proved worthwhile in helping the station explore the source of its popularity and in defining ways to better serve the information and educational needs of local people (see Mata, 1985).

Since that time, changes have occurred at the station with the departure of original staff members and the addition of new ones. Moreover, national elections brought about important political changes that had implications for the station and community organizations. As a result, in December 1988 the station staff decided to undertake another comprehensive self-evaluation to examine its achievements, limitations, and problems. The evaluation began in August 1989 and concluded in March 1990. It showed some deficiencies in the work of Radio Enriquillo, and changes were put through to improve the situation (see Camilo, Mata, & Servaes, 1990). The next evaluation was planned for 1997.

The participation and other development communication methods employed include:

1. *A participatory approach to evaluation:* Because Radio Enriquillo had always emphasized democratic participation in its operations, the station staff has always been inclined toward a participatory approach to evaluation. Everyone agreed that if staff were directly involved in the determination of evaluation results, they would also be more committed to carrying out the recommendations. Thus, the staff was involved at various stages of the evaluation process—selection of objectives, development of the methodology, data collection, and analysis. However, the process attempted to balance their in-depth knowledge of the station's operations with the research experience and independent perspective of "outside" coordinators of the evaluation.

2. *A participatory approach to research:* Data collection was carried out with the involvement of station staff and village correspondents. Five methods were used to collect data: surveys, community meetings, analysis of radio programming, document analysis, and participatory observation.

3. *Quantitative and qualitative research methods:* The research methods employed focused on a combination and interpretation of quantitative and qualitative data. For quantitative data, clear-cut conventions exist as to what can be done with data and how data should be collected. In the 1989 evaluation, some of these conventions (e.g. intercoder reliability) could not be met, due to the specific situations in which the research was executed (for instance, the inexperience of the interviewers with the data collection methods). However, most of these methodological problems in the quantitative part of the research could be corrected through the .qualitative research findings. The collection of qualitative data assisted in formulating the specific content of the questionnaires by identifying the most important key variables under which more specific data could be explored. It also aided in controlling the quantitative data. And, even more significantly, qualitative data enlivens and makes more concrete the statistical pictures that come out of survey information.

Some standards of data collection, such as a high degree of statistical reliability, could not be met because most data were gathered by associates of Radio Enriquillo, rather than by independent observers and because many of them were inexperienced in the protocols of data collection, although there was a provision of training. It was agreed that problems with quantitative measurements could be corrected through more in-depth qualitative research and careful data analysis and interpretation. The researchers also believed that the qualitative data would broaden the findings suggested by the statistical data.

4. *A community based approach:* Why does the community have such trust and support for Radio Enriquillo? "Because the people that work with it are valuable resources." "Because they have the support and acceptance of the people." "Because they make continual efforts toward improvement, as in this evaluation." These were the three answers most frequently cited by respondents during the evaluation. They are the three basic elements through which an organization like Radio Enriquillo can transcend its limitations and redefine its vision: a team that values people, works to revise its practice, and ensures that the listeners recognize this radio as their own.

5. *Edu-tainment:* Educative programs are aired in order to help the poor population develop. But the programs also have to appeal to popular

tastes in music, so that listeners do not switch to the commercial radio stations.

6. *Community participation:* The audience needs to express their needs and wishes. The organization of the radio is democratic. This means that the population can cooperate in the development of radio programs. Access for anyone to the radio microphones is all important. People express their feedback and their own ideas. Access for farmers in remote villages is made easier through the "unidad movil" (the mobile recording unit).

Until now Radio Enriquillo has reached the people who were the target audience, the farmers. They have become more conscious of their own situation and its possibilities for change. Radio Enriquillo has gained the trust of the farmers.

SYNTHESIS

1. One can distinguish among three phases the Latin-American radio movement went through: (a) Radio schools: Radio as a medium to support education of the population; (b) Democratization movement: Radio as a propaganda medium against the military dictatorships; and (c) Radio as a communication medium : Radio is part of the communication process as a whole, that is, radio is there for the people and made by the people.

2. The World Association of Community Radio Broadcasters (AMARC) characterizes community radio as: (a) radio that responds to the needs of the community which it serves and contributes to its development in a progressive manner, favoring social change; and (b) radio that offers a service to the community it serves or to which it broadcasts, while promoting the expression and participation of the community in the radio.

3. There is a diversity and variety of participatory communication projects. Each particular project can be evaluated along technical, cultural, linguistic, and social lines. General characteristics include: (a) small technologies, (b) local or community projects, (c) projects of the new social movements/media for empowerment, (d) defense of language, (e) communication and dialogue, (f) access and participation, and (g) defense of culture.

4. Radio Enriquillo is an audience-centered, participatory project. Radio Enriquillo recognizes that the public or "audience" is in fact made up of tendencies, tastes, and class interests that are often antagonistic to each other. Therefore, Radio Enriquillo does not pretend to be neutral. It

takes the side of the majority of the people. It respects and helps to strengthen the people's own political organizations, without making an explicit option for one ideological or political party. The basic philosophical position of Radio Enriquillo is not a theory of underdevelopment or dependency, but a diagnosis of the actual situation in the region.

5. Participation and evaluation are the main concepts of Radio Enriquillo. To encourage participation, the audience should be known. It is also an obligation for the radio station to make itself known and to know how the programs rate with the audience in terms of its needs and aspirations. Therefore, regular participatory self-evaluations, by which several methodologies are applied, have been organized since the the start of the station.

12

Conclusions

People cannot be developed; they can only develop themselves. For while it is possible for an outsider to build a man's home, an outsider cannot give the man pride and self-confidence in himself as a human being. Those things a man has to create in himself by his own actions. He develops himself by what he does; he develops himself by making his own decisions by increasing his understanding of what he is doing, and why; by increasing his own knowledge and ability, and by his own full participation—as an equal—in the life of the community he lives in.
—Julius Nyerere (1973: 60)

In this book I have overviewed three paradigms on communication for development. They can be summarized as follows:

The Modernization Paradigm

1. One of the oldest of western concepts, development in the modernization paradigm is seen as inevitable. It is a spontaneous and irreversible process inherent in every single society. Like the linear models of communication also formulated in the

West, it understands development as primarily unilinear, from the developed "source" to the underdeveloped "receiver."

2. Progressing through discernible, predetermined stages assessed primarily by industrial base and economic criteria, development of this genre implies structural differentiation and functional specialization—capital-centered modes of production. The concept is defined by and for those nations that are developed. And it was also accepted by the elites in developing countries. In a word, development is the state of being or becoming "westernized."

3. The process of development can be divided into distinct stages that show the level of development achieved by each society. Whereas the cause of underdevelopment in this paradigm lies in the "backwardness" of the developing society, the stimulus to change and development or growth is exogenous. Hence, culture and social structure, the essence of society, are seen as the primary impediments to its "progress."

4. Development can be stimulated by external, endogenous factors—the transfer of capital and technology, expertise and technique from industrialized nations—and by internal measures that support modernized sectors and modernize traditional sectors.

The Dependency Paradigm

1. Criticism of the modernization paradigm originated chiefly in Latin America. The most basic reason was that it did not work. Rather than underdevelopment being a stage on the road to development, the dependistas saw it as two sides of the same coin: an underdeveloped Periphery was prerequisite for the existence of the developed Center. Due to the fact that the Periphery is deprived of its surplus, development in the Center implies underdevelopment in the Periphery. Thus, the process of development is analyzed in terms of relations between regions, central and peripheral.

2. Dependency theory asserts that the causes of underdevelopment are external to the underdeveloped nation, that is, they are base on global economic structures, whereas the cure could be found in the nation itself, chiefly through economic and cultural dissociation from world markets and through self-reliance.

3. The dependency paradigm, both in theory and policy, focused almost exclusively on analysis at the international level and

bypassed analogous relations of exploitation and inequity intra-nationally, serving to enhance the positions of the many Third World bourgeoisie handsomely, as well as failing to prescribe any concrete solution.

4. Both the modernization and dependency paradigms employ an overwhelmingly economic, technological framework of analysis, ignoring cultural, aesthetic, environmental or other more holistic considerations.

5. Dependency theory is much more a description of structures than a prescription for sustainable growth or significant social change.

The Multiplicity Paradigm

1. All nations, in one way or the other, are dependent on one another. Consequently, internal as well as external factors inevitably influence the development process.

2. Development has to be studied in a global context, in which both Center and Periphery, as well as their interrelated subdivisions, have to be taken into consideration.

3. More attention is being paid to the content of development, which implies a more normative approach. Another development questions whether "developed" countries are in fact developed and whether this genre of progress is sustainable or desirable. It favors a multiplicity of approaches based on the context, the basic, felt needs, and the empowerment of the most oppressed sectors of various societies at divergent levels. A main thesis is that change must be structural and occur at multiple levels in order to achieve these ends.

4. There is no universal model for development. Each society must develop its own development strategy.

Table 12.1 presents the main characteristics regarding the theoretical and methodological origins and strengths and the policy consequences of the modernization, dependency, and multiplicity paradigms.

These "developments" have also affected communication research, as is reflected in the fascinating assessments and surveys by many communication scholars. The former hierarchical, bureaucratic, and sender-oriented communication model has been replaced by a more horizontal, participative, and receiver-oriented approach. The present vision is based fundamentally on interactive, participatory, and two-way communication at all levels of the society. A series of developments seem to have taken shape:

Table 12.1. Main Characteristics of the Modernization, Dependency, and Multiplicity Paradigm.

	MODERNIZATION	DEPENDENCY	MULTIPLICITY
PERIOD ORIGINS	1940-1960 Western neo-liberalism Keynes - functionalism behaviorism	1960-1980 Latin-American neo-marxism - structuralism	since 1980 diverse origins postmodernism - anthropology - psychoanalysis - pedagogy
LEVEL OF ANALYSIS	Nation-State	International: Center-Periphery	Multidimensional: Interdependency
CAUSE PROBLEM	INTERNAL (traditional society)	EXTERNAL (First World)	INTERNAL & EXTERNAL
	ECONOMIC VARIABLES	ECONOMIC & POLITICAL VARIABLES	CULTURAL VARIABLES
EMPHASIS ON ECONOMIC	Endless growth in linear stages (Rostow) - capital intensive - GNP	development & underdevelopment (Frank) global exploitation	end of growth - world system analysis - coupling of modes of production -
SOCIOCULTURAL	dualism (traditional-modern) - structural differentiation - functional specialization - socio-psychology - harmony model	class struggle - holism - subjectivism conflict model - regional contradictions	new social movements - empowerment - participation - ecology - culture normative approach
POLITICAL	Western democratic system -	Third World elitism -	participatory democracy
TECHNOLOGICAL	ethnocentric Technology Transfer - value free technological determinism	Technology creates dependency	

T
H
E
O
R
Y

Table 12.1. Main Characteristics of the Modernization, Dependency, and Multiplicity Paradigm (con't).

		MODERNIZATION	DEPENDENCY	MULTIPLICITY
T H E O R Y	COMMUNICATION		cultural imperialism/synchronization - institutional & structural constraints - professional values - imbalance of flow and content	ideology & culture - modes of communication / cultural identity - participatory communication / receiver oriented - exchange of meanings
	SCHOLARS		Beltran - Bordenave - Hamelink - Mattelart - Schiller - Somavia	Barbero - Dissanayake - White
RESEARCH	METHODOLOGY ASSUMPTIONS		Quantitative + Qualitative quantity equals quality -	Quantitative + Qualitative + Participatory contextual analysis - participatory observation
POLICIES	COMMUNALITIES "SOLUTION" COMING		TOP DOWN FROM "INSIDE" (THIRD WORLD)	BOTTOM UP NO UNIVERSAL MODEL AVAILABLE
	INTERNAL Domestic EXTERNAL International		INTEGRATION Implicit DISSOCIATION/SELF-RELIANCE Explicit	DISSOCIATION Explicit SELECTIVE PARTICIPATION Explicit
	PRINCIPLES NORMATIVE MEDIA THEORIES		FREE AND BALANCED FLOW media dependency theory authoritarian/marxist-leninist	RIGHT TO COMMUNICATE democratic-participatory theory

1. *The growth of a deeper understanding of the nature of communication itself:* Early models in the 1950s and 1960s saw the communication process simply as a message going from a sender to a receiver (that is, Laswell's classic S-M-R model). The emphasis was mainly sender- and media-centric; the stress was on the freedom of the press, the absence of censorship, and so on. Since the 1970s, however, communication has become more receiver- and message-centric. The emphasis is more on the process of communication (i.e., the exchange of meaning) and on the significance of this process (i.e., the social relationships created by communication and the social institutions and context that result from such relationships).

2. *A new understanding of communication as a two-way process:* The "oligarchic" view of communication implied that freedom of information was a one-way right from a higher to a lower level, from the Center to the Periphery, from an institution to an individual, from a communication-rich nation to a communication-poor one, and so on. Today, the interactive nature of communication is increasingly recognized. It is seen as fundamentally two-way rather than one-way, interactive and participatory rather than linear.

3. *A new understanding of culture:* The cultural perspective has become central to the debate on communication for development. Consequently, it has moved away from a more traditional mechanistic approach that emphasized economic and materialistic criteria to a more multiple appreciation of holistic and complex perspectives.

4. *The trend toward participatory democracy:* The end of the colonial era has seen the rise of many independent states and the spread of democratic principles, even if only at the level of lip-service. Though often ignored in practice, democracy is honored in theory. The world's communication media are still largely controlled by governments or powerful private interests, but they are more attuned to and aware of democratic ideals than previously. At the same time, literacy levels have increased, and there has been a remarkable improvement in people's ability to handle and use communication technology. As a consequence, more and more people can use mass media and no longer be denied access to and participation in communication processes because of a lack of communication and technical skills.

5. *Recognition of the imbalance in communication resources:* The disparity in communication resources between different parts of the world is increasingly recognized as a cause for concern. As the Center nations

develop their resources, the gap between Center and Periphery becomes greater. The plea for a more balanced and equal distribution of communication resources can only be discussed in terms of power at national and international levels. The attempt by local power elites to totally control modern communication channels—press, broadcasting, education, and bureaucracy—no longer ensures control of all the communication networks in a given society. Nor does control of the mass media ensure support for the controlling forces, nor for any mobilization around their objectives, nor for the effective repression of opposition.

6. *The growing sense of globalization and cultural hybridization:* Perhaps the greatest impetus toward a new formulation of communication freedoms and the need for realistic communication policies and planning have come from the realization that the international flow of communication has become the main carrier of transnational cultural synchronization. This cultural synchronization can take place without perceptible dependent relationships.

7. *A new understanding of what is happening within the boundaries of the so-called nation-state:* One has to accept that "internal" and "external" factors inhibiting development do not exist independently of each other. Thus, in order to understand and develop a proper strategy one must have an understanding of the class relationships of any particular peripheral social formation and the ways in which these structures articulate with the Center on the one hand, and the producing classes in the Third World on the other. For example, to dismiss Third World ruling classes as mere puppets whose interests are always mechanically synonymous with those of the Center is to ignore the realities of a much more complex relationship. The very unevenness and contradictory nature of the capitalist development process necessarily produces a constantly changing relationship.

8. *Recognition of the 'impact' of communication technology:* Some communication systems (e.g., audio- and videotaping, copying, radio broadcasting) have become so cheap and simple that the rationale for regulating and controlling them centrally, as well as the ability to do so, is no longer relevant. However, other systems (e.g., satellites, remote sensing, transborder data flows) have become so expensive that they are beyond the means of smaller countries and may not be "suitable" for local environments.

9. *A new understanding towards an integration of distinct means of communication:* Modern mass media and alternate or parallel networks of folk

media or interpersonal communication channels are not mutually exclusive by definition. Contrary to the beliefs of diffusion theorists, they are
more effective if appropriately used in an integrated fashion, according
to the needs and constraints of the local context. The modern mass
media, having been mechanically transplanted from abroad into Third
World societies, enjoy varying and limited rates of penetration. They are
seldom truly integrated into institutional structures, as occurs in
Western societies. However, they can be effectively combined, provided
a functional division of labor is established between them and the limits
of the mass media are recognized.

10. *The recognition of dualistic or parallel communication structures:*
Governments or rulers are no longer able to operate effectively, to control, censor, or play the role of gatekeeper with regard to all communications networks at all times in a given society. Both alternate and parallel
networks, which may not always be active, often function through political, sociocultural, religious, or class structures or can be based on secular,
cultural, artistic, or folkloristic channels. These networks feature a highly
participatory character, high rates of credibility, and a strong organic
integration with other institutions deeply rooted in a given society.

It should be obvious by now that no all-embracing view on communication for development is being offered. No theory has achieved
and maintained explanatory dominance. Each of the three theoretical
perspectives still finds support among academics, policymakers, international organizations, and the general public. In general, adopted and
updated versions of the ideas on which the modernization theory is
built—economic growth, centralized planning, and the belief that underdevelopment is rooted in mainly internal causes that can be solved by
external (technological) "aid"—are still shared by many development
agencies and governments. A revitalized modernization perspective, in
which some of the errors of the past are acknowledged and efforts are
made to deal in new ways (as outlined in the multiplicity view), remains
the dominant perspective in practice, but becomes increasingly more difficult to defend in theory. Consequently, the diffusion model continues
to be adopted as the most important communication perspective. On the
other side, while the multiplicity theory and the participatory communication model are gaining ground in academic spheres, in practice they
are still looked on as a sympathetic though idealistic side-show.

Shifts in theory are the results of specific policy choices.
Political, economic, juridical, or ethical conditions often interfere with
the implementation of a policy. This applies to local situations no less
than to world problems in which solutions seem to be unattainable more

because of the political obstinacy of powerful organizations or governments than a lack of knowledge. As a consequence, every policy recommendation has also implications for the practice of the policy and
research process.

As argued, my sympathy is with the multiplicity perspective. In
contrast to the more economic and politically oriented policy options in
the modernization and dependency paradigms, the central idea in the
multiplicity paradigm is that there is no universal development model
and that development is an integral, multidimensional, and dialectic
process that can differ from society to society. This implies that the
development problem is a relative problem and that no one nation can
contend that it is "developed" in every respect. Consequently, I believe
that the scope and degree of inter(in)dependency must be studied in
relationship with more content-related qualitative aspects of the development problem. In other words, each society or community must
attempt to delineate its own strategy to development, based on its own
ecology and culture. Therefore, it should not attempt to blindly imitate
programs and strategies of other countries with totally different historical and cultural backgrounds. Rigid and general strategies for participation are neither possible nor desirable. It is not an innovative formula
that "experts" diffuse to the masses. It is a process that unfolds in each
unique situation, and to prescribe how that unfolding should occur is
not only counterproductive, it is often the antithesis of authentic participation. Authentic participation, though widely espoused in the literature, is not in everyone's interest. Such programs are not easily implemented, highly predictable, or readily controlled, nor do they lend themselves to quick name-enhancing results. Behavioral response to an
exogenous stimulus of the passive reception of messages from the elite is
not participation. Neither is it a strategy to make "target audiences" feel
more involved and therefore more acquiescent to manipulative agendas.
It is not a means to an end, but legitimate in its own right.

* * *

Even though participation and social development are mam-
moth, complex issues, we believe complexity that would be too overwhelming for one person to handle can be figured out by all of us
together. We will need a new kind of school; not a school for teaching
writing and arithmetic, but a school for problems. This type of "school"
necessitates a latitude for participation, for the appropriate attitudes and
structures on the part of exogenous personnel and institutions: a school
that gives people the opportunity to identify their problems, deal with
their problems, and learn from their problems. Analysis should begin at

the level of the people within their own experience and level of understanding. This ensures people's collective initiative and participation in the direct development process.

Trust can foster or inhibit communication and participation between and among all groups regardless of education, culture, social, or economic status. It is "an a priori requirement for dialogue . . . without this faith . . . dialogue is a farce which inevitably degenerates into paternalistic manipulation" (Freire, 1983:79). It may be more important to know about trust than about educational standards, pedagogical methods, media technology or communication benchmarks.

Trust is egalitarian. We may succumb to superiors and condescend to subordinates, but these are not manifestations of genuine trust. Freire (1983:53) contends those who do not trust others "will fail to initiate (or will abandon) dialogue, reflection and communication, and will fall into using slogans, communiques, monologues, and instructions." Trust is not manifest in positions or labels, but in persons. In contrasting the "professional" and rural world, Fuglesang (1982: 20) writes "a judgement of reality made by a technical expert is more trusted than a judgement by the village farmer. We disrespect the ideas and opinions of people who happen to have their knowledge from sources other than books."

If we do not trust, we deem others untrustworthy. But is that quality within them, or in our own attitudes of insecurity and aspirations of superiority? More often than not, it may be the latter. Again, to the extent we trust, we are equals. We often do not trust those we want and are socialized to feel above, those "lower on the ladder."

We erect elaborate status symbols, orate eloquent speeches, and conduct meetings with much pomp and formality, all in the name of credibility and integrity. Yet it often seems more akin to an injudicious pageant of unbridled egos. In promoting "expertise," trust is destroyed. A fundamental distrust therefore often exists on the part of the officials, which is manifested in their opinions and actions.

Hence, participatory research and planning requires, first of all, changes in the thinking of development workers and policymakers themselves. The needles, targets, and audiences of communication and development models, combined with self-righteousness, titles, and insecurities, and perhaps sprinkled with a dash of misdirected benevolence, often renders "experts" a bit too verbose and pushy. Perhaps this is because it requires much more imagination, preparation, and hard work to have dialogical learning. It is far easier to prepare and give lectures.

There is possibly a valid reason why we have two ears, but only one mouth. Communication between people thrives not on the ability to talk fast, but the ability to listen well. People are "voiceless" not because they have nothing to say, but because nobody cares to listen to them. In this perspective it is legitimate to say that development begins with listening. It is so simple and yet we fail often because of an egocentric attitude. For instance, Fuglesang and Chandler (1987: 3) maintain that in the oral culture of the Massai "no one dare talk before learning the art of listening. Perhaps the best advice to the modern development communicators is to shut up for awhile." Authentic listening fosters trust much more than incessant talking. Participation, which necessitates listening, and moreover, trust, will help reduce the social distance between government leaders and villagers as well as facilitate a more equitable exchange of ideas, knowledge, and experiences. However, the need to listen is not limited to the local people. It must involve the governments as well as the citizens, the poor as well as the rich, and the planners and administrators as well as their "targets." This is not to imply that lack of trust is limited to the "experts." Trust, or the lack thereof, is reciprocal.

Participation can involve the redistribution of power at local and national levels. As such, it directly threatens those whose position and/or very existence depends on power and its exercise over others. Reactions to such threats are sometimes overt but most often are manifested as less visible, yet steady and continuous resistance.

Such barriers are not limited to government-populace relationships, but are prevalent both among bureaucratic organizations and communities as well. As a result of this, participation does not always entail cooperation or consensus. It can often mean conflict and usually poses a threat to extant structures. Because of this, the question can be raised if participation is appropriate in all contexts.

Attitude is paramount for the facilitator. He or she must truly believe the participants are not only capable, but are indeed the most qualified persons for the task at hand. Therefore, beyond class and organizational interests, perhaps the major obstacles to participation are large egos and self-righteousness. The most important expertise, technique, or methodology cannot be operationalized. What is needed is a change of attitude, the patient fostering of trust, and the ability to listen.

* * *

Finally, social scientists create robust structures in the knowledge that they may be standing on quicksand. And still they go on because this is the only way to create some order in disorder and to discern pattern, without denying the ultimate uncertainty that makes the study of human communication so challenging. Moreover, I would again argue that a combination of all the previously mentioned factors must consist not only of the formulation of knowledge but the influencing of those who can do more with knowledge than the researchers themselves because they have more power at their disposal. The political relevance of the multiplicity paradigm as a realistic counter-strategy has a chance to succeed only if an organic bond can be forged internationally between the grass-roots movement in the west and the Third World. In other words, this paradigm can demonstrate its reality value only in practice. Ultimately, this is the criterion against which every theory must be tested because, as Owen and Sutcliffe (1972: 12) stated, "to reveal the truth about the world is to lay a foundation for changing it."

List of Acronyms

ABU: Asia-Pacific Broadcasting Union
ACCE: African Council for Communication Education
ACCT: Agence de Cooperation Culturelle et Technique (Agency of Cultural and Technological Co-operation).
AED: Academy for Educational Development
AIBD: Asia-Pacific Institute for Broadcasting Development
ALAIC: Asociación Latinoamericana de Investigadores de la Comunicación (Latin American Association of Communication Researchers)
ALER: Asociación Latinoamericana de Educación Radiofonica (Latin American Association of Educative Radio Broadcasters)
AMARC: Association Mondiale des Radiodiffuseurs Communautaires (World Association of Community Radio Broadcasters)
AMIC: Asian Mass Communication Research and Information Center
APDC: Asian and Pacific Development Center
ASBU: Arab States Broadcasting Union

BRIDGES: Basic Research and Implementation in Developing Educational Systems

CANA: Caribbean News Agency
CARIMAC: Caribbean Institute of Mass Communication

CBD: Community-based Distribution System
CBU: Caribbean Broadcasting Union
CEBEMO: Catholic Agency for Development Aid
CEESTEM: Centro de Estudios para el Tercer Mundo
CIDA: Canadian International Development Agency
CIESPAL: Centro International de Estudios Superiores de Communicación
(International Centre for Graduate Communication studies for Latin
America)
COMNET: International Network of Documentation Centres on Communication
Research and Policies
CRS: Christian Relief Services

DAC/OECD: Development Assistance Committee of the Organization for
Economic Cooperation and Development
DANIDA: Danish International Development Agency
DCFRN: Developing Countries Farm Radio Network
DCR: Development Communication Report
DECU: Development and Educational Communication Unit
DSC: Development Support Communication
DSCS: Development Support Communication Service
DTCP: Development Training and Communication Planning

EBU: European Broadcasting Union
ECLA: Economic Commission for Latin America
ECOSOC: United Nations Economic and Social Council
EPI: Expanded Programme on Immunization
ESCAP : Economic and Social Commission for Asia and the Pacific of the United
Nations

FAO: Food and Agriculture Organisation of the United Nations
FELAFACS: Federación Latinoamericana de Facultades de Comunicación (Latin-
American Federation of Communication Faculties)
FES: Friedrich Ebert Stiftung
FIEJ: Féderation Internationale des Editeurs de Journeaux et Publications
FNS: Friedrich Neumann Stiftung

HSS: Hans Seidel Stiftung

IAMCR: International Association for Media and Communication Research
IAPA: Inter-American Press Association
ICA: International Communication Association
ICDR: Institute for Communication Development and Research
IDRC: International Development Research Centre
IEC: Information Education, and Communication
IEM: Information, Education and Motivation
IFAD: International Fund for Agricultural Development
IFDA: International Foundation for Development Alternatives

IFJ: International Federation of Journalists
IIC: International Institute of Communications
ILET: Instituto Latinoamericana de Estudios Transnacionales
ILO: International Labour Organisation
IMF: International Monetary fund
ININCO: Instituto de Investigaciones de la Comunicacion de la Universidad Central de Venezuela
INODEP: Institut pour le Développement des Peuples
INTELSAT: International Communications Satellite Organisation
IOJ: International Organisation of Journalists
IRI: Interactive Radio Instruction
IPAL: Instituto para America Latina (Institute for Latin America)
IPDC: International Programme for the Development of Communication
IPI: International Press Institute
IPS: Inter Press Service
ISRO: Indian Space Research Organization
ITU: International Telecommunication Union
IT: Information Technology

KAP: Knowledge, Attitudes and Practice
KAS: Konrad Adenauer Stiftung
KCP: Kheda Communications Project

MCR: Mahaweli Community Radio
MMHP: Mass Media and Health Practices

NANAP: Non-Aligned News Agencies Pool
NFB: National Film Board
NGO: Non-governmental organisation
NIEO: New International Economic Order
NIIO: New International Information Order
NORAD: Norwegian Agency for Development Cooperation
NTC: New Communication Technologies
NWICO: New World Information and Communication Order

OAS: Organization of American States
OAU: Organisation of African Unity
ODA: Overseas Development Assistance
OECD: Organisation for Economic Cooperation and Development
ORT: Oral Rehydration Therapy

PANA: Panafrican News Agency
PHRD: Population and Human Resources Development
PPP: Participatory People Projects
PR: Participatory Research
PROA: Latin-American association of Group Media

RAPID: Resources for the Awareness of Population Impacts on Development
RCT: Rural Communication Team
RCU: Regional Communication Unit
R&D: Research and Development
RNTC: Radio Nederland Training Centre
RSP: Rural Satellite Project

SAARC: South Asian Association for Regional Coorperation
SID: Society for International Development
SIDA: Swedish International Development Authority
SITE: Satellite Instructional Television Experiment

TCDC: Technical Cooperation between Developing Countries
TDF: Trans-border Data Flow
TDRI: Thailand Development Research Institute
TELESAT: Telecommunications Satellite
TSS: Technical Support Services

UCI: Universal Child Immunisation
UNCTAD: United Nations Conference on Trade and Development
UNDA: Catholic Association of Broadcasting Stations
UNDP: United Nations Development Programme
UNFPA: United Nations Population Fund
UNICEF: United Nations Children's Emergency Fund
UNIDO: United Nations Industrial Development Organisation
UNESCO: United Nations Educational, Scientific and Cultural Organisation
UN: United Nations
UNU: United Nations University
UPU: Universal Postal Union
URTNA: Union of National Radio and Television organisations of Africa
USAID: United States Agency for International Development

WACC: World Association for Christian Communication
WANAD: West and Central Africa News Agencies Development
WARC: World Administrative Radio Conference
WCARRD: World Conference on Agrarian Reform and Rural Development
WFS: Women's Features Service
WHO: World Health Organisation
WIF: Worldview International Foundation
WIPO: World Intellectual Property Organisation
WPFC: World Press Freedom Committee

Bibliography

ABEL, E. (1979). *Communication for an Independent, Pluralistic World*, Unesco, Paris.

ABEL, E. (1985). "International communication: A new order?", ROGERS, E.M. & BALLE, F. (eds.), *The Media Revolution in America and Western Europe*, Ablex, Norwood.

ADDO, H. (1985). "Beyond Eurocentricity: Transformation and transformational responsibility", ADDO, H., AMIN, S., ASENIERO, G. et al. (eds.), *Development as Social Transformation. Reflections on the Global Problematique*, Hodder and Stoughton, London.

ADELMAN, I. & C. T. MORRIS (1967). *Society, Politics and Economic Development*, John Hopkins Press, Baltimore.

ADKINS, G. (1985). "Commercial television: Blessing or blight? What commercial TV can mean to a country"., *Media Asia, Singapore*, 12(1).

AGUIRRE-BIANCHI, C. & G. HEDEBRO (1980). *Another Information: The Next Step After the MacBride Report*, Paper IAMCR Conference, Caracas, August.

ALBROW, M. & E. KING (eds.) (1990). *Globalization, Knowledge and Society*, Sage, London.

ALDER, P. (1985). "Beyond cultural identity: Reflections on cultural and intercultural Man", SAMOVAR, L. & PORTER, R. (eds.), *Intercultural Communication: A Reader*, Wadsworth, Belmont, CA.

ALGER, C. (1984). "Bridging the micro and the macro in international relations research", *Alternatives*, 10(3).

ALISJAHBANA, S.T. (1974). *Values as Integrating Forces in Personality, Society, and Culture*, University of Malaya Press, Kuala Lumpur.

ALMOND, G. & J. COLEMAN (eds.) (1960). *The Politics of the Developing Areas*, Princeton University Press, Princeton.

AMBROSE, S. (1983). *Rise to Globalism. American Foreign Policy Since 1938*, Penguin, Harmondsworth.

AMIN, S. (1979). *Classe et Nation dans L'histoire et la Crise Contemporaine* [Class and nation in history and the current crisis], Minuit, Paris.

AMIN, S. (1985). "A propos the 'green' movements", ADDO, H., AMIN, S., ASE-NIERO, G. et al. (eds.), *Development as Social Transformation: Reflections on the Global Problematique*, Hodder and Stoughton, London.

AMIT-TALAI, V. & H. WULFF (eds.) (1995). *Youth Cultures: A Cross-cultural Perspective*, Routledge, London.

ANDERSON, B. (1983). *Imagined Communities: Reflections on the Origin and Spread of Nationalism*, Verso, London.

ANDERSON, J. & T. MEYER (1988). *Mediated Communication: A Social Action Perspective*, Sage, Newbury Park.

ANDERSON, J. (ed.) (1985). *In the Mirror: Literature and Politics in the American Era*, DK Books, Bangkok.

ANG, I. (1996). *Living Room Wars: Rethinking Media Audiences for a Postmodern World*, Routledge, London.

ARCHER, M. (1988). *Culture and Agency: The Place of Culture in Social Theory*, Cambridge University Press, Cambridge.

ARGYRIS, C., PUTNAM, R. & D. SMITH. (1985). *Action Science*, Jossey Bass, San Francisco.

ARIYARATNE, A. (1986). "Asian values as a basis for Asian development", KORTEN, D. (ed.), *Community Management: Asian Experience and Perspectives*, Kumarian Press, West Hartford.

ASANTE, M.K. & K. L. KIM (1984). "Realizing a New Information Order : Alternative strategies", *Journal of Communication*, 34(3).

BAGGULEY, P. (1992). "Social change, the middle class and the emergence of 'new social movements': A critical analysis", *The Sociological Review*, 40(1), February, 26-48.

BALLE, F. (1985). "The communication revolution and freedom of expression redefined", ROGERS, E.M. & BALLE, F. (eds.), *The Media Revolution in America & Western Europe*, Ablex, Norwood.

BANERJEE, D. (ed.) (1985). *Marxian Theory and the Third World*, Sage, New Delhi.

BANGSAPAN, S. (1984, May 3). "A bleak future for good films", *Far Eastern Economic Review*, Hong Kong.

BARAN, P. (1957). *The Political Economy of Growth*, Monthly Review Press, New York.

BARENDT, E. (1985). *Freedom of Speech*, Clarendon Press, Oxford.

BARTON, D.L. & E. M. ROGERS (1981). *Horizontal Diffusion of Innovations. An Alternative Paradigm to the Classical Diffusion Model*, Massachusetts Institute of Technology, Cambridge.

BAUMGARTNER, M.P. (1984). "Social control from below", BLACK D. (ed.), *Toward a General Theory of Social Control*, Academic Press, Orlando.

BBS Seventh Plan Proposal 1992-1997, BBS, Thimpu.

BECK, U. (1986). *Risikogesellschaft: Auf dem Weg in eine andere Moderne* [Risk society. On the road to another modernization], Suhrkamp, Frankfurt am Main.

BECK U., GIDDENS, A. & S. LASH (1994). *Reflexive Modernization: Politics, Tradition and Aesthetics in the Modern Social Order*, Polity Press, Cambridge.

BECKER, J., HEDEBRO, G. & L. PALDAN (eds.) (1986). *Communication and Domination*, Ablex, Norwood.

BELTRAN L.R. (1976). *TV Etchings in the Minds of Latin Americans: Conservatism, Materialism and Conformism*, Paper IAMCR Conference, Leicester, September.

BELTRAN, L.R. (1993). "Communication for development in Latin America: A forty years appraisal", NOSTBAKKEN, D. & MORROW, C. (eds.), *Cultural Expression in the Global Village*, Southbound, Penang.

BERGER, P. & LUCKMANN, T. (1967). *The Social Construction of Reality: A Treatise in the Sociology of Knowledge*, Doubleday, New York.

BERQUE, P., FOY, E. & B. GIRARD (1993). *La Passion Radio. 23 Expériences de Radio Participative et Communautaire á Travers le Monde* [A passion for radio. 23 experiments of participatory and community radios around the world], Syros, Paris.

BERRIGAN, F. (1977), *Access: Some Western Models of Community Media*, UNESCO, Paris.

BERRIGAN, F. (1979), *Community Communications: The Role of Community Media in Development*, UNESCO, Paris.

BETZ, M., McGOWAN, P. & R. WIGAND (eds.) (1984). *Appropriate Technology: Choice and Development*, Duke Press Policy Studies, Durham.

BLAIR, H. (1981). *The Political Economy of Participation in Local Development Programs: Short Term Impasse and Long Term Change in South Asia and the United States from the 1950's to the 1970's*. Rural Development Committee, Center for International Studies, Cornell University, Ithaca.

BLOMSTROM, M. & B. HETTNE (1984). *Development Theory in Transition. The Dependency Debate and Beyond*, Zed, London.

BOAFO, K. (1989). *Communication and Culture: African Perspectives*, ACCE, Nairobi.

BOEREN A. (1994), *In other words . . . The Cultural Dimension of Communication for Development*, CESO, The Hague.

BOGAERT, M.V.D., BHAGAT, S. N.B. BAM. (1981). "Participatory evaluation of an adult education programme", in FERNANDES, W. & TANDON, R. (eds.), *Participatory Research and Evaluation: Experiments in Research as a Process of Liberation*, Indian Social Institute, New Delhi.

BOND M. H. (1991). *Beyond the Chinese Face. Insights from Psychology*, Oxford University Press, Hong Kong.

BOONYAKETMALA, B. (1982). "Influence of the transnational media in Thailand", GUBACK, T. & VARIS, T. (eds.), *Transnational Communication and Cultural Industries*, UNESCO, Paris.

BOONYAKETMALA, B. (1985). *The political economy of cultural dominance, dependence and disengagement: The transnationalized film industry in Thailand (1897-*

1984), PhD Dissertation, Department of Political Science, University of Hawaii, Honolulu.

BOOTH D. (ed.) (1994). *Rethinking Social Development: Theory, Research & Practice*, Longman, London.

BORDENAVE, J.D. & H. DE CARVALHO (1978). *Planificacion y Comunicacion* [Planification and communication], CIESPAL, Quito.

BORDENAVE J.D. (1977). *Communication and Rural Development*, UNESCO, Paris.

BORDENAVE, J.D. (1994). "Participative communication as a part of building the participative society", WHITE, S., NAIR, K.S., & J. ASCROFT (eds.), *Participatory Communication. Working for Change and Development*, Sage, New Delhi.

BOUDON R. (1991). *Theories of Social Change*, Polity Press, Cambridge.

BOURDIEU, P. (1979). *La Distinction: Critique Sociale du Jugement* [The distinction: Social critique of judgment], Minuit, Paris.

BOURDIEU, P. (1980). *Questions de Sociologie* [Sociological Questions], Minuit, Paris.

BOURDIEU P. (1981). *Ce que Parler veut Dire: l'économie des échanges Linguistiques* [What talking means: The economy of linguistic exchanges], Fayard, Paris.

BOUTROS-GHALI, B. (1995). *An Agenda for Development*, United Nations, New York.

BOYD D., & J. STRAUBHAAR (1985). "Developmental impact of the home video cassette recorder on Third World countries", *Journal of Broadcasting & Electronic Media*, 29(1), Winter.

BOYD, D., STRAUBHAAR, J. & J. LENT (1989). *Videocasette Recorders in the Third World*, Longman, New York.

BOYD-BARRETT, O. (1977). "Media imperialism : Towards an international framework for the analysis of media systems", CURRAN, J., GUREVITCH, M. & J. WOOLLACOTT (eds.), *Mass Communication and Society*, Arnold, London.

BOYD-BARRETT, O. (1982). "Cultural dependency and the mass media", GUREVITCH, M., BENNETT, T., CURRAN, J. & J. WOOLLACOTT (eds.), *Culture, Society and the Media*, Methuen, London.

BRANDT, T. (December 2-22, 1990). *Report on Radio Production Training*, DaniCom, Copenhagen.

BRANDT, W. (ed.) (1980). *North-South: A Programme for Survival*, Pan Books, London.

BRESNAHAN, M., CAI, D. & A. RIVERS (1994). "Saying no in Chinese and English: Cultural similarities and differences in strategies of refusal", *Asian Journal of Communication, Singapore*, 4(1).

BROWN, A. (1979). *The Dialectics of Mass Communication in National Transformation*, Paper presented at the Conference on Human Development Models in Action, Mogadishu, June.

BRUMMELHUIS, TEN H. & J. KEMP (eds.) (1984). *Strategies and Structures in Thai Society*, Antropologisch-Sociologisch Centrum, Amsterdam.

BRYMAN, A. (1984). "The debate about quantitative and qualitative research: A question of method or epistemology?", *The British Journal of Sociology*, 35(1), 75-92.

BRYMAN, A. & R. BURGESS (eds.) (1994). *Analyzing Qualtative Data*, Routledge, London.

BUDDHADASA, B. (1986). *Dhammic Socialism*, Thai Interreligious Commission for Development, Bangkok.

BUNBANGKORN, S. (1983). "Thailand", ATAL, Y. (ed.), *Dynamics of Nation-Building* (with particular reference to the role of communication), UNESCO, Bangkok.

BUNZLOVA A. (1986). "Some thoughts about the New International Information Order", *The Democratic Journalist, Prague*, 33(9).

BURKE, K. (1968). *Language as Symbolic Action*, University of California Press, Berkeley.

BURUMA, I. (1989). *God's Dust: A Modern Asian Journey*, Jonathan Cape, London.

CABEZAS, A., ROSARIO, A., LLORENTE, P. G., CONTRERAS, E. & J. ROS (1982). *La Emisora Popular* [The popular radio], Editora Andina, Quito.

CABRAL, A. (1980). *Unité de Lutte* [Unity in struggle], Maspero, Paris.

CAMILO, M., MATA, M.C. & J. SERVAES (1990). *Autoevaluacion de Radio Enriquillo* [Self-evaluation of Radio Enriquillo], Cebemo, Oegstgeest.

CAMPBELL, J. (1988). *The Power of Myths*, Doubleday, Garden City, NY.

CAMRE, H., GIESE, S. et al. (1982). *Bridging the Gap: Towards a Policy and Strategy for Film and Television Training in the Developing World*, The Danish National Film School, Copenhagen.

CANCLINI, N.G. (1982). *Las Culturas Populares en el Capitalismo* [Popular cultures in capitalism], Nueva Imagen, Mexico.

CANCLINI, N.G. (1993). *Transforming Modernity: Popular Culture in Mexico*, University of Texas Press, Austin.

CANINI, G. (1994). "Public participation in decision-making in science and technology", *Communicatio*, 20(1), 15-25.

CARDOSO, F.H., & E. FALETTO (1969). *Dependencia y Desarrollo en América Latina* [Dependency and development in Latin America], Siglo XXI, Mexico.

CAREY J. (ed.) (1988). *Media, Myths and Narratives: Television and the Press*, Sage, London.

CASMIR, F. (ed.) (1991). *Communication in Development*, Ablex, Norwood.

CHALOEMTIARANA, T. (1983). *Kanmang, Rabop Phokhun Uppatham bp Phadetkan* [Thailand, the politics of despotic paternalism], Thammasat University, Bangkok. (in Thai)

CHAMARIK, S. (1993). *Democracy and Development: A Cultural Perspective*, Local Development Institute, Bangkok.

CHANTANA, P., & S. WUN GAEO (1985). "Participatory research and rural development in Thailand", FARMER'S ASSISTANCE BOARD (ed.), *Participatory Research: Response to Asian People's Struggle for Social Transformation*, Farmer's Assistance Board, Manila.

CHAROENSIN-O-LARN, C. (1988). *Understanding Postwar Reformism in Thailand*, Editions Duang Kamol, Bangkok.

CHESNAUX, J. (1983). *De la Modernité* [About modernity]. Maspero, Paris.

CHEUNG, Y. (1996), "Gezinsplanningscampagnes in China", SERVAES, J. & R. LIE (eds.), *Communicatie in Sociale Verandering: Een Culturalistisch Perspectief* [Family planning campaigns in China) (Communication in Social Change. A culturalist perspective], ACCO, Louvain.

CHILCOTE, R., & D. JOHNSON (eds.) (1983). *Theories of Development: Mode of Production or Dependency?*, Sage, Beverly Hills.

CHOUDHARY, B.N., & C. PRASAD (1986). "Predictive values of the selected factors in contributing towards the variation in the effectiveness of communication", *Interaction*, 4(1-2).

CHRISTIANS, C., & J. CAREY (1981). "The logic and aims of qualitative research", STEMPEL, G. & WESTLEY, B. (eds.), *Research Methods in Mass Communication*, Prentice Hall, Englewood Cliffs.

CIESPAL (1983). *Comunicacion Popular Educativa* [Educative popular communication], CIESPAL, Quito.

CINCO (1987). *Comunicacion Dominante y Comunicacion Alternativa en Bolivia* [Dominant communication and alternative communication in Bolivia], Cinco/IDRC, La Paz.

CLARKE, J., CRITCHER, C., & R. JOHNSON (eds.) (1979). *Working Class Culture: Studies in History and Theory*, Hutchinson, London.

COMMISSION ON GLOBAL GOVERNANCE (1995). *Our Global Neigbourhood*, Oxford University Press, New York.

CONTRERAS, E. (1980), "Brazil and Guatemala: Communications, rural modernity and structural constraints", McANANY, E. (ed.), *Communications in the Rural Third World: The role of Information in Development*, Praeger, New York.

CONTRERAS, E. (1993). *Evaluación de Proyectos de Comunicación* [Evaluation of communication projects], CIESPAL, Quito.

COOPER, R., & N. Cooper (1982). *Culture Shock!*, Times Books, Singapore.

COQUERY-VIDROVITCH, C. & S. NEDELEC (eds.) (1991). *Tiers Monde: L'informel en Question* [The Third World: The informal sector under question), l'Harmattan, Paris.

CRITICOS, C. (ed.) (1989). *Experiential Learning in Formal & Non-formal Education*, University of Natal, Durban.

CRUSH, J. (ed.) (1995). *Power of Development*, Routledge, London.

CUEVA, A. (1977). *El Desarrollo de Capitalismo en America Latina* [The development of capitalism in Latin America], Siglo XXI, Mexico. .

CURRY, J.L., & J. R. DASSIN (eds.) (1982). *Press Control Around the World*, Praeger, New York.

D'ABREO, D. (1981), "Training for participatory evaluation." in FERNANDES, W. & TANDON, R. (eds.) *Participatory Research and Evaluation: Experiments in Research as a Process of Liberation*, Indian Social Institute, New Delhi.

D'ARCY J. (1969). "Direct broadcast satellites and the right to communicate", *EBU-Review*, 118.

DAGNINO, E. (1980). "Cultural and ideological dependence : Building a theoretical framework", KUMAR, K. (ed.), *Transnational Enterprises: Their Impact on Third World Societies and Cultures*, Westview, Boulder.

DAHLGREN, P. (1995). *Television and the Public Sphere: Citizenship, Democracy and the Media*, Sage, London.

DAVIS, J. (1993). *Poles Apart? Contextualising the Gospel*, Kanok Bannasan, Bangkok.

DE LA COURT, T. (1990). *Beyond Brundtland: Green Development in the 1990s*, Zed Books, London.

DE SCHUTTER, A. (1983). *Investigacion Participativa: Una Opcion Metodologica Para la Educacion de Adultos*, CREFAL, Mexico.

DE SOUSA, E. (1974). *Portuguese Colonialism in Africa*, UNESCO, Paris.

DE VILLERS, G. (ed.) (1992). "Le pauvre, le hors la loi, le métis: La question de l'économie informelle en Afrique" [The poor and illegal: The question of the informal sector in Africa], *Les Cahiers du CEDAF-ASDOC Studies, 6*.

DEMAS, W.G. (1953). "The development of backward areas", *Social and Economic Studies, 2*(2-3).

DERVIN, B. (1980). "Communication gaps and inequities. Moving toward a reconceptualization", DERVIN, B. & VOIGT, M. (eds.), *Progress in Communication Sciences*, Ablex, Norwood.

DERVIN B. (1982). "Citizen access as an information equity issue", SCHEMENT J.R., GUTIERREZ, F., & M. SIRBU (eds.), *Telecommunications Policy Handbook*, Praeger, New York.

DHILLON, H.S., & L. PHILIP (1991). *Health Promotion in Developing Countries*, WHO, Geneva.

DISKUL, S. (1986). *Art in Thailand: A Brief History*, Amarin Press, Bangkok

DISSANAYAKE, W., & A.R. SAID (eds.) (1983). *Communications Research and Cultural Values*, AMIC, Singapore.

DISSANAYAKE, W. (ed.) (1994). *Colonialism and Nationalism in Asian Cinema*, Indiana University Press, Bloomington.

DISSANAYAKE, W. (1986). "The need for the study of Asian approaches to communication," *Media Asia, 13*(1).

DOS SANTOS, T. (1970). "The structure of dependency", *American Economic Review, 60*(21), May.

DOWMUNT, T. (ed.) (1993). *Channels of Resistance: Global Television and Local Empowerment*, BFI Publishing, London.

DROR, Y. (1973). "The planning process: A facet design", FALUDI, A. (ed.), *A Reader in Planning Theory*, Pergamon, Oxford.

EKINS, P. (1992). *A New World Order: Grassroots Movements for Global Change*, Routledge, London.

ESCOBAR, A. (1994). *Encountering Development: The Making and Unmaking of the Third World*, Princeton University Press, Princeton.

ESCOBAR, A., & S. ALVAREZ (eds.) (1992). *The Making of Social Movements in Latin America: Identity, Strategy and Democracy*, Westview, San Francisco.

ESTEVA, G. (1987). "Regenerating people's space", *Alternatives, 12*, 125-152.

EURICH, C. (1980). *Kommunikative Partizipation und Partizipative Komunikationsforschung* [Participatory communication and participatory communication research], Rita G. Fischer Verlag, Frankfurt.

EWEN, S. (1983). "The implications of empiricism", *Journal of Communication, 33*(3).

EYERMAN, R., & A. JAMISON (1991). *Social Movements: A Cognitive Approach*, Pennsylvania State Press, University Park.

FALS BORDA, O. & H. A. RAHMAN (eds.) (1991). *Action and Knowledge: Breaking the Monopoly with Participatory Action Research*, Intermediate Technology Pubs, London.

FALS BORDA, O. (ed.) (1985). *The Challenge of Social Change*, Sage, London.

FALS BORDA, O. (1988). *Knowledge and People's Power: Lessons with Peasants in Nicaragua, Mexico, and Colombia*. New Delhi: Indian Social Institute.

FARMERS ASSISTANCE BOARD (ed.) (1985). *Participatory Research: Response to Asian's People's Struggle for Social Transformation*, Farmers Assistance Board, Manila.

FARRINGTON, J. (1988). "Farmer participatory research: Editorial introduction", *Experimental Agriculture*, 24.

FAULLIMMEL, J. (1987, August 7), "Research and development: Cooperation needed between academics, private sector", *The Nation*, pp. 4-5.

FAY, B. (1987). *Critical Social Science*, Cornell University Press, Ithaca.

FERNANDES, W., & R. TANDON (eds.) (1981). *Participatory Research and Research and Evaluation: Experiment in Research as a Process of Liberation*, Indian Social Institute, New Delhi.

FISCHER, D. (1982). *The Right to Communicate: A Status Report*, Unesco, Paris.

FISCHER, D., & L.S. HARMS (eds.) (1983). *The Right to Communicate: A New Human Right*, Boole Press, Dublin.

FORESTER, J. (1989). *Planning in the Face of Power*, University of California Press, Berkeley.

FORESTER, J. (1992). "Critical ethnography: On fieldwork in a Habermasian way", ALVESSON M. & WILLMOTT H. (eds.), *Critical Management Studies*, Sage, London.

FORESTER, J. (1993). *Critical Theory, Public Policy and Planning Practice*, State University of New York Press, Albany.

FORESTER, J. (ed.) (1988). *Critical Theory and Public Life*, MIT Press, Cambridge.

FOUCAULT, M. (1977). *Language, Counter-Memory, Practice*, Cornell University Press, Ithaca.

FOUCAULT, M. (1980). *Power/Knowledge: Selected Interviews and Other Writings 1972-1977*, The Harvester Press, Brighton.

FOX, E. (1988). *Media and Politics in Latin America. The Struggle for Democracy*, Sage, London.

FRANK, A.G. (1969). *Latin America : Underdevelopment or Revolution*, Monthly Review Press, New York.

FREIRE, P. (1970a). "Cultural action and conscientization", *Harvard Educational Review*, 40(3).

FREIRE, P. (1970b). *Cultural Action for Freedom*, Penguin, Harmondsworth.

FREIRE, P. (1973). *Extension o Comunicacion? La Concientizacion en el Medio Rural* [Extension or communication? Conscientization in the rural sector], Siglo XXI, Mexico.

FREIRE, P. (1974). *Education for Critical Consciousness*, Seabury Press, New York.

FREIRE, P. (1983). *Pedagogy of the Oppressed*, Seabury Press, New York.

FREIRE, P. (1993). "Foreword", McLAREN, P. & LEONARD, P. (eds.), *Paulo Freire. A Critical Encounter*, Routledge, London.

FREIRE, P. (1994). *Pedagogy of Hope. Reliving Pedagogy of the Oppressed*, Continuum, New York.

FREUD, S. (1951). *Civilization and its Discontents*, Norton, New York.

FRIBERG, M., & B. HETTNE (1985). *The Greening of the World: Development as Social Transformation*, Westview, Boulder.

FRIEDMAN, J. (1988). "From social to political power: Collective self-empowerment and social change", *Journal für Entwicklungspolitik*, 4(2), 63-74.

FRIEDMAN, J. (1994). *Cultural Identity & Global Process*, Sage, London.

FRIEDMANN, J. (1992). *Empowerment: The Politics of Alternative Development*, Cambridge, Blackwell.

FUGLESANG, A., & D. CHANDLER (1987). *The Paradigm of Communication in Development: From Knowledge Transfer to Community Participation—Lessons from the Grameen Bank*, Bangladesh, FAO, Rome.

FUGLESANG, A. (1982). *About Understanding: Ideas and Observations on Cross-Cultural Communication*, The Dag Hammarskjøld Foundation, Uppsala.

FUGLESANG, A. (1984). "The myth of people's ignorance", *Development Dialogue, Uppsala*, 1(2).

GALLAGHER, M., & L. QUINDOZA-SANTIAGO (eds.) (1994). *Women Empowering Communication*, WACC-Isis International, London-Manila.

GALTUNG, J. (1980). *The True Worlds. A Transnational Perspective*, Free Press, New York.

GALTUNG J., O'BRIEN, P. & R. PREISWERK (eds.) (1980). *Self-Reliance. A Strategy For Development*, Bogle-L'Ouverture, London.

GALTUNG, J. (1994). *Human Rights in Another Key*. Cambridge: Polity Press.

GARCIA-ZAMOR, J. (ed.) (1985). *Public Participation in Development Planning and Management: Cases From Africa and Asia*, Westview, Boulder.

GEERTZ, C. (1973). *The Interpretation of Cultures*, Basic Books, New York.

GEERTZ C. (1983). *Local Knowledge: Further Essays in Interpretive Anthropology*, Basic Books, New York.

GERBNER, G., MOWLANA, H., & K. NORDENSTRENG (eds) (1993). *The Global Media Debate. Its Rise, Fall, and Renewal*, Norwood, Ablex

GIDDENS, A. (1976). *New Rules of Sociological Method*, Hutchinson, London.

GIDDENS, A. (1979). *Central Problems in Social Theory*, MacMillan, London.

GIDDENS, A. (1984). *The Constitution of Society: Outline of the Theory of Structuration*, University of California Press, Berkeley.

GIDDENS, A. (1991), *The Consequences of Modernity*, Polity Press, Cambridge.

GIRART, B. (ed.) (1992). Radio Apasionados. 21 Experiencias de Radio Comunitaria en el mundo, [Radios with a passion. 21 experiments of community radio in the world], AMARC, Montreal.

GIRLING, J. (1981). *Thailand: Society and Politics*, Cornell University Press, Ithaca.

GIRLING, J. (1984). "Hegemony and domination in Third World countries: A case study of Thailand", *Alternatives*, 10, Winter.

GOLDFARB, J. (1982). *On Cultural Freedom: An Exploration of Public Life in Poland and America*, University of Chicago Press, Chicago.

GOONASEKERA A. (1990). "Mass media campaigns for development: Some practical guidelines", *Journal of Development Communication, 1*(1), June, 47-54.

GORDON, D., & J. MERRILL (1988). *A Power Theory of Press Freedom*, Paper ICA Conference, New Orleans, May.

GOULET, D. (1971). *The Cruel Choice: A New Concept in the Theory of Development*, Atheneum, New York.

GOULET, D. (1977). "Development-experts: The one-eyed giant", *World Development, 8.*

GRAN, G. (1983). *Development by People. Citizen Construction of a Just World*, Praeger, New York.

GUNDER, F., & M. FUENTES (1988). "Nine theses on social movements", *IFDA Dossier, 63*, 27-44.

HABERMANN P., & G. DE FONTGALLAND (eds.) (1978). *Development Communication—Rhetoric and Reality*, AMIC, Singapore

HABERMAS, J. (1981). *Theorie des Kommunikativen Handelns: Vol. I: Handlungsrationalitat und Gesellschaftliche Rationalisierung, Vol. II: Zur Kritik der Funktionalistischen Vernunft* [Theory of Communicative Action], Suhrkamp, Frankfurt.

HABERMAS, J. (1985). *Der Philosophische Diskurs der Moderne. Zwolf Vorlesungen* [A philosophical discussion of modernity], Suhrkamp, Frankfurt.

HABERMAS, J. (1986). *Die neue Unubersichtlichkeit* [The new chaos], Suhrkamp, Frankfurt.

HABERMAS, J. (1988)., *Nach Metaphysisches Denken. Philisophische Aufsätze* [Toward metaphysic thinking. Philosophical explorations], Suhrkamp Verlag, Frankfurt. .

HACHTEN, W. (1981). *The World News Prism: Changing Media, Clashing Ideologies*, The Iowa State University Press, Ames.

HALL, E. (1973). *The Silent Language*, Doubleday, New York.

HALL, E. (1976). *Beyond Culture*, Doubleday, New York.

HALL, J., & M. NEITZ (1993). *Culture: Sociological Perspectives*, Prentice Hall, Englewood Cliffs.

HALL, S., & P. DU GAY (eds.) (1996). *Questions of Cultural Identity*, Sage, London.

HALL, S. (1985). "Signification, representation, ideology: Althusser and the post-structuralist debates", *Critical Studies in Mass Communication, 2*(2).

HALL S., HOBSON, D., LOWE, A., & P. WILLIS (eds) (1980). *Culture, Media, Language : Working Papers in Cultural Studies, 1972-79*, Hutchinson, London.

HALLINGER, P. (1994, November 21), "Challenge to think globally, act locally", *The Nation*, Bangkok, p. A4.

HALLORAN, J. D. (1981), "The context of mass communication research," in MCANANY, E., SCHNITMAN, J., & JANUS, N (eds.), *Communication and Social Structure: Critical Studies in Mass Media Research*, Praeger, New York.

HAMARSAA, S.,& K. EBBESEN (1992, June). *Management Training II. Development of Broadcasting in Bhutan*, DaniCom, Copenhagen.

HAMELINK, C. (ed.) (1977). *The Corporate Village*, IDOC, Rome.

HAMELINK, C. (ed.) (1980). *Communication in the Eighties: A Reader on the MacBride Report*, IDOC, Rome.

HAMELINK, C. (1981). *New Structures of International Communication. The Role of Research*, Institute of Social Studies, The Hague.

HAMELINK, C. (1982). *Finance and Information. A Study of Converging Interests*, Ablex, Norwood, NJ.

HAMELINK, C. (1983). *Cultural Autonomy in Global Communications: Planning National Information Policy*, Longman, New York.

HAMELINK, C. (1984). *Information Technology and the Third World*, Studentlitteratur, Lund.

HAMELINK, C. (1994a). *Trends in World Communication: On Disempowerment and Self-empowerment*, Southbound, Penang.

HAMELINK, C.J. (1994b). *The Politics of World Communication. A Human Rights Perspective*. London: Sage.

HAMILTON, J. (1990). *Entangling Alliances: How the Third World Shapes Our Lives*, Seven Locks Press, Washington.

HANCOCK, A. (1981). *Communication Planning for Development: An Operational Framework*, UNESCO, Paris.

HANCOCK, A. (ed.) (1984). *Technology Transfer and Communication*, UNESCO, Paris.

HANCOCK, A. (1992). *Communication Planning Revisited*, UNESCO, Paris.

HANNERZ, U. (1987). "The world in creolisation", *Africa*, 57(4), 546-559

HANNERZ, U. (1992). *Cultural Complexity: Studies in the Social Organization of Meaning*, Columbia University Press, New York.

HARMS, L.S., RICHSTAD, J., & K. KIE (eds.) (1977). *Right to Communicate: Collected Papers*, University Press of Hawaii, Honolulu.

HARRIS, M. (1980). *Cultural Materialism: The Struggle for a Science of Culture*, Vintage, New York.

HARRISON, D. (1988). *The Sociology of Modernization and Development*, Unwin Hyman, London.

HARRISON, R. (1994), "Introduction: Sidaoru'ang and the radical tradition in contemporary Thai fiction", SIDAORU'ANG, *A Drop of Glass and Other Stories*, Editions Duang Kamol, Bangkok.

HARTWELL S., ARNALDO, C., & G. BOSTON (June 1992). *Computerization of BBS News and Archive Procedures*, UNESCO, Paris.

HEDEBRO, G. (1982). *Communication and Social Change in Developing Countries: A Critical View*, Iowa State University Press, Ames.

HEIM, F., RABIBHADANA, A., & C. PINTHONG (1983). *How To Work With Farmers: A Manual for Field Workers*, Research and Development Institute, Khon Kaen University, Khon Kaen.

HELD, D. (1987). *Models of Democracy*, Stanford University Press, Stanford.

HELD, D. (ed.) (1993). *Prospects for Democracy*, Polity Press, Cambridge.

HELD, D. (1995). *Democracy and the Global Order: From the Modern State to Cosmopolitan Governance*, Polity Press, Cambridge.

HERNDON, S., & G. KREPS (eds.) (1993). *Qualitative Research. Applications in Organizational Communication*, Hampton, Cresskill.

HETTNE, B. (1982). *Development Theory and the Third World*, SAREC, Stockholm.

HETTNE, B. (1990). *Development Theory and the Three Worlds*, Longman, New York.

HILL, M. (ed.) (1993). *The Policy Process: A Reader*, Harvester Wheatsheaf, New York.

HOFSTEDE, G. (1980). *Culture's Consequences: International Differences in Work-Related Values*, Sage, Beverly Hills.

HOFSTEDE, G. (1991). *Cultures and Organizations: Software of the Mind. Intercultural Cooperation and its Importance for Survival*, McGraw-Hill, London.

HOLDGATE, M. (1996). *From Care to Action: Making a Sustainable World*, Earthscan, London.

HOLMES, H., & S. TANGTONGTAVY (1995). *Working with the Thais*, White Lotus, Bangkok.

HOOK S. (1987). *Paradoxes of Freedom*, Prometheus Books, Buffalo.

HOOVER, S., VENTURELLI, S., & D. WAGNER (1993). "Trends in global communication Policy-making: Lessons from the Asian case", *Asian Journal of Communication*, 3(1), 103-132.

HORNIK, R. (1988). *Development Communication: Information, Agriculture, and Nutrition in the Third World*, White Plains, Longman

HOSTETLER, J. (1980). *Amish Society*, John Hopkins University Press, Baltimore.

HOWARD, M. (1986). *Contemporary Cultural Anthropology*, Little, Brown, and Co, Boston.

HSIUNG, J. (ed.) (1985). *Human Rights in East Asia: A Cultural Perspective*, Paragon House, New York.

HUIZER, G. (1983). *Guiding Principles for People's Participation Projects*, Food and Agricultural Organization (FAO), Rome.

HUIZER, G. (1989). *Action Research and People's Participation: An Introduction and Some Case Studies*, Third World Centre, Nijmegen.

HULME, D., & M. TURNER (1990). *Sociology and Development*, Harvester Wheatsheaf, New York.

HUSBAND, C. (ed.) (1994). *A Richer Vision: The Devlopment of Ethnic Minority Media in Western Democracies*, UNESCO, Paris.

INKELES, A., & D. SMITH (1974). *Becoming Modern: Individual Change in Six Developing Countries*, Harvard University Press, Cambridge.

ISHII, S. (1985). "Thought patterns as modes of rhetoric: The United States and Japan," SAMOVAR L. & PORTER R. (eds.), *Intercultural Communication: A Reader*, Wadsworth Publishing, Belmont.

ITTY, C. (ed.) (1984). *Searching for Asian Paradigms*, Asian Cultural Forum on Development, Bangkok.

JACOBSON ,T. (1993), "A pragmatist account of Participatory Communication Research for National Development", *Communication Theory*, 3(3), 214-230.

JAKUBOWICZ, K. (1993). "Stuck in a groove: Why the 1960s approach to communication democratization will no longer do", SPLICHAL, S. & WASKO, J. (eds.), *Communication and Democracy*, Ablex, Norwood.

JAMESON, F. (1981). *The Political Unconscious*, Cornell University Press, Ithaca.

JANDT, F. (1995). *Intercultural Communication*. Sage, Thousand Oaks.

JANOS, A. (1986). *Politics and Paradigms: Changing Theories of Change in Social Science*, Stanford University Press, Stanford, CA.

JAYAWEERA, N. (1986). *The Political Economy of the Communication Revolution and the Third World*, AMIC, Singapore.

JAYAWEERA, W. (20 June 1991a). *Farm Broadcasting: A Strategy for BBS*, DaniCom, Copenhagen.

JAYAWEERA, W. (3 July 1991b). *Radio Programme Formats for BBS*, DaniCom, Copenhagen.

JAYAWEERA, W. (5 June 1992a). *Performance Discrepancies of BBS Producers and Recommended Remedies*, Danida, Copenhagen.

JAYAWEERA, W. (1 July 1992b). *A Rationale for a Morning Transmission*, DaniCom, Copenhagen.

JAYAWEERA, N., & S. AMUNAGUMA (eds.) (1987). *Rethinking Development Communication*, AMIC, Singapore

JENSEN, J. (1990). *Redeeming Modernity: Contradictions in Media Criticism*, Sage, Newbury Park.

JOHNSON, F. (1985). "The Western concept of self", MARSELLA A., DEVOS G., & HSU S. (eds.), *Culture and Self: Asian and Western Perspectives*, Tavistock, London.

JORGENSEN, L. (1981). *The Freedom of the Press and the Right to Information*, PhD Thesis, Faculty of Theology, Louvain.

JOUET, J. & S. COUDRAY (1991). *New Communication Technologies: Research Trends*, UNESCO, Paris.

KABRA, K.N. (1995). "The informal sector: A reappraisal", *Journal of Contemporary Asia*, 25(2), 197-232.

KAPLUN M. (1992). *A la Educacion por la Comunicacion: La Practica de la Comunicacion Educativa* [Education for communication: The Practice of educative communication], UNESCO/Orealc, Santiago.

KASSAM, Y., & MUSTAFA K. (eds.) (1982). *Participatory Research: An Emerging Alternative Methodology in Social Science Research*, Society for Participatory Research in Asia, New Delhi.

KAY, C. (1989). *Latin American Theories of Development and Underdevelopment*, London, Routledge

KELSALL, T. (1995). "African development: Where to from here?", *Africa*, 65(2), 297-309.

KENNEDY, T. W. (1984). *Beyond Advocacy: An Animative Approach to Public Participation*. Dissertation, Cornell University.

KEUNE R. (1984). *An International Information Order?*, Friedrich Ebert Stiftung, Bonn.

KEYES, C. (1989). *Thailand: Buddhist Kingdom as Modern Nation-State*, Editions Duang Kamol, Bangkok.

KHAN, A. (1976). "The Comillia experience in Bangladesh—My lessons in communication", SCHRAMM W. & LERNER D. (eds.), *Communication and Change: The Last Ten Years—And the Next*, The East-West Center, Honolulu.

KIATIPRAJUK, S. (ed.) (1995). "After three decades of development: It's time to rethink", *Thai Development*, Bangkok, 27-28.

KIDD, R., & K. KUMAR (1981, January 3-10). "Co-opting Freire. A critical analysis of pseudo-Freirean adult education", *Economic and Political Weekly*, 27-36.

KIM, Y. (1985). "Communication and acculturation", SAMOVAR, L. & PORTER, R. (eds.), *Intercultural Communication: A Reader*, Wadsworth Publishing, Belmont.

KIN CHI, L. (1994). "Reunification", *Asian Exchange, Hong Kong*, 10(2).

KING, A. (ed.) (1991). *Culture, Globalization and the World-System*, MacMillan, London.

KIVIKURU, U. (1990). *Tinned Novelties or Creative Culture? A Study on the Role of Mass Communication in Peripheral Nations*, Department of Communication, University of Helsinki.

KLAPPER, J.T. (1960). *The Effects of Mass Communication*, Free Press, Glencoe, Illinois.

KLAUSNER W. (1980). *Conflict and Communication*, Business Information & Research, Bangkok.

KLAUSNER, W. (1983). *Reflections on Thai Culture*, Siam Society, Bangkok.

KLAUSNER, W. (1997). *Thai Culture in Transition*. The Siam Society, Bangkok.

KLOOS, P. (1984). *Antropologie als Wetenschap* [Anthropology as science], Coutinho, Muiderberg.

KLOPF, D., & M. S. PARK (1982). *Cross-cultural Communication: An Introduction to the Fundamentals*, Han Shin Publishing, Seoul.

KO, Y.B. (1979). "Principal-subordinate relationship", PARK M.S. (ed.), *Communication Styles in Two Different Cultures : Korean and American*, Han Shin, Seoul.

KOBJITTI, C. (1983). *The Judgement* (Kham Phi Phaksa), DK Books, Bangkok.

KOLM, S. (1984). "Marxisme et bouddhisme" [Marxism and bouddhism], *Cahiers Internationaux de Sociologie*, 77.

KOLOSOV, Y., & B. TSEPOV (1984), *The NIIO and the Problems of Maintaining Peace*, Nauka Publishers, Moscow.

KOMIN, S. (1988). "Thai value aystem and its implication for development in Thailand", SINHA D. & KAO H. (eds.), *Social Values and Development: Asian Perspectives*, Sage, New Delhi.

KOMIN S. (1991). *Psychology of the Thai People. Values and Behavioral Patterns*, National Institute of Development Administration, Bangkok.

KORTEN, D. (ed.) (1986). *Community Management: Asian Experience and Perspectives*, Kumarian Press, West Hartford.

KOTHARI, R. (1984). "Peace in an age of transformation", WALKER R. (ed.), *Culture, Ideology, and World Order*, Westview, Boulder, CO.

KOTHARI, R. (1986). "Masses, classes and the state", *Alternatives, New York*, 11(2), April.

KOTHARI, R. (1988). *Rethinking Development: In Search of Humane Alternatives*, Ajanta Publications, New Delhi.

KOZOL, J. (1975). *The Night is Dark and I Am Far From Home*, Houghton Mifflin, Boston.

KROEBER, A., &C. KLUCKHOHN (1952). *Culture: A Critical Review of Concepts and Definitions*, Vintage Books, New York.

KRONENBURG, J. (1986). *Empowerment of the Poor: A Comparative Analysis of Two Development Endeavours in Kenya*, Third World Center, Nijmegen.

KUHN, T. (1962). *The Structure of Scientific Revolutions*, University of Chicago Press, Chicago.

KUHN, T. (1970). *The Structure of Scientific Revolutions* (2nd ed., enlarged), University of Chicago Press, Chicago.

KUMAR, K. (ed.) (1993). *Rapid Appraisal Methods*, World Bank, Washington.

LACLAU, E. & C. MOUFFE (1985). *Hegemony and Socialist Strategy*, Verso, London.

LARRAIN, J. (1994). *Ideology & Cultural Identity: Modernity and the Third World Presence*, Polity Press, Cambridge.

LASWELL, H. (1948). "The structure and function of communication in society", L. Bryson (ed.), *The Communication of Ideas*. Harper & Brothers, New York.

LAZARSFELD, P., BERELSON, B. & H. GAUDET (1944). *The People's Choice*, Duell, Sloan & Pearce, New York.

LEE, C.C. (1980). *Media Imperialism Reconsidered: The Homogenizing of Television Culture*, Sage, London.

LEE, O.Y. (1967). *In This Earth and in That Wind*, Hollym, Seoul.

LEE, P. (ed.) (1995). *The Democratization of Communication*, WACC, London.

LERNER, D., & W. SCHRAMM (eds.) (1967). *Communication and Change in the Developing Countries*, University Press of Hawaii, Honolulu.

LERNER, D. (1958). *The Passing of Traditional Society: Modernizing the Middle East*, Free Press, New York.

LERNER, D. (1977). "Communication and development", LERNER D. & NELSON L. (eds.), *Communication Research: A Half-century Appraisal*, East-West Center, Honolulu.

LERNER, D. (1978). "Communication, development, world order", *Murrow Reports*, September.

LERTVICHA, P. (1987). "Political forces in Thailand", *Asian Review*, 1.

LEWIS, P. (1993). *Alternative Media: Linking Global and Local*, UNESCO, Paris.

LIEBES, T., & E. KATZ (1986). "Patterns of involvement in television fiction : A comparative analysis", *European Journal of Communication*, 1(2), 151-171.

LIMPRUNGPATANAKIT, A. (1989, January 17). "Loopholes allow export of complete benefits", *The Nation*, p. 15.

LIN, N. (1973), *The Study of Human Communication*, Bobbs-Merrill, Indianapolis.

LONG, N., & LONG A. (eds.) (1992). *Battlefields of Knowledge. The Interlocking of Theory and Practice in Social Research and Development*, Routledge, London.

LOWE, V. (1987). *Dependency within Bounds: Media and Information Technology Policies within the ASEAN Region*, Institute of Asian Studies, Chulalongkorn University, Bangkok.

LOZARE, B. (1994). "Power and conflict: Hidden dimensions of communication, participative planning, and action", WHITE, S., NAIR, K.S., & ASCROFT, J. (eds), *Participatory Communication: Working for Change and Development*, Sage, New Delhi.

LUBIS M. (1986). "Cultural integrity: Free and balanced information flow: Mutually exclusive terms or parts of the same thing?", *Media Asia*, Singapore, 13(2).

LULL, J. (1995). *Media, Communication, Culture: A Global Approach*, Polity Press, Cambridge.

MacBRIDE, S. (ed.) (1980). *Many Voices, One World. Communication and Society. Today and Tomorrow,* UNESCO, Paris.

MacBRIDE, S. (1981). "The most important of human rights", *IPI Report,* October 1981.

MACKIE, R. (ed.) (1981). *Literacy and Revolution,* Continuum, New York.

MADRID, J. (1983). *Los Medios de Comunicacion y la Construccion de la Hegemonia* [Communication media and the construction of hegemony], CEESTEM, Mexico. .

MAGDOFF, H. (1969). *The Age of Imperialism.* Monthly Review Press, New York.

MAHMUD, T. (1981). *Politics of the New International Information Order,* PhD Thesis, Political Science, University of Hawaii, Honolulu.

MAIR, L. (1984). *Anthropology and Development,* MacMillan, London.

MAJCHRZAK, A. (1984). *Methods for Policy Research,* Sage, London.

MALM, K., & R. WALLIS (1984). *Big Sounds from Small Peoples: The Music Industry in Small Countries,* Constable, London.

MANSELL, R. (1984). *Contradiction in National Communication/Information Policies: The Canadian Experience,* Paper IAMCR Conference, Prague, August.

MARCUS, G., & M. FISHER (1986). *Anthropology as Cultural Critique,* The University of Chicago Press, Chicago.

MARINI, R.M. (1973). *Dialectica de la Dependencia* [Dialectics of dependency], Era, Mexico.

MARSELLA, A., DEVOS, G., & F. HSU (eds.) (1985). *Culture and Self: Asian and Western Perspectives,* Tavistock, London.

MARTIN-BARBERO, J. (1987). *De los Medios a las Mediaciones: Comunicacion, Cultura y Hegemonia* [From the media to mediations: Communication, culture and hegemony], Ed. G. Gili, Barcelona.

MARTIN-BARBERO J. (1993a). *Communication, Culture and Hegemony: From the Media to Mediations,* Sage, London.

MARTIN-BARBERO, J. (1993b). "Latin America: Cultures in the communication media", *Journal of Communication,* 43(2), Spring, 18-30.

MASINI, E., & J. GALTUNG (eds.), (1979). *Visiones de Sociedades Deseables* [Visions of desirable societies]. CEESTEM, Mexico.

MASINI, E. (ed.) (1994). *The Futures of Cultures,* Unesco, Paris.

MASTERMAN, L. (1984). *Television Mythologies : Stars, Shows and Signs,* Comedia, London.

MATA, M.C. (1985). *Radio Enriquillo en Dialogo con el Pueblo* [Radio Enriquillo in dialogue with the people], Aler, Quito.

MATA M.C. (1990). *Nociones para Pensar la Comunicación y la Cultura Masiva,* La Crujia, Buenos Aires.

MATTA, F. R. (1986), "Alternative communication: Solidarity and development in the face of transnational expansion", ATWOOD, R. & McANANY, E. (eds.), *Communication and Latin American Society: Trends in Critical Research 1960-1985,* University of Wisconson Press, Madison.

MATTA, F.R. (1979). *La Comunicacion Transnacional y la Respuesta Alternativa* [Transnational communication and the alternative answer], ILET, Mexico.

MATTA, F.R. (1981). "A model for democratic communication", *Development Dialogue,* 2.

MATTELART, A. (1976). *Multinationales et Systèmes de Communication* [Multinationals and communication systems], Anthropos, Paris. .

MATTELART A. (1983). *Transnationals and the Third World: The Struggle for Culture*, Bergin & Garvey, Massachusetts.

MATTHEWS, B., & J. NAGATA (eds.) (1986). *Religion, Values and Development in Southeast Asia*, Institute of Southeast Asian Studies, Singapore.

MAYO, J., & J. CHIEUW (1993). *The Third Channel: Broadening Learning Horizons*, Unicef, New York.

MAYO, J., & J. SERVAES (eds.) (1994). *Approaches to Development Communication: A Resource and Orientation Kit. Volumes 1 & 2*, UNESCO/UNFPA, Paris/New York.

McANANY, E., & J. MAYO (1980). *Communication Media in Education for Low-income Countries. Implications for Planning*, Unesco, Paris.

McANANY, E. (1983). "From modernization and diffusion to dependency and beyond: theory and practice in communication for social change in the 1980s", *Development Communications in the Third World, Proceedings of a Midwest Symposium*, University of Illinois, April.

McANANY, E. (ed.) (1980). *Communications in the Rural Third World: The Role of Information in Development*, Praeger, New York.

McCREARY, D., & R. BLANCHFIELD (1986). "The art of Japanese negotiation", SCHWEDA-NICHOLSON, N. (Ed.), *Languages in the International Perspective*, Ablex, Norwood

MCKEE, N. (1994). "Beyond social marketing: A community-based learning model", WHITE, S., NAIR ,K.S., & J. ASCROFT (eds.), *Participatory Communication. Working for Change and Development*, Sage, New Delhi.

McKEE, N. (1992). *Social Mobilization & Social Marketing in Developing Communities: Lessons for Communicators*, Southbound, Penang.

McLAREN, P. (1995). *Critical Pedagogy And Predatory Culture*, Routledge, London.

McLAREN, P., & C. LANKSHEAR (eds.) (1994). *Politics of Liberation: Paths from Freire*, Routledge, London.

McLAREN, P., & P. LEONARD (eds.) (1993). *Paulo Freire. A Critical Encounter*, Routledge, London.

McLUHAN, M. (1964), *Understanding Media*, Signet Books, New York.

McPHAIL, T. (1987). *Electronic Colonialism*, Sage, Newbury Park.

McQUAIL, D. (1983). *Mass Communication Theory*, Sage, London.

McQUAIL, D., & K. SIUNE (eds.) (1986). *New Media Politics. Comparative Perspectives in Western Europe*, Sage, London.

McQUAIL, D., & WINDAHL S. (1993). *Communication ·Models for the Study of Mass Communication*, Longman, London.

MEHMET, O. (1995). *Westernizing the Third World: Eurocentricity of Economic Development Theories*, Routledge, London.

MELKOTE, S. (1991). *Communication for Development in the Third World: Theory and Practice*, Sage, New Delhi.

MERRILL, J. (1971). "The role of the mass media in national development: An open question for speculation", *Gazette*, 17(4).

MERRILL, J. (1974). *The Imperative of Freedom: A Philosophy of Journalistic Autonomy*, Hastings, New York.

MERRILL, J.C., & R. L. LOWENSTEIN (1979). *Media, Messages and Men: New Perspectives in Communication*, Longman, New York.

MEYER, W. (1988). *Beyond the Mask: Toward a Transdiciplinary Approach of Selected Social Problems Related to the Evolution and Context of International Tourism in Thailand*, Breitenbach Publishers, Saarbrucken.

MIDDLETON, J. (ed.) (1980). *Approaches to Communication Planning*, UNESCO, Paris.

MIDDLETON, J., & D. WEDEMEYER (eds.) (1985). *Methods of Communication Planning*, UNESCO, Paris.

MIDGLEY, J. (ed.) (1986). *Community Participation, Social Development, and the State*, Methuen, London.

MIGNOT-LEFEBVRE, Y. (ed.) (1994). "Technologies de communication et d'information au Sud: la mondialisation forcée" [Information and Communication Technologies in the South: Forced globalization], *Revue Tiers-Monde* (Special Issue), 35(138).

MILLER, D. (ed.) (1995). *Worlds Apart: Modernity Through the Prism of the Local*. Routledge, London.

MINOGUE K. (1980). "Between rhetoric and fantasy", *Encounter*, 55(6), December.

MITCHELL, J. (1978). "The appropriateness of satellite communication for the Third World", *Media Asia*, Singapore, 5(2).

MODY, B. (1991). *Designing Messages for Development Communication: An Audience Participation-based Approach*, Sage, New Delhi.

MOEMEKA, A. (ed.) (1994). *Communicating for Development. A New Pan-Disciplinary Perspective*, State University of New York Press, Albany.

MONGA, C. (1994). *Anthropologie de la Colère. Société Civile et Démocratie en Afrique Noire* [Anthropology of anger. Civil Society and democracy in Black Africa], l'Harmattan, Paris.

MOORE, S. (1986). "Participatory communication in the development process", *The Third Channel*, 2(2).

MOREHOUSE, W. (ed.) (1989). *Building Sustainable Communities. Tools and Concepts for Self-Reliant Economic Change*, The Bootstrap Press, New York.

MOTTA, G.L. (1984). "National communication policies : Grass roots alternatives", GERBNER G. & SIEFERT M. (eds.), *World communications*, Longman, New York.

MOUSTAKAS, C.E. (1974). *Individuality and Encounter*, Howard A. Doyle Publishing, Cambridge.

MOWLANA, H. (1984). "Communication for political change. The Iranian revolution", GERBNER G. & SIEFERT, M. (eds.), *World Communication*, Longman, New York.

MOWLANA H. (1986). *Development. A Field in Search of Itself*, American University, Washington.

MOWLANA, H. (1997). *Global information and World Communication: New Frontiers in International Relations*, Newbury Park, Sage.

MOWLANA, H., & L. WILSON (1987). *Communication and Development: A Global Assessment*, UNESCO, Paris.

MULDER, N. (1985). *Everyday Life in Thailand: An Interpretation*, DK Books, Bangkok.

MULDER, N. (1990). *Inside Thai Society: An Interpretation of Everyday Life*, DK Books, Bangkok.

MUMBY, D. (1982). *Two Discourses on Power and the Subject: Jürgen Habermas and Michel Foucault*, Paper ICA Conference, San Francisco, May.

NAKAMURA, H. (1985). *Ways of Thinking of Eastern Peoples*, University of Hawaii Press, Honolulu.

NANAVATTY, M. (1988). "The community sevelopment movement in South East Asian countries: An Asian perspective", *Community Development Journal*, 23(2).

NARULA, U., & W. BARNETT PEARCE (1986). *Development as Communication: A Perspective on India*, Southern Illinois University Press, Carbondale, Illinois.

NEGT, O. (1971). *Soziologische Phantasie und Exemplarisch Lernen* [Sociological Fantasy and exemplary learning], Suhrkamp, Frankfurt.

NG'WANAKILALA, N. (1981). *Mass Communication and Development of Socialism in Tanzania*, Tanzania Publishing House, Dar-es-Salaam.

NORDENSTRENG, K. (1981). "New international directions. A non-aligned viewpoint", HAIGH R.W., GERBNER, G., & BYRNE, R. (eds.), *Communication in the 21st Century*, Wiley, New York.

NORDENSTRENG, K. (1984), *The Mass Media Declaration of Unesco*, Ablex, Norwood.

NORDENSTRENG, K., & SCHILLER H. I. (eds.) (1979). *National Sovereignty and International Communication*, Ablex, Norwood.

NORDENSTRENG, K., & H. I. SCHILLER (eds.) (1993). *Beyond National Sovereignty: International Communication in the 1990s*, Ablex, Norwood.

NWOSU, I. (1985). "Building a new global economic and information order", *The Democratic Journalist*, Prague, 33(7-8), July-August.

NYAMNJOH, F. (1994). *Communication Reserarch and Sustainable Development in Africa: The Need for a Domesticated Perspective*, Paper ACCE Conference, Accra, October.

NYERERE, J. (1973). *Freedom and Development*, Oxford University Press, Dar-es-Salaam

NYONI, S. (1987). "Indigenous NGOs: liberation, self-reliance, and development", *World Development*, 15.

O'CONNER, A. (1990). "Radio is fundamental to democracy", *Media Development*, 37(4).

O'SULLIVAN-RYAN, J., & M. KAPLUN (1979). *Communication Methods to Promote Grassroots Participation*, UNESCO, Paris.

OEPEN, M. (ed.) (1995). *Media Support and Development Communication in a World of Change: New Answers to Old Questions?*, Horlemann, Bad Honnef.

OWEN, R., & B. SUTCLIFFE (eds.) (1972). *Studies in the Theory of Imperialism*, Longman, London.

PADMADIN, S. (1984). *Mass Communication in Thailand: An Overview*, Asian Mass Communication Research and Information Centre (AMIC), Singapore

PAKKASEM, P. (1988). *Leading Issues in Thailand's Development Transformation 1960-1990*, Office of the Prime Minister, Bangkok, March.

PALMER, M., & K. SIMMONS (1995). "Communicating intentions through non-verbal behaviors", *Human Communication Research*, 22(1), September, 128-160.

PARKER, E. (1977). "Planning communication technologies and institutions for development", RAHIM S. & MIDDLETON, J. (eds.), *Perspectives in Communication Policy and Planning*, East-West Center, Honolulu.

PARSONS, T. (1960). *Structure and Process in Modern Societies*, Free Press, Chicago.

PASEWARK, K. (1986). "Communicative irrationality and political discourse in Jürgen Habermas: A theological experiment", McLAUGHLIN M. (ed.), *Communication Yearbook. Vol. 9*, Sage, London.

PASQUALI, A. (1970). *Comunicacion y Cultura de Masas* [Mass communication and Culture], Avila, Caracas.

PASQUALI A. (1980). *Comprender la Comunicacion* [Understanding communication], Avila, Caracas.

PAVLIC, B., & C. HAMELINK (1984). *The Relationship Between the NIEO and the NIIO*, Unesco, Paris.

PEK, S. (27 November 1991). *BBS: A General Report*, BBS, Thimpu.

PEREZ De CUELLAR, J. P. (1995). *Our Creative Diversity: Report of the World Commission on Culture and Development*, UNESCO, Paris.

PERROUX, F. (1983). *A New Concept of Development*, UNESCO, Paris.

PHILIPPINE PARTNERSHIP FOR THE DEVELOPMENT OF HUMAN RESOURCES IN RURAL AREAS (1986), *Participatory Research Guidebook*, Philippine Partnership for the Development of Human Resources in Rural Areas, Laguna.

PHONGPAICHIT, P., & C. BAKER (1996). *Thailand's Boom!*, Silkworm Books, Chiang Mai.

PHONGPAICHIT, P., & S. PRIRYARANGSAN (1994). *Corruption and Democracy in Thailand*, Faculty of Economics, Chulalongkorn University, Bangkok.

PHONGPHIT, S. (1989). *Development Paradigm: Strategy, Activities and Reflection*, Thai Institute for Rural Development, Bangkok.

POOL I. de Sola. (1983). *Technologies of Freedom*, Belknap Press, Cambridge.

PRASERTKUL, S. (1989, July 24-30). "Samee Jiab lae Thai society" [Samee Jiab and Thai society], *Management Review*.

PRASITH-RATHSINT, S. (ed.) (1987). *Thailand's National Development: Policy Issues and Challenges*, Thai University Research Association, Bangkok .

PREISWERK, R. (1980). "Identité culturelle, self-reliance et besoins fondamentaux" [Cultural identity, self-reliance and basic needs], SPITZ, P., GALTUNG, J. et al. (eds.), *Il faut Manger pour Vivre* [One needs to eat to live], Presses Universitaires de France, Paris.

PUNYANUBHAH, S. (ed.) (1981). *Buddhism in Thai Life*, Samnakngan Kana Kammakan Raksa Ekalak Thai, Bangkok.

RABINOW, P., & W. SULLIVAN (eds.) (1987). *Interpretive Social Science: A Second Look*, University of California Press, Berkeley.

RAHIM, S., & J. MIDDLETON (eds.) (1977). *Perspectives in Communication Policy and Planning*, East-West Center, Honolulu.

RAHIM, S., & A. PENNINGS (1987). *Computerization and Development in Southeast Asia*, Asian Mass Communication Research and Information Centre, Singapore.

RAHIM, S., LAMBERTON, D., & D. WEDEMEYER (1978). *Planning Methods, Models, and Organization: A Review Study for Communication Policy Making and Planning*, East-West Center, Honolulu.

RAJADHON, A. (1968). *Essays on Thai Folklore*, DK Books, Bangkok.

RAJADHON, A. (1987). *Some Traditions of the Thai*, Sathirakoses Nagapradipa Foundation, Bangkok.

RAJAVARAMUNI, P. (1983). *Social Dimension of Buddhism in Contemporary Thailand*, Thai Khadi Suksa, Bangkok.

RAMANA, D.V. (1982). *A Monograph on Access Planning as an Essay on Explorations in Alternatives*, APDC, Kuala Lumpur.

RAMASHRAY, R., & R. K. SRIVASTAVA (1986). *Dialogues on Development: The Individual, Society, and Political Order*, Sage, New Delhi.

RAMIREZ, M. (1990). *Communication from the Ground Up*, Asian Social Institute, Manila.

RAO, S. (1986). "The agenda of Third World communication research: A critical review", *Media Asia, Singapore, 13*(4).

REDCLIFT, M. (1987). *Sustainable Development: Exploring the Contradictions*, Routledge, London.

REITOV, O. (1990, 30 May). *Report on Music Recordings, Music Programmes, and Music Policy* (2nd Consultancy Period), Danicom, Copenhagen.

RICOEUR, P. (ed.) (1986). *Philosophical Foundation of Human Rights*, UNESCO, Paris.

RIGGS, F. (1984). "Development", SARTONI, G. (ed.), *Social Science Concepts*, Sage, Beverly Hills.

RITZER, G. (1996). *The McDonaldization of Society: An Investigation into the Changing Character of Contemporary Social Life*, Pine Forge Press, Thousand Oaks.

ROACH, C. (1986). *Context and Contradiction of the United States Position on the NWICO*, Paper IAMCR Conference, New Delhi, August.

ROBERTSON, R. (1992). *Globalization: Social Theory and Global Culture*, Sage, London.

ROBINSON, D., BUCK E., & M. CUTHBERT (eds.) (1992). *Music at the Margins: Popular Music and Global Diversity*, Sage, Newbury Park.

ROCKHILL K. (1982). "Researching participation in adult education: The potential of the qualitative perspective", *Adult Education, 33*(1), Fall.

ROGERS, E.M. (1962). *Diffusion of Innovations*, Free Press, New York.

ROGERS, E. M. (ed.) (1976a). *Communication and Development*, Sage, Beverly Hills.

ROGERS E. M. (1976b). "The passing of the sominant paradigm. Reflections on diffusion research", SCHRAMM, W. & LERNER, D. (eds.), *Communication and Change: The Last Ten Years—And the Next*, East-West Center, Honolulu.

ROGERS, E. M. (1983). *The Diffusion of Innovations* (3rd ed.), The Free Press, New York.

ROGERS, E. M. (1986). *Communication Technology: The New Media in Society*, The Free Press, New York.

ROGERS, E.M., & D. L. KINCAID (1981). *Communication Networks. Towards a New Paradigm for Research*, MacMillan, London.

ROGERS, E. M., & F. SCHOEMAKER (1973). *Communication of Innovations*, Free Press, New York.

ROKEACH, M. (1966). "Attitude change and behavioral change", *Public Opinion Quarterly, 30*(4), Winter.

RONDINELLI, D. (1993). *Development Projects as Policy Experiments: An Adaptive Approach to Development Administration*, Routledge, London.

ROSENAU, J.N. (1980). *The Study of Global Interdependence*, Pinter, London.

ROSENGREN, K.E. (1981). "Mass media and social change : Some current approaches", KATZ, E. & SZECSKO, T. (eds.), *Mass Media and Social Change*, Sage, Beverly Hills.

ROSS, D., & P. USHER (1986). *From the Roots Up: Economic Development as if Community Mattered*, The Bootstrap Press, New York.

ROSTOW, W.W. (1953). *The Process of Economic Growth*, Clarendon Press, Oxford.

ROWAT, D. (1981). "The right to government information in democracies", *Journal of Media Law and Practice, 2*(3), December.

RUTNIN, M. (1988). *Modern Thai Literature*, Thammasat University Press, Bangkok.

SADIK, N. (1991). *Population Policies and Programmes: Lessons Learned From Two Decades of Experience*, New York University Press, New York.

SAID, E. (1985). *Orientalism*, Penguin Books, Harmondsworth.

SAID, E. (1993). *Culture and Imperialism*, Knopf, New York.

SALMEN, L.F. (1987). *Listen to the People: Participant-Observer Evaluation of Development Projects*, Oxford University Press, New York.

SAMARAJIVA, R. (1987). "The murky beginnings of the communication and development field: Voice of America and the passing of traditional society", JAYAWEERA N. & AMUNAGUMA, S. (eds.), *Rethinking Development Communication*, AMIC, Singapore.

SAMOVAR, L., & R. PORTER (eds.) (1988). *Intercultural Communication: A Reader*, Wadworth, Belmont, CA.

SAMOVAR, L., & R. PORTER (eds.) (1995). *Communication Between Cultures*, Wadworth Publishing, Belmont.

SANDERSON, S. (1995). *Social Transformations: A General Theory of Historical Development*, Blackwell, Oxford.

SARTI, I. (1981). "Communication and cultural dependency: A misconception", McANANY E., SCHNITMAN, J., & JANUS, N. (eds.), *Communication and Social Structure*, Praeger, New York.

SCHILLER, H. I. (1969). *Mass Communications and American Empire*, Kelly Publishers, New York.

SCHILLER, H. I. (1973). *The Mind Managers*, Beacon Press, Boston.

SCHILLER, H. I. (1976). *Communication and Cultural Domination*, International Arts & Sciences Press, New York.

SCHILLER, H. I. (1981). *Who Knows: Information in the Age of the Fortune 500*, Ablex, Norwood.

SCHILLER, H.I. (1984). *Information and the Crisis Economy*, Ablex, Norwood.

SCHILLER, H. I. (1989). *Culture Inc. The Corporate Takeover of Public Expression*, Oxford University Press, New York.

SCHRAMM, W., & D. LERNER (eds.) (1976). *Communication and Change: The Last Ten Years-and the Next*, University Press of Hawaii, Honolulu.

SCHRAMM, W., & W. RUGGELS (1967). "How mass media systems grow", LERNER D. & SCHRAMM W. (eds.), *Communication and Change in the Developing Countries*, University Press of Hawaii, Honolulu.

SCHRAMM, W. (1954). *The Process and Effects of Mass Communication*, University of Illinois Press, Urbana.

SCHRAMM, W. (1964). *Mass Media and National Development: The Role of Information in the Developing Countries*, Stanford University Press, Stanford.

SCHRAMM, W. (1982). "Preface", EDELSTEIN, A., *Comparative Communication Research*, Sage, Beverly Hills.

SEESAWAT, L. (1987). *Naew Noam Bot Bat Lae Stanapab khong Video Nai Pujjuban* [The role of video: present status and trends], Thesis, Chulalongkorn University, Dept. of Public Relations, Bangkok.

SEGALLER, D. (1981). *Thai Ways*, Allied Newspapers, Bangkok.

SEGALLER, D. (1982). *More Thai Ways*, Allied Newspapers, Bangkok.

SEGUIER, M. (1976). Critique Institutionelle et Créativité Collective, L'Harmattan, Paris. (Institutional Critique and Collective Creativity).

SERIKI, O. (1982). "Communication engineering education and practice in developing countries: Nigerian experience", KAISER, W. (ed.), *Telekommunikation und Bernchance*, Springer Verlag, Berlin.

SERVAES, J., & P. MALIKHAO (1989). "How 'culture' affects films and video in Thailand", *Media Development*, 36(4).

SERVAES, J. (1983). *Communication and Development: Some Theoretical Remarks*, Acco, Leuven.

SERVAES, J. (1987). *Media Aid. Naar een "Ander" Communicatie—En Ontwikkelingsbeleid* [Media Aid. Toward "another" communication and development policy], Acco, Leuven. .

SERVAES, J. (1989). *One World, Multiple Cultures: A New Paradigm on Communication for Development*, Acco, Leuven.

SERVAES, J. (1992). *Advocacy Strategies for Health and Development: Development Communication in Action*, WHO, Division of Health Education, Geneva.

SERVAES, J. (1993). *Evaluation of Bhutan Broadcasting Service*, Report prepared for the Government of the Kingdom of Bhutan, UNESCO, Paris..

SERVAES J., JACOBSON T., & WHITE S. (eds) (1996). *Participatory Communication for Social Change*, New Delhi, Sage.

SERVAES, J., & R. LIE (eds.). (1997). *Media and Politics in Transition. Cultural Identity in the Age of Globalization*, Acco, Louvain.

SHAW, B. (February 1992). "Bhutan in 1991. 'Refugees' and 'Ngolops'", *Asian Survey*, 184-188.

SIEBERT, F., PETERSON, T., & W. SCHRAMM (1956). *Four Theories of the Press*, University of Illinois Press, Urbana.

SILBERMAN, M. (1979). "Popular participation through communications", *Media Asia*, 6(2).

SILVERSTONE, R. (1981). *The Message of Television: Myth and Narrative in Contemporary Culture*, Heinemann, London.

SILVERSTONE, R. (1995). *Television in Everyday Life*, Routledge, London.

SIMBULAN, R. (1985). "Participatory research: A response to Asian people's struggle for social transformation", FARMER'S ASSISTANCE BOARD (ed.), *Participatory Research: Response to Asian People's Struggle for Social Transformation*, Farmer's Assistance Board, Manila.

SIMPSON, C. (1994). *Science of Coercion: Communication Research and Psychological Warfare 1945-1960*, Oxford University Press, New York.

SIRIYUVASAK, U. (1997). "Limited competition without re-regulating the media: The case of the broadacsting industry in Thailand", *Asian Journal of Communication*, 7(2).

SIVARAKSA, S. (1981). *A Buddhist Vision for Renewing Society*, Thai Wattana Panich, Bangkok.

SIVARAKSA, S. (1988). *A Socially Engaged Buddhism*, Thai Inter-Religious Commission for Development, Bangkok.

SKLAIR, L. (1991). *Sociology of the Global System*, Harvester Wheatsheaf, New York.

SLACK, J. (1984). *Communication Technologies and Society*, Ablex, Norwood.

SMITH, B. (1985). *Decentralization. The Territorial Dimension of the State*, George Allen & Unwin, London.

SMITH, J. (1981). "Freedom of expression and the market place of ideas", *Journal of Communication Inquiry*, 7(1), Summer.

SMITH, J. (1995). *Understanding the Media: A Sociology of Mass Communication*, Hampton Press, Creskill.

SMYTHE, D.W. (1981). *Dependency Road: Communication, Capitalism, Consciousness and Canada*, Ablex, Norwood.

SMYTHE, D. W., & T. VAN DINH (1983). "On critical and administrative research: A new critical analysis", GERBNER G. (ed.), "Ferment in the field", *Journal of Communication*, 33(3), Summer

SOMAVIA, J. (1977). *Third World Participation in International Communication: Perspective after Nairobi*, Paper symposium 'International Communication and Third World Participation', Amsterdam, September.

SOMAVIA, J. (1980). "Perspectivas del Informe MacBride [Perspectives of the McBride Report]", *Media Development, London*, 27(4).

SOMAVIA, J. (1981). "The democratization of communication : From minority social monopoly to majority social representation", *Development Dialogue*, 2.

SOUCHOU, Y. (1994). "The predicament of modernity: Mass media and the making of the west in Southeast Asia", *Asian Journal of Communication*, 4(1).

SPYBEY, T. (1992). *Social Change, Development and Dependency: Modernity, Colonialism and the Development of the West*, Polity Press, Cambridge.

SRISOOTARAPAN, S (1976). *Chom Nar Sakdina Thai* [The face of Thai Sakdina], Agsorn Sampan, Bangkok.

STAVENHAGEN, R. (1966). "Siete tesis equivocados sobre América Latina" [Seven misleading theses about Latin America], *Desarrollo Indoamericano*, 4.

STEWART, E.C. (1972). *American Cultural Patterns: A Cross-Cultural Perspective, Intercultural Network*, La Grange.

STOHR W., & F. TAYLOR (eds.) (1981). *Development from Above or Below? The Dialectics of Regional Planning in Developing Countries*, Wiley, Chichester.

STOVER, W. (1984). *Information Technology in the Third World: Can I.T. Lead to Humane National Development?*, Westview Press, Boulder.

STRATHERN, M. (ed.) (1995). *Shifting Contexts: Transformations in Anthropological Knowledge*, Routledge, London.

SUKIN, K. (1994, November 20). "The overlooked panacea", *The Nation*, Bangkok, p. B6.

SUNKEL O. (ed.) (1993). *Development from Within: Toward a Neostructuralist Approach for Latin America*, Lynne Rienner, Boulder.

SUNKEL, O., & E. FUENZALIDA (1980). "La transnacionalizacion del capitalismo y el desarrollo nacional" [The transnationalization of capitalism and national development], SUNKEL O., FUENZALIDA E., CARDOSO F.H. et al. (eds.), *Transnacionalizacion y dependencia*, Cultura Hispania, Madrid.

SUNKEL, O., & P. PAZ (1970), *El Subdesarrollo Latinoamericano y la Teoria del Desarrollo* [The subdevelopment of Latin America and the development theory], Siglo XXI, Mexico. .

SUSANTO, A., ALFIAN, S. B., & H. SUWARDI (1981). *Impact of Modern Communication Technology: Indonesia*, Unesco, Paris.

SUU KYI, A.S. (1994, November 22). "Empowerment for peace and development", *The Nation*, Bangkok,A4.

SWEEZY, P. (1981). *Four Lectures on Marxism*, Monthly Review Press, London.

SZTOMPKA, P. (1993). *The Sociology of Social Change*, Blackwell, Oxford.

TANDON, R. (1981). "Participatory evaluation and research: Main concepts and issues," in FERNANDES, W. & TANDON, R. (eds.), *Participatory Research and Evaluation: Experiments in Research as a Process of Liberation*, Indian Social Institute, New Delhi.

TANDON, R. (1985). "Participatory research: Issues and prospects", FARMER'S ASSISTANCE BOARD (ed.), *Participatory Research: Response to Asian People's Struggle for Social Transformation*, Farmer's Assistance Board, Manila.

TAYLOR, J. (1979). *From Modernization to Modes of Production*, Macmillan, London.

TEHRANIAN, M. (1977). "Communication and national development", TEHRANIAN M., HAKIMZADEH F., & VIDALE M. (eds.), *Communications Policy for National Development*, Routledge & Kegan, London.

TEHRANIAN, M. (1979). "Development theory and communication policy. The changing paradigm", VOIGT, M. & G. HANNEMAN (eds.), *Progress in Communication Sciences. Vol. 1*, Ablex, Norwood.

TEHRANIAN, M. (1985). *Communitarian Democracy: From Utopia to Reality*, Paper ICA Conference, Honolulu, May.

TEHRANIAN, M. (1996). "Communication and empowerment: The dialectics of technology and mythology", SERVAES, J., JACOBSON, T., & WHITE, S. (eds.), *Participatory Communication for Social Change*, Sage, New Delhi.

TERWIEL, B. (1984). "Formal structure and informal rules: An historical perspective on hierarchy, bondage and patron-client relationship, TEN BRUMMELHUIS, H. & KEMP, J. (eds.), *Strategies and Structures in Thai Society*, Anthropologisch-Sociologisch Centrum, Amsterdam.

THAILAND DEVELOPMENT RESEARCH INSTITUTE. (TDRI). (1994). *Thailand Economic Information Kit*, TDRI, Bangkok.

THAYER, L. (1983). "On 'doing' research and 'explaining' things", GERBNER G. (ed.), Ferment in the Field, *Journal of Communication*, 33(4).

THERNBORN, G. (1980). *The Ideology of Power and the Power of Ideology*, Verso, London.

THOMAS, P. (1993). "Communication and development: Freirean cultural politics in a post-modern Era", *PCR-Newsletter*, 1(1), 2-3

THOMAS, S. (1982). "Some problems of the paradigm in communication theory", WHITNEY, D.C. & WARTELLA, E. (eds.), *Mass Communication Review Yearbook 3*, Sage, London.

THOMPSON, J. (1984). *Studies in the Theory of Ideology*, Polity Press, Cambridge.

THOMPSON, J. (1990). *Ideology and Modern Culture: Critical Social Theory in the Era of Mass Communication*, Polity Press, Cambridge.

THOMPSON, J. (1995). *The Media and Modernity: A Social Theory of the Media*, Polity Press, Cambridge.

THOMPSON, M., ELLIS, R., & A. WILDAVSKY (1990). *Cultural Theory*, Westview Press, Boulder.

THUNBERG, A-M., NOWAK, K., ROSENGREN, K. E., & B. SIGURD (1982). *Communication and Equality: A Swedish Perspective*, Almqvist & Wiksell International, Stockholm.

TING-TOOMEY, S. (1984). "Qualitative research: An overview", GUDYKUNST W. & KIM Y. (eds.), *Methods for Intercultural Communication Research*, Sage, Beverly Hills.

TOBIAS, K.J. (1982). *Participatory Research: An Introduction*, Participatory Research Network, New Delhi.

TODARO, M. (1977). *Economic Development in the Third World: An Introduction to Problems and Policies in a Global Perspective*, Longman, New York.

TOFFLER, A. (1985). *Previews & Premises*, Bantam, Toronto.

TRACEY, M. (1985). "The poisoned chalice? International television and the idea of dominance", *Daedulus*, 114(4), Fall.

TRI, H. (ed.), *Participer au Développement* [Participation in development], Unesco, Paris.

TUAZON, R. (ed.) (1983). *Planning the Use of Communication Technology: A Course Guide*, Asian Institute of Journalism, Manila.

TUNSTALL, J. (1977). *The Media are American*, Constable, London.

TUNSTALL, J. (1984). "Media policy dilemmas and indecisions", *Parliamentary Affairs*, 37(3), Summer.

TURNER, B. (1994). *Orientalism, Postmodernism & Globalism*, Routledge, London.

UGBOAJAH, F.O. (ed.) (1985). *Mass Communication, Culture and Society in West Africa*, Saur, München.

UNESCO (1971). *Proposals For an International Programme of Communication Research* (Doc. COM/MD/20), Unesco, Paris.

UNESCO (1972). *Report of the Meeting of Experts on Communication Policies and Planning* (Paris, 17-28 July 1972), Unesco, Paris.

UNESCO (1989). *World Communication Report*, Unesco, Paris.

UNESCO (1995). *The Cultural Dimension of Development: Towards a Practical Approach*, Unesco, Paris.

VAN BEEK, S. (ed.) (1983). *Kukrit Pramoj: His Wit and Wisdom. Writings, Speeches and Interviews*, DK Books, Bangkok.

VAN DEN BERGH, G. (1975). *The Interconnection Between Processes of State and Class Formation: Problems and Conceptualizations*, Institute of Social Studies, The Hague.

VAN NIEUWENHUIJZE, C.A.O. (1982). *Development Begins at Home: Problems and Projects of the Sociology of Development*, Pergamon Press, Oxford.

VARMA, R., GHOSAL, J., & R. HULLS (1973). *Action Research and the Production of Communication Media*, Paper All India Field Workshop, Udaipur, September.

VILANILAM, J., & J. LENT (eds.) (1979). *The Use of Development News*, AMIC, Singapore.

VIRULRAK, S. (1975). *Li-ke, Traditional Folk Media of Central Thailand*, Paper Seminar on Traditional Media, East-West Center, Honolulu, July-August.

VITALE, L. (1979). *La Formacion Social Latino Americana* [The Latin American social systems], Fontamora, Barcelona.

VOGLER, C. (1985). *The Nation State: The Neglected Dimension of Class*, Gower, Hants.

VOORHOOF, D. (1985). *Recht op Informatie, Garingsvrijheid en een Zwijgrecht voor de Journalistiek* [Right of information, right to collect, and right to abstain in journalism], Liga voor Mensenrechten, Gent. .

WALLERSTEIN, I. (1979). *The Capitalist World Economy*, Cambridge University Press, Cambridge.

WALLERSTEIN, I. (1983). *Historical Capitalism*, Verso, London.

WALSH, J. (1973). *Intercultural Education in the Community of Man*, University of Hawaii Press, Honolulu.

WANG, G., & W. DISSANAYAKE (eds.) (1984). *Continuity and Change in Communication Systems: An Asian Perspective*, Ablex, Norwood.

WANG, G. (ed.) (1994). *Treading Different Paths: Informatization in Asian Nations*, Ablex, Norwood.

WARR, P. (ed.) (1993). *The Thai Economy in Transition*, Cambridge University Press, Cambridge.

WEBER, M. (1983). *On Capitalism, Bureaucracy and Religion*, Allen & Unwin, London.

WEDEL, Y., & P. WEDEL (1987). *Radical Thought, Thai Mind: The Development of Revolutionary Ideas in Thailand*, Assumption Business Administration College, Bangkok.

WENZEL, H., & U. HOCHMUTH (1989). "Die Kontingenz von Kommunikation. Zur kritischen Theorie des kommunikativen Handelns von Jürgen Habermas" [A critique on Habermas' Theory of Communicative Action], *Kölner Zeitschrift für Soziologie und Sozialpsychologie, 41*(2), 215-240.

WHITE, R. (1976). *An Alternative Pattern of Basic Education: Radio Santa Maria*, Unesco, Paris.

WHITE, R. (1982). *Contradictions in Contemporary Policies for Democratic Communication*, Paper IAMCR Conference, Paris, September.

WHITE, R. (1984). *The Need for New Strategies of Research on the Democratization of Communication*, Paper ICA Conference, San Francisco, May.

WHITE, R. (1985), "Christians building a New Order of Communication", LEE P. (ed.), *Communication for All: The Church and the New World Information and Communication Order*, Satprakashan Sanchar Kendra, Indore.

WHITE, R. (1988). *Media, Politics and Democracy in the Developing World* [draft], Center for the Study of Communication and Culture, London, April.

WHITE, S., NAIR, K.S., & J. ASCROFT (eds.) (1994). *Participatory Communication: Working for Change and Development*, Sage, New Delhi.

WHYTE, W. F. (ed.) (1989). *Learning From the Field: A Guide from Experience*, Sage, Beverly Hills.

WHYTE, W.F. (ed.) (1991). *Participatory Action Research*, Sage, Newbury Park.

WIGAND, R., SNIPLEY, C., & D. SHIPLEY (1984). "Transborder Data Flow, informatics and national policies", *Journal of Communication*, 34(1), Winter.

WIGNARAJA, P. (1986). *Lessons for Sustainable Development in Asia*, Paper UNU Asian Regional Perspectives Project, Beijing, May.

WIGNARAJA, P. (ed.) (1993). *New Social Movements in the South: Empowering the People*, Zed Books, London.

WILCOX, D.L. (1975). *Mass Media in Black Africa: Philosophy and Control*, Praeger, New York.

WILLIAMS, R. (1981). *Culture*, Fontana, Glasgow.

WONG, S. (1979). *Sociology and Socialism in Contemporary China*, Routledge & Kegan Paul, London.

WOODCOCK, G. (1986). *Planning, Politics and Communications*, Gower, Vermont.

WORLD ASSOCIATION FOR CHRISTIAN COMMUNICATION (WACC). (1991). *Statements on Communication*, WACC, London.

WORLD COMMISSION ON ENVIRONMENT AND DEVELOPMENT (1987). *Our Common Future*, Oxford University Press, Oxford.

XAVIER INSTITUTE (1980). *Development from Below: Notes for Workers Engaged in Rural Development and Adult Education*, Xavier Institute for Social Service, Ranchi.

YADAVA J. (ed.) (1984). *Politics of News: Third World Perspective*, Concept Publishing, New Delhi.

ZASSOURSKY, Y. (1997). *Media in transition and politics in Russia*, SERVAES, J. & LIE, R. (eds.), *Media and Politics in Transition: Cultural Identity in the Age of Globalization*, Acco, Louvain.

Author Index

Subject Index